NUMEROLOGY & SUN SIGNS

NUMEROLOGY
&
SUN SIGNS

P. KHURRANA

RUPA

Published by
Rupa Publications India Pvt. Ltd 2007
161-B/4, Gulmohar House,
Yusuf Sarai Community Centre,
New Delhi 110049

Sales centres:
Bengaluru Chennai
Hyderabad Kolkata Mumbai

P-ISBN: 978-81-291-1249-1
E-ISBN: 978-81-291-2788-4

Fourth impression 2026

10 9 8 7 6 5 4

Printed in India

Those who know Astrology only indicate in a way
what will take place in the future.
Who else, except the Creator Brahma,
can say with certainty what will definitely happen?

Dedicated to Her Holiness my mother
late Smt. Raj Khurrana

CONTENTS

ACKNOWLEDGEMENT

I express my gratitude to my guru, Swami S. Chandraji, who selflessly set my bearings right, who baptised and ushered me completely into the depths of Hindu as well as western astrology.

I thank Ramikka Thakur for her hard work, devotion and efficient management of my work schedule and office.

I owe a lot to my father, Shri R.D. Khurrana, for his blessings and good Sanskaraas, in every sense of the word. I am grateful for the help and support I received from my wife, Poonam and my children, Ayushmaan and Aparshakti, who made it possible for me to lead a fairly normal life and to be a successful astrologer.

I thank my friends, brothers and their wives for their encouragement and continued patience during my hectic work schedule.

My heartfelt thanks to Tomms Babrrani Bravocorr, whose unconditional love and emotional support eased my adjustments to a strange way of life and who made the writing of this book a joyous task.

And last, yet not the least, I express my thanks to Rupa & Co., New Delhi for making this work a complete and wholesome success.

PREFACE

Astrology is a divine subject of the study of nine planets and their effect on the body. Astrology has been used to determine one's nature and the direction of one's life. Each Sun Sign represents a different character ...the capacity for love, intelligence, work, emotions, expressions, etc.

I have written one book titled *SUN SIGNS*. This is a simple form of astrology that can provide you with some interesting but rather general information about you and your personality. In the present book, we take a step further to reveal how your sun sign influences your date of birth.

One may define one's sun sign as that sign of the Zodiac which was occupied by the Sun when one was born. The world of astrological literature is filled with a plethora of books that explain the significance of sun signs. These books touch merely the surface of the science and give us but a glance at the intriguing, yet general characteristics associated with the individual and his personality. Our book goes deeper and shows numerologically how the Number, one to nine, in conjunction with your Sun Sign, impact your approach to your life.

The question, 'What's your sun sign?', is often used as an icebreaker in many conversations and once the answer is given, leads into animated discussions about the characteristics of that particular sign. For instance, if you are a Scorpio by your Sun Sign, you should be a confident, energetic and independent person. Yet, if born on 4, 13, 22 or 31 under the period from 24 October to 22 November, then you will be mysterious, creative and critical, something that is alien to the Scorpion nature. How can all sun signs have the same characteristics? It is a topic generally debated in parties and public. One person who is Taurus is wealthy, learned and well educated; the other is poor, ignorant and uncouth. The Sun Signs could not show these differences at first; that's why the date of birth in a particular Sun Sign plays a significant role in fortune telling. The destiny of a child varies according to the influence of the Numbers when he was born.

Linking numerology to astrology is a very difficult task but a very interesting science, which requires studying the science of Numbers 1 to 31 in a particular Sun Sign. Both are empirical sciences which should be studied by competent people.

In order to gain a detailed insight into your personality, your date of birth plays an important role in moulding your personality.

Astrology can affect the way you think and behave when you are in association with a person of different sun sign. But your date of birth in a particular sun sign provides you with fascinating information about the complete characteristics of others. When you meet someone to whom you are attracted, sun signs and numerology can provide you with a valuable insight into his or her personality. It may even reveal unattractive characteristics that your prospective partner is trying to conceal.

This book is a complete manual on numerology & sun signs, and it is my sincere attempt to give my lay readers an understanding and in-depth meaning of every character they possess. The book contains all the necessary information on general astrological knowledge pertaining to the influence of Numbers on your Sun Sign.

The book throws light on Numbers and their aspects in different sun signs. Numerology is a very important part of astrology and it helps people, if applied accurately. The book will help the serious readers to have a detailed information about their career, health, marriage and various aspects of life. The subject of Astrology in combination with Numerology has been dealt with in an simple manner by which a commoner can find out the basics of fortune telling. Students of astrology can use it as a textbook.

If at any point in your life you feel you need help please do not hestate to contact me at, Hotel Shivalikview, Sector 17, Chandigarh (India) ph: (0172) 2703018, 2712280, 9810349900, (Delhi) 09819807558 (Mumbai)

P. KHURRANA
Astrologer

ARIES

(21ST MARCH TO 20TH APRIL)

Aries in General

Aries is the sign which rules the month of April. It starts on March 21st. However, it assumes total influence and control around the 27th of March, since before that, for the preceding seven days, it is overlapped by the 'cusp' of the previous sign. It is from the 27th of March that Aries exercises complete influence till the 19th of April, after which for the next seven days, it slowly loses strength because of being overlapped by the 'cusp' of the next sign, that is, Taurus.

There are certain defining characteristics that mark the individuals who are born during this period. Arians are known to be stubborn, unwavering and strong-minded. As a matter of fact, they are known to battle all odds and overcome most hurdles that stand in their path. Generally, most Arians have a gift for being natural leaders and have a flair for managing people.

Self-reliant and persistent, they enjoy working on their own and also need to have things done according to their tastes and preferences. When they feel that their way is being meddled with, they often step back and let the other person take over, not because they are submitting, but simply because they cannot have someone else run the show for them.

Arians have a strong and insistent streak that enables them to scale to great heights of material wealth and power. However, it is important that they remain grounded and stable. They at times, have a tendency to get swayed by success and flattery. This results in them being egotistical, and when something like this happens, their pride leads to their downfall.

Blessed with immense enthusiasm and imagination, they are gifted individuals when it comes to planning, strategising and innovating. However, it is important that they have an inclination for the subject. They have determination and grit; however, it takes only strong logic and reasoning to make them consider a point of view other than their own.

Arians are also known to have a reckless temperament and this tends to be reflected in their spontaneous enthusiasm and their rapid thought processes and actions. Moreover, they tend to swing to the extremes in nearly everything. Straightforward and blunt to a fault, they speak their mind more often than not. As a result, they tend to step on a few toes and hurt quite a few people, mostly unintentionally.

Driven by ambition and desire, they have their goals clear. They need to either have plenty of money or immense responsibility or better still, both. There are certain Arians who, for their desire for money, let their scruples and good sense take second place. They can be cruel and oppressive masters and nearly always meet a similar end. The more superior Arians are good masters. However, even they are extremely rigid and demanding in their standards.

Both types of Arians have a strong wish to find out what the future holds for them. The main reason for this is their inherent eagerness to see movement and change. As a result, they also have an uncanny knack of perceiving things and are quite often successful.

Arians often want to be looked upon with respect and admiration by their family members, friends, colleagues and even superiors.

As far as their love life is concerned, the men face some difficulties since they often misunderstand women and as a result, create problems for themselves romantically.

For both Arian men and women, the greatest high comes from the work they do and their ability to conquer hardships and difficulties.

The planet Mars, with its characteristics of courage, fire, and power is concentrated in this part of the zodiac. It is also referred to as the House of Exaltation of the Sun. Mars is also the traditional icon for War and Action and as a result, it is not surprising to see the combative tendency present in most Arians. They love to battle things out and hardly ever succumb to pressure. They enjoy the thrill of change and newness and hurdles are treated as mere stepping stones towards better avenues.

The temperament of an Arian is marked by optimism, vigour and courage. They refuse to be held down by the adversities of life and nearly always rise to the occasion. A word of caution is that if they truly wish to attain success, they should try to keep a check on their reckless nature. It is their naturally impulsive temperament that often puts them in the midst of undesirable action.

It will be incorrect for us to state that Arians do not think their decisions through. It is just that they get swayed in the heat of the moment and hence, act rashly. On the other hand, while it may seem contradictory, Arians are also extremely adept at organising and managing people and situations. They never hesitate to be innovative and deal with situations with practicality and sensibility.

Finance

Arians are ruled by the planet Mars and due to most of their inherent traits, they have the ability to make a good amount of money and earn a decent living. However, they also have the tendency to spend money in an equally flamboyant way. Although most Arians have exemplary organisational skills as far as people and situations are concerned, yet when it comes to financial management, they display an unusual amount of recklessness. They tend to plunge head on into schemes that seem promising even if they lack reason and logic.

Single-minded and unwavering, Arians display the same grit and willpower when it comes to accumulating their wealth and riches. However, there is no doubt about the fact that they will make higher profits by wise investments and sensible businesses than by relying on luck and fate.

April-born individuals have a tendency to be involved in court cases and disputes that may lead to court cases. While some of them may come out triumphant in such disputes, there may also be instances where fate may not favour them. Hence, it will be in their best interests to avoid getting embroiled in complicated and unnecessary arguments and conflicts.

Health

The intense impact of Mars on Arians can be seen in most of their health-related issues. Nearly all Arians are blessed with an intense amount of stamina and good health. However, this stamina can often prove to be their undoing since they might become workaholics and go overboard trying to do too many things at one time. As a result, most of the illnesses they suffer from are due to over-work and stress.

Their inherent stubbornness also often makes them somewhat prone to distress and discontent. This leads to some amount of annoyance and exasperation which brings about mental exhaustion and fatigue which could even lead to ulcers and stomach problems.

It is important for Arians to live in relatively serene and mild environments. Otherwise, they are prone to inflammatory infections and fevers. Regular exercise and proper diets have a beneficial impact. They should avoid indulging in alcohol or any sort of drugs, since with their temperament, a calming rather than stimulating influence is needed.

Owing to their restless nature and being constantly on the move, Arians nearly always wound or bruise easily. Also, the head is a particularly sensitive area and headaches, ear-aches, irritation in the eyes and such ailments are often a part of their lives.

Along with the head, the stomach, kidneys and liver are also prone to disorders resulting more from stress and work than from anything else. Surgery, for this sign, is somewhat inevitable at some point.

ARIES

Born on 1st, 10th, 19th, 28th

Individuals born on any of the above dates are influenced by the vibes from the Sun and Mars. This alliance is indeed, an influential one, which plays a significant role in attaining the goals and objectives so desired.

The dominant characteristics of Arians are felt earlier than normal in the case of those individuals born on these dates. Also, the individual generally has an immensely gifted imagination and does not hesitate to take a great number of risks in order to achieve a goal or desire. There is no doubt, that this individual can be fiercely ambitious and driven by a strong sense of purpose in everything they do. There are also strong chances that they will scale to great heights and achieve a high degree of fame and repute.

These individuals are more comfortable working independently, rather than as a member of a team or partnership. Rules, regulations and restrictions irritate them and they often try to find a way out of them rather than give in to them. As a result, they often have quite a few adversaries and some amount of obstacles in their path to success. Obstinate and determined, they are extremely appreciative if they are allowed to do things the way they please, however, if someone dares to oppose them, they could be quite harsh and relentless.

As far as family life is concerned, there will be instances where they might face problems with their children and also their partners. This could be owing to their stubborn temperament. However, they desire to be loved and cared for. They may face difficulties in being able to find a partner who will suit their tastes and preferences.

Nature holds a strong attraction for them. Spending time outdoors and involvement in a sport may help in keeping them energetic and happy. Hunting and guns are something that they should be wary of. It will be wise to protect oneself from the risk of car accidents.

Finance

When it comes to finances, people born on these dates will have to handle quite a bit of uncertainty. This will primarily be due to their recklessness in investing their money. However, in most situations, they will be able to get out and start afresh with renewed enthusiasm and energy.

Individuals born on these dates are gifted with inherent charisma and as a result are quite successful in selling ideas and views to the public. People will be drawn towards them and will willingly buy into their views and products.

Although, they possess the art of making money, they need to exercise prudence in making that money last. They need to be tactful and diplomatic so as to avoid hurting people in the process of attaining their goals.

Health

These individuals possess a lot of energy and resilience as well as a strong disposition. However, there are chances that they might ruin this blessing by overloading it with work and pressure. In fact, hypertension, heart problems and high blood pressure will be the greatest threats. It is advisable for these individuals to find a way to relax, unwind and enjoy life. Follow a regular exercise routine and a simple and wholesome diet. Avoid indulging in too much of alcohol and stimulants of any sort. Serenity and peace is essential.

Born on 2nd, 11th, 20th and 29th

Individuals born on any of the above dates are influenced by the vibes of the Moon and Neptune with Mars. This is a profound and complex alliance, the effects of which will be seen in their general personality and disposition.

These individuals are endowed with a complicated and strong personality. Although they are highly independent and indomitable, they are also greatly influenced by dreamy thoughts and idealistic notions. This is an example of the incongruity of their personality. In other words, they may have ground-breaking and thought provoking ideas which will have a tinge of creativeness and idealism in them.

It is not possible for anyone or anything to bind them down. They are free spirited, wanting to soar free and liberated through the world and life, in general. Their enthusiasm is contagious. It is advisable that they do not be too impulsive.

It is important that they learn to walk the tight-rope of reality and romanticism. Otherwise, chances are that they might have to face some hardships in their married or love life. There are also quite a few possibilities that marriage will not be quite a cakewalk for these individuals. It is essential that expectations are set in the very beginning of the relationship, to avoid unnecessary trouble at a later stage. Also, these individuals will need to learn to manage their feelings and decide to lead a settled life.

As far as career is concerned, those born on these dates do not want to be limited to one particular area of expertise. Moreover, their thirst for additional responsibilities will often end up making them look for alternate job opportunities to satisfy them.

In nearly every area, they are dominating, independent and authoritative. They stand out in a crowd and more often than not, have a strong inclination towards politics and the army. Even if they do not follow either one of these lines, they demonstrate their forcefulness in the way they carry themselves, speak or even write. If engaged in conventional areas of trade, business or industry, they are often appreciated for their unique, out of the box thoughts and there are strong chances that they might even reach the top of the corporate ladder at a young age. There are chances of excelling in the fields of writing and arts.

Finance

If born on the above mentioned dates, they will be quite prosperous in matters of money and wealth. However, the possibility will be more if self-employed, rather than in a partnership.

Health

Blessed with an inherently strong disposition, these individuals are energetic and full of life. Nevertheless, they have the tendency to tire themselves when extremely happy or charged up. Fevers and ailments of the blood will often be a cause of concern and the main reason for this is the tendency to stress oneself out. Regarding the parts of the body, the intestines will be a cause of concern. And, so will the mouth, teeth, gums, ears and sinuses. Surgery may be required for one or the other reasons.

It is essential that these individuals curb their reckless nature and in doing so, are able to protect themselves from mishaps and enmity.

Born on 3rd, 12th, 21st and 30th

Individuals born on any of the above-mentioned dates are influenced by the vibes from the planet Jupiter in addition to Mars.

They are gifted with a strong sense of authority and this aspect of their personality ensures that they succeed in nearly everything that they attempt to do. It will be somewhat beneficial if the tendency to dominate and dictate is curbed.

Extremely self-reliant and self-respecting, they do not enjoy being obligated to anyone. What these individuals truly enjoy doing is administering authority and control over others. As a result, they are often highly successful in fields of law and administration. The armed forces is also a suitable career choice for someone born on these dates.

Another career option might be the handling of high profile government posts, only because of the exceptional administrative skills these individuals possess.

These individuals are fortunate to have a circle of influential friends and acquaintances. However, their instinct to dominate at times earns them the enmity and envy of quite a few people. Irrespective of the amount of wealth and prosperity that they attain, they are generous and do not hesitate to help those who are in need.

Regarding home life, in all likelihood, they will want to be at the helm of all affairs. In other words, they want to be the figure of authority. It is essential that they remember that commanding respect is not the only important thing; they must earn the love and affection of their dear ones.

Although they are somewhat forceful and controlling, they are also in a strange way, liberal and progressive. These individuals always have the 'greater good' in mind when deciding on anything or anyone. Individuals born on these dates, also have extraordinary abilities to judge and evaluate situations and people correctly. They also possess a strong sense of equality.

There is a strong possibility that they are fortunate enough to be spared from mishaps, accidents and other unforeseen, unfortunate dangers.

Blessed with a taste for literary works, science and analysis, they spend quite a bit of time honing their already sharp mental skills and abilities. There is also a strong chance that they will be the trendsetters in whichever field they are engaged in.

Finance

In money matters, Arians born on the 3rd, 12th, 21st and 30th have quite a bit of luck. Due to their judicious nature, they will in all likelihood, be able to build a decent fortune for themselves. They will, at the very least, live a comfortable life and be well provided for.

Health

Arians born on the above dates have a strong and healthy physique. These individuals enjoy being outdoors. Sports and games will be a pastime. However, these individuals have to ensure that they play safe and do not get hurt by the roughness of some sports. Animals will also have to be dealt with caution.

Despite the fact that they have an inherently tough constitution, they might be prone to gastric disorders and may also put on weight due to irregular eating habits. In case they are susceptible to weight problems, they should be careful, especially around middle age, when these might lead to heart problems.

Born on 4th, 13th, 22nd and 31st

Arians born on the above-mentioned dates are influenced by the vibes from the planets Mars, Uranus and the Sun. This particular alliance is quite powerful and complex. As a result, the personality of these individuals is intriguing in a way that enables them to stand apart from the crowd.

These individuals have to undergo a reasonable amount of change and turmoil in life. This should not imply that life will be tough. On the contrary, it will toughen them up. Events that are unforeseen rather than forecasted will have to be dealt with. Destiny has a strong role to play here.

There will be a number of variations in the professional life. Changes in jobs and career lines are expected. Moreover, these individuals find it somewhat tough to find and keep loyal friends.

The friends that they have will be somewhat strange in character and habits. Opinions are creative and unusual.

Due to the fact that they are highly independent and unique, they often have many opponents and foes who try to disrupt their peace of mind and normal course of activities. Their belief in their significant principles and ideas tend to rub people the wrong way. However, this should not be a cause to demoralise. A positive spirit will always stand in good stead.

These individuals are gifted with a mechanical bent of mind. As a result, they often tinker around with machinery and electrical devices, such as the television, radio, stereos, etc.

Since they are extremely self-reliant and individualistic, they are not open to advice and suggestions from other people. They trust their own instincts and opinions. They have more faith in themselves as compared to the people around them. This has both positive and negative outcomes. Therefore, it will be advantageous if a proper balance is obtained.

Their strong views and tendency to support the losing side in an argument tends to put them in a difficult spot most of the times. Also, more often than not, they forget about diplomacy and state their verdict in a blunt and unconventional fashion. They could win themselves more admirers if they learn to use tact and consideration, so as to avoid hurting people's feelings and emotions. This will also ensure that people view them as more approachable and lovable.

Finance

In matters concerning finance and trade, they do well working on their own rather than when in partnership with others. They are also sensible and wise when handling money, as a result, ensuring that they always have a decent amount in savings and investments. Again, the element of balance has to be implemented, otherwise, they might be known as miserly people. Therefore, it is advisable to learn to balance saving with spending so as to enjoy all the benefits that life has to offer.

If engaged in a business, there will be an inclination to retire early and enjoy the savings.

There is an inherent tendency to brood too much about the future. It is imperative to realise that the past is gone; the future is yet to come and all that is there is today. It is, indeed, prudent to prepare for the future years, yet it should not be done at the cost of the present.

Health

Individuals born on these dates are a bundle of contradictions as far as health is concerned. There are times when they are filled with immense energy and enthusiasm and push themselves to the limit in terms of work and pressure. These will be alternated with occasions when they will be the picture of indolence and listlessness. Hence, it will be difficult to judge the disposition of these individuals.

Although they will mostly enjoy a healthy and fruitful life, there will be times when they will be affected with some vague and unknown illnesses. At these times, they should relax and enjoy quiet moments in the lap of nature and eat simple, nourishing food.

Born on 5th, 14th and 23rd

Arians born on the above dates are influenced by the vibes from the planets Mercury along with Mars. This distinct alliance can have both positive and negative influences since a lot depends upon the overall character and determination of these individuals. It is an alliance that can bring great fortune if used to the right advantage.

These individuals are gifted with a mind that is sharp and adaptable. They are intelligent, possessing a quick grasping power. It is essential that this intelligence is channeled in the right direction to derive the maximum benefit. In the conditions that it is used for good and noble purposes, their minds will be able to accomplish the most difficult of tasks and activities.

Orthodox thoughts and norms incite a spirit of rebellion and considering that these individuals possess an inherently independent mind, they should refuse to bow down to thoughts and ideas that have no logic behind them.

Individuals born on these dates are highly impressive. Their oration or writing skills could sway the masses and give them the popularity that they deserve. Reading and history holds a special fascination for these individuals. Therefore, it will not be surprising that these individuals are able to remember numbers, dates and facts with ease and precision.

Although these individuals often win the love and attention of those around them, as individuals, they are somewhat distant and cool in their behaviour. It will be advisable for them to bring more warmth into life, and to be able to express their emotions with sincerity and depth.

While they often have many friends, they might also have a fair amount of jealous opponents who could stand in their path to success. These people will not appreciate straightforwardness and candid temperament and will sometimes be an obstruction.

It will be immensely beneficial if these individuals are able to build their self-control and determination. This will enable them to achieve all that their heart desires and will lead to their ascendancy to a position of power and influence.

On the other hand, if they were to give into the temptations of life and let the weaker side of their personality take over, they might be prone to addictions and wastefulness. Therefore, it is extremely important that their intelligence and abilities be directed and used with care and prudence.

As far as marital relations are concerned, if these individuals were to learn the art of compromise and tact, they will have great happiness in their homes. If not, there are chances that these individuals may marry more than once and relationships on the domestic front will be strained and difficult.

Finance

As far as money matters are concerned, these individuals will, to a large extent, be the creators of their own fortunes. They will aim to succeed and more often than not, will prosper and flourish.

In the event that they lead a moral and righteous life, they will always have enough resources for themselves and their family. Their needs will always be met and they will have a comfortable life throughout.

On the other hand, if they have given into addictions and such, they will surely lose their money and possessions to these addictions of drinks, drugs, and gambling. Not only that, they might not even take advantage of the various opportunities that are presented to them. As a result, life will become difficult. Hence, it will be wise to adopt the higher path and enjoy the fruits of life, love and living.

Health

Since they are gifted with a mind that is constantly working, they will often tire it out. They should learn to still their thoughts and enjoy moments of calm and peace. These will refresh and rejuvenate them and prepare them to take on the hectic activities of daily life. If they do not do so, there is the chance that they will suffer from nervous illnesses, mental and physical exhaustion.

The digestive system will also be susceptible to problems such as acidity and indigestion as well as some other illnesses.

Born on 6th, 15th and 24th

Arians born on the above-mentioned dates will be influenced by the vibes from Venus along with Mars. This alliance is, indeed, a positive one and will bring harmony in the native's life.

Individuals born on these dates have benevolent and amiable temperaments as well as a strong passion and zeal for life in general.

Loving, expressive, intense and compassionate, they have a strong affinity for the opposite sex. They are quite sociable and enjoy the company of a wide circle of friends. Also, they are generous and willing to share all that they have with those who are deprived and needy. Charity and benevolence is innate in them. Their compassion and tenderness is aroused whenever they will see someone who lacks something that they are able to provide.

On the other hand, they also ensure that they too, have a comfortable and lavish lifestyle. They enjoy leading a life that has all the comforts in it and will also want to show off to their contemporaries and peers. There is also the slight danger that they may live beyond their means and this may lead to some difficulties. However, as long as they remember to provide for the future and not go overboard with generosity, there should not be too many problems in their path.

These individuals achieve success in creative fields such as music, poetry, writing, sculpture, painting, etc. Even the theatre and cinema appeals to them and they stand a good chance of making a name for themselves in that field as well.

As far as family and married life is concerned, they will in all likelihood, marry at an early age. As a result, they will have to make adjustments and use tactfulness in order to retain peace and harmony on the domestic front.

Since they are sociable and cheerful, they will enjoy the company of many friends, however, it will be wise not to waste too much time and money on friends. Devoting themselves to study and work will yield rich dividends. On the whole, maintaining a balance in everything is essential.

Distant places and foreign cultures intrigue these individuals and hence they enjoy travelling immensely and undertake many interesting and educative journeys.

Finance

When it comes to financial matters, these individuals are quite fortunate during their early years, which is when they will make the major chunk of life's earnings. However, owing to their lavishness and reckless spending, chances are that they might squander a fair amount of their hard-earned money. Therefore, it will be wise if they save some and spend some. On the whole though, they will have a well provided for life and will have access to quite a few luxuries of their time.

Health

These individuals are blessed with a strong constitution and hardly ever remain ill for too long. Also, they bounce back from any illness with renewed energy and enthusiasm.

However, they are prone to infections and illnesses of the respiratory system, the throat, nose and ears as well as headaches.

Born on 7th, 16th and 25th

Arians born on the above dates will be influenced by the planet Neptune, the Moon along with Mars. This is indeed, a unique combination and as a result, these individuals possess complex personalities and a life that is interesting and as unique as the alliance of the planetary influences themselves.

These individuals are enigmatic and this results in them being intrigued by spiritual, secretive and mysterious groups and clubs. Also, they have a keen interest in witchcraft, astrology, occult and the like.

They also have a creative side to their personality and this is reflected in their love for music. In fact, chances are that they will be proficient in playing a particular musical instrument as well. Also, their creative temperament is responsible for their interest in business endeavours which will have some innovation and imagination involved in it. If involved in mundane business, they will witness many variations and it is quite probable that they will have a life that will not be one with a set of routines, rules, and regulations.

Deep and passionate, their emotions are profound especially in matters of religion and society. They are not easily understood and their ideas are sometimes derided by other people. However, this does not matter to them in the least and they are proud to stand for what they believe in.

Also, the influence of Neptune makes their emotions stronger, yet they do not have a particularly materialistic view of life. What is more likely is that they will not be the ones to live a traditional, orthodox life.

These individuals have a keen interest in new and exotic lands and hence, spend quite a bit of time and money-making trips to such places and learning about them.

Due to their inherent restless and impatient nature, it is advisable that these individuals think through their actions before executing them.

There is also a strong streak of generosity in these individuals. As a result, they enjoy being involved with charitable institutions and societies.

One of the quirks attached to individuals born on these dates will be to either like or dislike people strongly without much reason. However, it will be beneficial to try and keep this habit in check, otherwise it will result in them getting misinterpreted.

Finance

These individuals will always face some amount of vagueness and ambiguity with finances. There will be lean periods followed by good times when some investments will pay off and bring in good fortune and prosperity.

It is important that all forms of gambling and risky ventures be avoided. Think carefully before investing in any schemes.

Health

Individuals born on these dates are endowed with a constitution that is as variable as their life, in general. They are the kind who will be affected with their environs. Therefore, it is important that they stay in cheerful and warm areas. Any overwork or stress on the body makes them susceptible to infections and tiredness. Also, the occasional colds, fevers, chills will bring them down every once in a while.

Born on 8th, 17th and 26th

If born on any of the above-mentioned dates, these Arians will be influenced by the vibes from the planet Saturn along with Mars. This particular alliance is not a highly positive one. Yet, it has its own unique benefits.

However, if they are born on the 26th of March, they will be influenced by the sign Taurus and the planet Venus. Therefore, they will have quite a few traits that are distinctly different from Arians born on the 8th and 17th .

Ambitious and driven, they will find that the path to success is not easy. Therefore, they will have to tackle these difficulties in order to prosper. They will also have strong bonds with their family and relatives. They might be put in the position of a provider before they are ready for it. However, this will make them more responsible and independent.

They are gifted with immense endurance, willpower and they ensure that they overcome all odds in order to reach their goals and aims.

As far as partnerships are concerned, both on the business and personal fronts, they have to work hard at being amicable and maintaining the peace. It will be beneficial if they do not rush into anything and wait for the right time and the right person.

They also have a gifted imagination and as a result, they have great ideas for business and entrepreneurship. It will take them sometime to find someone who will be able to match their imagination and foresight.

There will be people who think that they tend to be too lofty in their plans and ideas. However, considering the fact that they have exceptional strength of mind, fortitude, and endurance, they will be able to accomplish nearly everything that they set your mind to.

As far as materialism is concerned, individuals born on these dates are not very money-minded. However, they worry about the future. As a result, they might be cautious in the way they spend. People might even consider that they are miserly. But that is not the true picture.

Your tendency to accumulate also reflects in your habit to hold on to things, clothes and other possessions despite the fact that you hardly ever use them or even take them out.

As a person, they are happier on their own and tend to keep their distance from new acquaintances. They do not open up easily and take time to trust people.

Those Arians born on the 8th or the 17th of April are skilful and do very well in the fields of medicine, science, or any kind of line which needs administration.

For individuals who are born on the 26th of March, the influence of Taurus, which is the next sign, will be marked. As a result, quite a few of the above-mentioned features will be reduced in intensity by the influence of the planet Venus. Let us now discuss the traits that are unique to these Arians.

You are quite a fighter when they find that their path is obstructed. However, when the fight is over, they will be filled with remorse over their words and actions. Impatience is your key feature. They do not have much patience with others and are quick to lose their cool.

Since they are on the cusp of Taurus, they are quite fortunate when investing in land, real estate, property and the like. Everything that is linked to the planet Venus is beneficial for them and they could make a business out of perfumes, flowers, and the arts. As a matter of fact, music, poetry and painting will interest them and they might even have a flair for them.

There is also the possibility that they will be quite free with money and will enjoy spending it on comforts to surround their self. Life will be quite a happy affair and probably the one thing that they could work on is their stubbornness. Try listening to others and there is a chance that they might learn something new.

Independent and confident, they will be successful on their own and will manage to make the best of any situation, good or bad. Even tough times will not get them down; rather, they will battle out things and come out a winner.

Considering the planetary influences on their date of birth, the life that them lead will have its own uniqueness and many inconsistencies. Despite all that, they will be able to overcome odds and reach their goals.

Finance

These individuals have quite an advantage over others as far as determination and stubbornness are concerned. These two features benefit them in money matters. However, it might be somewhat tough for them to find partners who are able to keep pace with them.

In all likelihood, they will be responsible for their own success and will work best independently, either in a profession or in a business. This does not imply that they will not receive assistance from others. They will get help from many unexpected quarters; however, it will be they themselves who will eventually use the help in the right manner and create a financially secure present and future for themselves.

Health

For all Arians born on 8th, 17th or 26th, health is something that they don't have to worry much about. However, they might be prone to some unusual medical experiences. It will also be extremely beneficial for you to keep away from drugs and addictive substances.

By following a healthy diet and exercise regime, they will be able to take care of most things. Common ailments such as boils, skin allergies and infections, constipation, etc, will come and go.

As far as their dental health is concerned, they might have to get some surgery done. The throat, nose and ears might also give them some cause for concern.

On the whole, though, their health will be relatively be good and they are blessed with a strong constitution.

Born on 9th, 18th and 27th

All Arians born on the above-mentioned dates are influenced by the planet Mars except for those born on 27th of March, which is influenced by Venus, since it is on the cusp of Taurus.

They have a strong sense of self- reliance and are high on self-esteem. Moreover, they have an aversion to following rules and regulations of any sorts. They will, as a matter of fact, enjoy being different and unconventional.

Despite the fact that they are not someone who follows a routine, they somehow enjoy the life of the defense forces and chances are that they might even take it up as a profession. Also, since they are excited by the thrill of adventure, the idea of being on the war-front will send the adrenalin rushing through them.

Spontaneous and social, they are talkative and entertaining. However, it is important for them to get to know people well before they actually open up.

Impulsive and impatient, they want to rush head-long into things and at times, lose their temper with people who are unable to either understand them or keep up with them.

Since they are the kind who enjoy a good challenge or risk, there are chances that they might get involved in mishaps and accidents. So, it is advisable for them to think before they get into anything. They enjoy being outside and therefore nature, outdoor sports and anything that keeps them in the fresh air appeals to them. They also enjoy both playing and watching sports. These will be an outlet for all the energy that they have within them and also gives them a chance to learn more about team spirit and sportsmanship.

Their strong independence leads them to excel whenever they are working on their own. As a result, even professionally, they do better by being on their own, especially in business matters.

If they have inculcated the habits of teamwork early on, they find themselves quite popular in teams at work, since they are innovative and them willing to take risks.

There will be instances when they might over-indulge in drinks and such, however, this will only be when socialising and will not become an addiction; the reason being that they are smart enough to realise that it will become a hindrance in their path to prosperity.

In matters of the heart and romance, they have a charm that attracts members of the opposite sex to them and as a result, they will be the centre of attention. However, when it will come to marriage, it is important that they marry someone who is willing to compromise and adjust to their independent, rebellious temperament.

Finance

Arians born on the 9th, 18th and 27th are gifted with unusual financial skills. They have the ability to earn and make a profit from nearly every form of business, trade or job.

If they are born on any of these dates, they will find that their sense of independence ensures that they emerge from all difficulties as a stronger and wiser person. Their openness to danger and risk also assists they in making investments where others might not and hence, them stand to gain more.

There is no doubt about the fact that they like to speculate and hypothesise about financial situations. They easily and bravely get into deals based on their own instinct. For them, life is a gamble in which their win some and you lose some. On the whole, they find that fortune smiles upon them and their days will be well provided for. They will have a comfortable life and will enjoy all that they want to.

Health

Strong and healthy, they are blessed with a good constitution. Hence, they have a great deal of energy and enthusiasm, which enables them to take on a lot more than usual. Not only that, whenever they fall ill, they recuperate quickly and are on their feet in no time.

However, they are prone to disorders caused due to overwork and pressure, such as high blood pressure, hypertension, and anxiety. If they learn to relax and take things easy, these too will disappear.

Since they are adventurous in spirit, it is important that they learn to protect them from any mishap or injury that may occur during such endeavours.

TAURUS

(21ST APRIL TO 21ST MAY)

Taurus in General

The sign of Taurus, symbolised by the Bull, begins on the 19th of April and continues till the 20th of May. However, it attains complete strength only around the 26th of April, since before that it is preceded by the cusp of the previous sign. This sign is also known as the House of Venus (Positive). Taurus has many characteristics and hence, their lives are altered accordingly. We will go through the next few pages understanding the strength and the power of this sign and what is it that distinguishes this sign from all the rest.

Since the sign is one of the fixed signs of the zodiac, the features that it exudes are also fixed and solid. Determination, perseverance and stubbornness are just some of them. Taureans are noted for their ability to hold their ground and not budge till they get their way. Like the Bull, they are solid and steadfast.

Everything they do reflects this tendency of theirs. However, it may also be said that this sign has the predisposition of being somewhat paradoxical, especially in certain traits.

Most of the characteristics of the Taureans are similar to those of the Bull. Like the Bull, they are quite enduring, uncomplaining and determined. They set their eyes on what they want and then, steadily and slowly, move closer towards their goal. They also have a strong sense of faith in their abilities and hence, are pretty much self-motivated. Not the kinds to lose their temper quickly, they will however, be a force to reckon with when pushed against a wall. To see a Taurean enraged is one of the most daunting sights ever. They will amaze you with their force and latent power.

Known for being stubborn and 'bullish', they do not give in to anyone or anything easily. Even as children, they are extremely obstinate and do not budge from their stance. The only way they will change is when they feel the need to do so. It will be unfair for us to say that the Taurean can never change or adapt. They can, however, they just need a strong enough reason to do so. Once they see logic, they can be extremely flexible and malleable.

It is a fact that Taureans have immense stamina and strength. Whether they seem physically strong or not, is another question. However, they have the ability to take on a lot of pressure and stress and deal with it in an effective and resourceful manner. As long as they are unwavering and resolute, they are able to take on anything that life throws at them. Hurdles, obstacles, pressures and stress are all handled with capability and competence.

Taureans have the inclination to be fond of friends and family. They are in their element when in the company of friends and loved ones. Socialising and entertaining comes naturally to them. However, even if they have many friends, they only have a few intimate and close friends. These will be the people who will be allowed to see the real Taurean. Behind the solid façade, is someone who is gentle and tender, sensitive and intuitive. Creative and imaginative, they are able to make homes that are beautiful and inviting. They are also good cooks and enjoy taking care of their family. Everything they do bears an artistic touch. Even their clothes and overall appearance is appealing. They do not need money to create pleasurable surroundings and things. All they require is their own creative flair and a strong belief in themselves.

Irrespective of what section of society they belong to, Taureans have the knack of creating a perception about themselves. They are able to create an appearance and an appeal that is unique, but at the same time, fits in with any role that life has to offer them. Their imagination is truly fertile and they are able to yield beautiful results that help them to carve a niche in the larger fabric of society.

Despite the fact that they are known for the practicality and realistic approach to life, Taureans are also quite emotional and sensitive. They are loyal and devoted to those whom they consider their friends. However, they can be fiery and dangerous when crossed.

When in love, they are willing to do anything for their loved ones and are not scared to sacrifice anything for the person they truly care about. Hence, to say that a Taurean is incapable of change will not be true. They are open to change, provided they feel that they are doing it for a good cause. Taureans have the tendency to be possessive and overly protective about their partners. They are also known for their streaks of jealousy and the anger that comes with it. However, once they see their mistakes, they are willing to make up and apologise with grace and genuineness.

When arguing and fighting for their cause and convictions, they will do it with all fairness and will not be mean and sly. However, they are tenacious and will not rest till they get their due. They are not willing to give in and admit defeat simply because they are tired. If they believe in something strongly, they will keep on fighting till they have made their point. In all likelihood, they will win and earn more respect for themselves. Although they lose their temper and get angry, they are also extremely forgiving and are willing to mend relationships, provided they are convinced about the sincerity of the individual.

Taureans also have temperaments that are influenced by their surroundings. Therefore, when in unhappy and dismal environs, their spirits droop and they become despondent. On the other hand, when in a happy and cheerful atmosphere, they are at their energetic and enthusiastic best.

They possess all the qualities that make a leader. They are capable of putting in several hours of hard work and always try to take a fair and balanced approach. Moreover, they have a natural compassion for people in distress and always try to help out in some way or the other. It is not surprising that they often win the respect of their peers and the admiration of their subordinates. Even their superiors see the potential in them and are willing to support them in their journey to success.

Taureans, inherently, have a flair for maintaining balance and harmony in their lives and their environment. They are quite successful in a variety of fields and are able to bring a sense of solidity and stability to everything that they do, without being boring and dull.

It is quite a well-known fact that they have a strong, creative streak and are good at writing, poetry, drama and the like. Yet, they will not be able to cash in on these talents and make money out of them. They will go in for more conventional professions and will do well in them. Nursing, teaching, administrative jobs and positions of responsibility suit them well and they will create a name for themselves in their circle.

Finance

Taureans, in matters related to finance, are intelligent and sensible. They are able to make money in whatever field they are in. However, they are also quite generous and are willing to share their resources with those who really need it. They will also come into money through unexpected sources, such as marriage, inheritances, etc.

They also have the inclination to want money and have a lot of it. However, they will not be greedy or selfish about it. Like in most other things, they will be straightforward and upfront about it. The main reason why they want money will be to have a life that is comfortable and well-settled.

More Taurean women than men have an acumen for business and they will be quite good at generating profits and establishing a solid set-up. They also have the ability to organise and administrate affairs while at the same time, retain their creativity and sensibility. Even the Taurean man will be quite successful in business and administration. However, they could become too driven by profits and numbers and may lose focus of the goal.

Irrespective of their gender, Taureans will do well in a diverse range of fields and will be able to earn a good living for themselves and their family. They will do well in fields such as construction, management, real estate and similar businesses. They will also be able to climb up the ladder to success and create an impact when entrusted with positions where they get a chance to exhibit their diligence and conscientiousness.

Health

Since the Taureans are ruled by the planet Venus, they are fortunate to be gifted with plenty of strength, stamina and energy. They are able to take on a lot in life and deal with it without putting undue stress on their systems. Their enthusiasm for life and living is contagious and at times, reflects in a tendency to over-indulge in food, alcohol or similar substances. Therefore, it is of prime importance that they learn to make exercise and diet control an integral part of their lives.

They have somewhat of an inclination towards respiratory ailments and disorders of the reproductive and digestive system. Although their constitutions are equipped to cope with a great deal of stress, they should not push it to the limit and should try to take things easy every now and then. Moreover, too much of anything, including stress, is bad for health and increases their tendency to develop cardiac ailments as well.

They should also try and live in cheerful and vibrant surroundings, since their temperaments are most likely to be affected by their environment and the atmosphere that surrounds them.

Taurus

Born on the 1st, 10th, 19th and 28th

Taureans born on these dates are strongly influenced by the planet Venus and the Sun. This combination has several effects on their personality and enables them to make the most of the potential that being a Taurean endows them with.

Highly independent and artistic, they are able to bring their own special touch to everything that they do. All their ideas and plans are imaginative, yet realistic. They tend to think things through and do not jump into something recklessly or rashly. They always have the tendency to work their plans through and not just plan their work.

They are tender and empathetic and have a lot of patience with people around them. They are not the sort to lose their temper easily, however, when they get angry, they are formidable. In nearly every case, they lose their temper when they have to deal with slyness, cheating, dishonesty and such things. Even when people try and obstruct their progress by unfair means, they are unstoppable and will not tolerate anything.

Since they are meticulous in all that they do and also go out of their way to build relationships with people, they naturally do well in any professional field that they choose. They are a warm and compassionate person and a good friend, guide and advisor. They believe in standing up for their values and their friends. They are not scared of taking a firm approach when the need arises and it is important that people are not fooled by their calm and gentle demeanor.

They are known for lending a helping hand and are generous with their time and other resources. Also, they have strong attachments to family and others who have supported them during their difficult times. They are loyal and dedicated in their relationships. They also have a fondness for travel and exploration. However, they do it more from a relaxation point of view than an academic interest.

Their intelligence and wisdom is profound and not merely confined to bookish knowledge. They learn from their experiences and try and apply that knowledge to their daily life. It is this education that makes them a strong and more self-reliant person.

Finance

Taureans born on the 1st have the good fortune of being influenced by Venus and the Sun. As a result, in money matters, they are successful and fortunate. They have the ability to make money where others don't see potential and they make the most of their talents and skills. At the same time, they also have a fondness for living a comfortable and lavish life. If born into money, this will not be too much of a problem. However, if born in a modest society, they will need to work hard and long in order to achieve the lifestyle that they truly crave for.

Health

For them, health will be just as strong as everything else. They will be gifted with a robust constitution and plenty of energy and stamina, which will enable them to do much more than most other people. They radiate good health and liveliness. However, it is essential that they get a good amount of sleep and rest, so as to keep their body in the best condition possible. They have a tendency to contract colds and coughs easily. Therefore, they should try to keep building their immune system strong by taking good care of their chest and respiratory system.

Born on the 2nd, 11th, 20th and 29th

The vibrations of the planets Neptune and Venus, along with the Moon are critical in shaping their personality, if they were born on any of the above-mentioned dates. As a matter of fact, the effect of the Moon is stronger on their personality, since it is in the 'House of its Exaltation'.

Their personality and temperament is beautiful, idealistic and creative. They are able to weave artistic dreams and have the energy and the enthusiasm to realise those dreams. There are strong indications that they have an interest in studying the unknown and the inexplicable. Occult, astrology, mysticism intrigue them and they make attempts to understand them and master them. These subjects also play an important role in their life and its happenings.

Their love for beauty and creativity is seen in many facets; their home and appearance being one such dimension. They will want a home that is not only warm and inviting, but also pleasing to the eye. They have an inherent flair for creating beauty and aesthetically pleasing environments. Their temperament is affected by their surroundings; therefore, they strive to maintain balance and tranquillity all around them. They function at your best when in a harmonious and peaceful environment.

They have a fondness for the arts, music, painting, literature and similar fields. Whether they take them up professionally is not essential, however, they have an interest in them and often turn to them for recreation and relaxation.

There is a seemingly strong undercurrent of restlessness in their personality. They often get tired or bored of the same place or situation and crave for change and newness. It is this desire for novelty that motivates you to travel and explore the world. Even if they lack the resources of time and money for travelling, they try and sate the desire by reading about places. However, if they have the resources, they will spend a great deal of their time, money and energy in seeing the world and the wonders it has to offer.

Their inclination for change also reflects itself in their desire to change houses as often as possible. Again, this particular occurrence depends on their circumstances. Given a choice, they will not want to spend their entire lifetime in the same house. Another advantage of having such a temperament is their ability to adjust to new people and surroundings with ease and comfort. As a result, they have a wide and diverse social circle and are able to mingle with people from all walks of life.

Sociable and warm, they enjoy entertaining and being in the company of friends and loved ones. They thrive on good humour, food and overall, a good life. There could also be times when they do not want the hustle-bustle of too many people around them. However, these instances serve as welcome breaks.

Compassion is another dominant feature of their personality. They are touched by the sadness and misery of another person and try to do everything to alleviate the same. However, it will be better for their emotional health if they learn to discriminate between genuine and fake sorrow. This should not be too much of a problem, since they are blessed with astute perception and are able to make accurate judgments and react appropriately.

They often enjoy a life of comfort and have an inclination to over-indulge in certain pleasures. Therefore, it is advisable for them to practise moderation in everything that they do, so as to derive greater satisfaction from all that life has to offer.

Finance

Finance, for them, is quite an interesting subject. They experience several ups and downs in money matters. However, they have the strength to be able to endure everything and also to make the most of the good times. If they are able to keep a control on their tendency to splurge, they will be able to save quite a lot and hence, provide for a comfortable future.

Professionally, they do well in most fields, since they have the aptitude for hard work. Intelligence and diligence will pay off and they will be able to earn a comfortable living for themselves and their family.

Health

Although they have a strong constitution and immune system, they have to protect themselves from common ailments such as colds, coughs and respiratory infections. They may also have a tendency to contract sinus infections. Other than that, they are at their very best in surroundings that appeal to their senses and give a sense of balance. Discord and disharmony jars their senses and makes them feel despondent and sad.

Born on the 3rd, 12th, 21st and 30th

It is the influence of Venus along with Jupiter that will change their personality so that it stands apart from all the other Taureans born on different dates. Certain features are enhanced while others are played down. This planetary alliance is special and it brings prosperity into their life, as long as they keep a close watch on the Venusian side of their personality.

The presence of Jupiter endows them with a strongly ambitious temperament, and it should be their earnest endeavour to express this ambition and use it to motivate them to achieve great things. They have a strong inclination to socialise with people who are of a higher status than themselves; the reason behind this being that they want to be part of a circle of people that they aspire to be like. With their ambition, this will not be a problem.

They have a strong sense of balance and fairness and always try to do what seems right to them. There is always the possibility that they will support worthy causes and bravely stand up for their convictions, even if it means that others will disapprove of them or not support them. They are also quite unconventional and original in the way they think. Therefore, their opinions on religion and other such matters are different from others. As a matter of fact, they have their own definite way of life.

They are steadfast in everything that they do and have a strong willpower. In fact, in certain things, they are stubborn and do not want to see any other viewpoint than their own. As far as relationships are concerned, they are loyal and will probably find a suitable life partner early on. However, they need to learn to make adjustments and compromises in order to have a successful and stable marriage. There are possibilities that they may fall in love more than once before they finally marry.

It is the influence of Venus that endows them with an idealistic, creative temperament. They will do well in music, arts, literature and will be able to take the limelight with grace and ease. Venus also endows them with a romantic nature and that accounts for their attractiveness and appeal for the opposite sex.

Everything they do bears their own stamp. Their social life includes people from varied fields. Consciously or subconsciously, they try and interact with people who belong to a stratum above their own. They always want to rise above and be someone famous and prosperous. So strong is they ambition that they will devote themself to this purpose and focus on it all the time. Therefore, it is no surprise that they succeed and do well.

Generosity is something that is close to their heart and they try and support the needy and the worthy whenever and however they can. Even if they lack the money, they try and give their time and energy to such people and organisations. It will only be a matter of time before, they become known for their work and efforts. Life for them is a constant journey for improvement and growth. With their persistence, drive and focus, there will be little difficulty in their achieving all of this and much more.

Finance

Overall, they have a planetary combination that is fortunate and this is reflected even in their financial affairs. Therefore, they do not have to worry too much about money and investments. Since they are open to working hard for their goals, their efforts will surely pay off and they will be able to achieve a life that they want. It is advisable for them to stay away from speculation and gambling, since they will not bring great returns to them. They have the knack of making the most of opportunities and hence are able to gain from the most unexpected sources.

Health

They are blessed with good health, energy and stamina. During their childhood, they may be perceived as weak or ill; however, they gain in strength with age. They have good resistance and are able to recover from most illnesses with speed and ease. The one thing that they need to guard themselves against is too much work and stress. In all likelihood, they place too much pressure on achievement and forget rest and relaxation in the process. Therefore, stress-related disorders could become a bane for them. Also, their lungs require some attention and care.

Born on the 4th, 13th, 22nd and 31st

Taureons born on any of the dates given above, are strongly influenced by the planets Venus, Uranus and the Sun. This alliance is indeed, unusual and therefore indicates that their life will be filled with surprising and unconventional experiences.

They will have a life that will be different, to say the least. Nothing that they do will have the stamp of the usual and ordinary about it. In most aspects of life, they will opt for the offbeat and unusual. They find it interesting to experiment and explore. They also have an intelligent and sharp mind that comes up with creative and original ideas and thoughts. As a result, they do well in fields such as drama, philosophy, writing and similar areas. There are strong indications that they will do well in unconventional fields, however, everything that they do bears their unique, individual touch and appeals to those of a similar thought pattern.

They are always prepared for change and that is probably the reason why they will do well in crises and emergencies. Their true strength and mettle shines through in such times. They are not fazed by difficult times. Firm and committed, they stand up for their beliefs and do not waver from the goal. Since they are confident, there are chances that they could be somewhat obstinate and even critical or judgmental of others.

Since they are so often unusual and unconventional, there are chances that they might find it difficult to find friends and acquaintances that are of the same wave length as them. Therefore, they have a select and small circle of close friends who are able to understand and accept their quirks and eccentricities. As far as marriage is concerned, they will have an unusual marriage in the eyes of other people. However, the views and opinions of others do not make a difference to them. They believe in doing that which they feel is right and they have the strength to stand on their own.

They are not afraid of voicing their views and they support whatever they feel is right and feel strongly for. There could be instances where they may not be too vocal but still manage to get their point across in a way that is firm and yet discreet.

Adjusting to others is something that is not easy for them. They are resolute and only believe in themselves. As a result, compromising does not come naturally to them. However, when they have a strong enough reason, they are willing to make a change and do so with grace and dignity. They carry themselves with a certain charm, without being aloof and snobbish. In fact, they are thought of as a warm yet quirky individual with a strong mind of his or her own.

They take life as it comes. Planning every single move and action is not their cup of tea. They enjoy uncertainty and gladly take the good times with the bad times.

Finance

The streak of unusualness is reflected even in their financial life. They come into money through unusual sources and even their professional line will not be something that is deemed as traditional or ordinary. Even if they do take up a traditional profession, such as teaching, the circumstances will not be ordinary. However, they will always have a life that has all the comforts in it. Even if they have to struggle during their initial years, they will be able to enjoy the benefits later on. Their mind is filled with creativity and expresses itself in various ways. This will bring them success and prosperity and make their life complete and fruitful.

Health

Although they have a strong disposition, they are prone to vague and mysterious ailments, which will be difficult to diagnose and treat. However, nothing will be too serious. Aches and pains, cramps in the stomach, colds, coughs and fever will be the most common ailments. If they keep a check on their diet and exercise, they will be able to combat most ailments and keep them at bay.

Born on the 5th, 14th and 23rd

The effect of Mercury along with Venus (Positive) molds and alters their personality, if they were born on any of the dates given above. This particular alliance is favourable and constructive as far as their intelligence and mental development is concerned.

They are gifted with a sharp and perceptive mind that is able to pick up the finest nuances and grasp the most complex of concepts. They are able to rationalise and argue with logic, however, they also have the tendency to be somewhat critical and judgmental of others. They have the ability to observe people and situations with great insight and depth.

Although they are self-reliant and high on confidence, they also possess the ability to adjust and adapt to various situations and people. They are open to change, as long as it has some goodness in it. They know the art of being able to maintain their identity without being difficult or uncompromising. They have strong views on subjects such as religion, politics and money. However, they listen to other's views as well and then decide for themselves if what they say holds more weight than their own views. They are not the sort to reject another opinion or view, simply because it differs from their own.

They are sensitive and perceptive without being overly emotional. They do not get unduly attached to things and people and as a result, are always open to new places, people and professions. At the same time, they have a respect and regard for relationships and do their best to nurture and nourish them. This brings us to the question of their marriage. They will, most likely, want to marry early in life. However, this will depend on whether or not they find the right person, someone who will understand and accept their intelligence and uniqueness. While they will be drawn towards the opposite sex, they will also not want to be tied down. Hence, they may have to make adjustments and changes when married.

Influenced by Mercury and Venus, they have a keen mind and agile body. They also enjoy travelling and if they have the resources, they will spend a great deal of time and money on travelling to lands far and near that will help them to sate their curious nature and also widen their perspective of the world around them.

Professionally, they will succeed in virtually any field as long as they are fascinated by it and gain enough mental and financial benefits from it. Since they are adaptable and flexible, as well as intelligent, they will be comfortable doing just about anything.

Finance

They can be quite a bundle of contradictions in terms of money matters. Even they, themselves, will not be able to understand their financial situation, most of the times. They will make money through unusual sources and will be quite fortunate in profiting from assets, such as land, house, and stocks and shares. If they opt for a profession that is unconventional and different, they have strong chances of greater prosperity and fame than otherwise.

Health

As far as health-related matters are concerned, they will be prone to suffering from nervous ailments and injuries to the facial structure. However, nothing is too serious for them and they will be able to recuperate with strength. They need to take special care of their teeth, jaws and bones of the head. The reproductive system is also delicate and needs special attention. If they follow a good diet and exercise regimen, they will be able to keep most illnesses and injuries away.

Born on the 6th, 15th and 24th

If they were born on any of the dates given above, they will be influenced by the combined effects of the Moon and the planet Venus. This particular combination enhances the sensitive, idealistic aspects of their personality. They have a strong affinity for fellow-human beings and even for nature and animals. In either case, their attachment to mankind and nature is strong and prominent.

They are strongly attached to people and all those things which play a dominant role in their life. They have a passionate and emotional temperament and in order to fulfil the emotional side of their personality, they are willing to do just about anything. They also have a high amount of energy and enthusiasm and view life with eagerness and optimism.

They are ruled by their feelings and sentiments. They may even have a strong spiritual side and have an unwavering faith in a Superior power. Even though they may seem fragile, they have great strength and do not hesitate in taking firm steps to realise their goals and ambitions. Whether they realise them using force or quiet strength remains to be seen. However, the bottom line is that if they believe in something strongly, they will go for it and give it their one hundred per cent.

They have a wonderful combination of strength and weakness in their personality and are able to make the most of both. Since they have the essential traits of Taurus and the specific features that Venus endows on them, they have a personality that is unique and they are capable of great things.

The backbone of their character is their emotions. They either love or hate someone and do so with passion. None of their feelings can be termed as moderate or lukewarm. In fact, emotionally, they are at their best or their worst, without even realising it. This is good when pursuing a goal or ambition. However, this intensity could create some problems in relationships. They could become extremely possessive and hence, stifle their partner completely. Therefore, while it is good for them to be passionate, they should maintain some balance and keep a control on their feelings.

One thing that should be noted here is that once they are convinced about doing something, no one and nothing can stand in their way. They leave no stone unturned in attempting to bring about change. Though this kind of passion is admirable, it is advisable for them to devote their energy and sentiments to noble, lofty ideals and not get swayed by anti-social elements. Their efforts will not go unnoticed and they will be rewarded socially.

Creative, idealistic and sensitive, they are deeply moved by natural beauty and simplicity. Their home and surroundings reflect their creative temperament and will be warm, inviting and comfortable. Music, painting and literature find a place in their life and will comfort them whenever they are feeling sad or lonely. They are sociable and amiable. Making friends comes easily to them and they enjoy entertaining and organising get-togethers and celebrations. They often get along better with members of the opposite sex; however, the relationships will be mainly platonic and will not become serious, unless they will want them to take that direction.

Marriage and children will be one of their priorities and they will devote their energy and efforts to make a success of these relationships. They are loyal and dependable and support their partner with faithfulness and dedication. Children also have a special place in their life and they shower their love, attention and time on them.

One of the best things about them is their ability to remain youthful and energetic for the maximum part of their life. Their good humour and ability to look at the positive side of life always account for their high energy levels and stamina. Life for them should be lived with passion and enthusiasm with a fair amount of optimism thrown in for good measure.

Finance

Financial matters will not worry them too much. They will often come into money or will be able to make the most of the opportunities that come their way. Whether they go into a business or a profession, they will be able to succeed and make great profits from both. While they are able to do well in most professions, they will do exceedingly well in those which tap into their creative potential and let them explore their aesthetic sensibilities. They will do well in businesses and professions that are related to clothes, luxuries, perfumes, food, and such areas. Another facet of their personality will make them a success in fields of teaching, writing, drama and similar lines.

Health

They are gifted with a sound disposition and a robust temperament that will be able to withstand a lot of stress and strain. However, owing to their fondness for good food and life, they will bring illnesses on themselves. They need to make conscious lifestyle changes in order to enjoy good health for the rest of their life. In all likelihood, they will have a slim physique; however, if they do not keep an eye on their diet, they could harm it and take it in the opposite direction.

The usual ailments will not harm them as much as their tendency to splurge on an easy life and good food. Heart disease and liver problems could mar their well-being in later years and they will also need to take special care of their respiratory system.

Born on the 7th, 16th and 25th

Number seven Taureans are influenced by the radiations from the planets Venus, Neptune and the Moon. This combination of planetary influences brings about a softer, philosophical orientation in their personality. At the same time, they retain the fundamental Taurean traits and are able to use all of them to achieve all that they want from life.

They are fascinated by the unusual and the unknown. Astrology, occult, mysticism, all have a special place in their life and even if they do not take them up professionally, they will still be deeply interested in them. Their perceptive skills will be remarkable and they will be able to make relatively accurate judegments about people and situations.

Intelligent and keen, they will have the knack of coming up with creative, offbeat yet productive ideas that will be appreciated and recognised. They may also have a mechanical bent of mind and will be able to do well with wireless systems, radios, televisions. They will also have a fondness for novelty and hence, will get bored with routine and humdrum things. They will not want to be bogged down with the same things day in and day out. That is the reason they will want to change professions, residences or relationships.

Their intelligence and creative temperament will make them a success in fields such as writing, teaching, painting, music, science and research. Even management and administration will suit them and they will be able to succeed in them.

They will be generous and tender at heart. If they have the resources, they will want to devote them to helping the needy and weak. They are moved by sadness and sorrow in the lives of other people and will sincerely want to make a difference to them. They are not the sort to be pleased with the usual comforts and will often get pleasure from unusual sources. Their originality and individuality will be their trademark. As a result, they will make friends with people who understand and accept their point of view.

As far as marriage and children are concerned, they should probably wait till they meet the right person; one who will be able to accept and acknowledge their independence and individualism. Once they find the right person, they will be a devoted and loyal partner with a gentle yet passionate nature. Marriage will mean commitment and sacredness to them and they will sincerely give it their hundred per cent. However, it will be important that they are compatible with their partner and are happy with the choices they made. That is why, it will be better if their take they time in settling down.

They will go through the journey of life with a maturity that will belie their years and at the same time, will have the spontaneity and enthusiasm that will be infectious and charming. They will be able to create a balance between the two dimensions of their personality and will use their talents and potential to create the best outcome.

Finance

There are indications that they will have to work hard during the start of their professional life. However, they are intelligent and sincere and nothing can stop them from reaching the goals they've set for themselves. They will be able to earn a good income and will also win a reasonable position for themselves in society. They have more faith in their own abilities than in luck or fate. That is one of the reasons why they will tirelessly work for their dreams and aspirations and will also be able to realise them. It is important that they invest their money with care and take the guidance only of trusted sources.

Health

While they will be keen to work hard for their aims and dreams, chances are that they will not be extremely strong and will get exhausted every now and then. That is the reason they should take breaks and relax every once in a while. Their mental strength will be greater than their physical strength and their nerves will be in a better position to withstand stress and strain. It will be favourable for them to take good care of their diet and rest routine, especially since their digestive and intestinal system will be prone to infections.

It is also advisable to surround themselves with positive and cheerful elements since their moods will be deeply influenced by their environment. To lift their spirits, they should indulge in meditation and exercise and stay away from all sorts of drugs, stimulants and such things. If they manage to keep a watch on their diet and also not tire themselves out physically, they will remain in relatively good shape and will lead a fruitful life.

Born on the 8th, 17th and 26th

The planetary combination of Venus, Saturn and the Moon is responsible for modifying and shaping their personality, if they were born on any of the dates given above. This particular combination is potent and will endow them with a life that will be filled with interesting and unique occurrences.

In their life, the Hand of Fate will be relatively important and a great deal will be dependent on chance, luck or fortune. While they possess the ability to make or mar their life by virtue of their own efforts, fate plays a dominant role in determining the circumstances of their life. They will be someone who will have either extremely good fortune or the complete opposite. However, it is important to remember that nothing is forever. So, if they are experiencing some ill-luck today, it will be followed by good fortune tomorrow.

They have a personality that will be influenced by Venus and Saturn. The presence of Venus indicates that they have a temperament that will want affection, love and gentleness. They are thoughtful and often, suppress their own desires for the sake of those they care for. However, chances are that they may not feel secure in those relationships; rather they will feel ignored, neglected or alone. It will be as if all that they do is not being reciprocated. The best thing for them to do in such cases will be to spend some time alone and introspect and reflect on their life and what can be done to better it.

They should not think that all their relationships will be the same. They will enjoy the warmth and love of some close and wonderful relationships which will add greatly to the quality of their life. Temperamentally, they are insightful, thoughtful and will often like to be alone rather than in the company of people. They enjoy solitude and will use it to better themselves and also to focus on their goals in life. They are focused and will be driven by a deep desire to improve their standing in society. Irrespective of the background that they are from, they will wish to rise higher.

They are not the sort who like to blow their own trumpet; rather they like their achievements to speak for themselves. They often, win the admiration and respect of those around them and even though they may seem too mature for their age, they still have a childish innocence about many things.

Adaptable to an extent, they believe in standing up for what they feel is right and at the same time, will be open to listening to others and evaluating their point of view. They are firm and decisive and even if they do take time in arriving at a decision, they will do so with thought and caution. Professionally, they will do well in fields that suit their train of thought and that are not temporary or fickle. They believe in opting for more traditional occupations rather than unconventional ones, simply because they are not sure about their reliability.

Nearly everything that they do will be out of emotion and feeling. They are often, swayed by their sentiments and then will have to rethink their actions. While this is not a bad approach, they should also try and incorporate more practicality in their life. Being realistic about people and situations will help them to cope better with the ups and downs of life, particularly since in their life, fate will play a strong hand.

Finance

They are able to make maximum profits by adopting a strategy that is sound, solid and judicious. Speculation, risk-taking and the like do not suit their financial affairs. They will benefit from investing in or adopting professions that are safe and secure rather than speculative and risky. They also benefit from investing in real estate, land and mining industries.

Health

They are gifted with a constitution that, like their temperament, is strong and stable. They are able to take on activities of physical endurance with ease and are also in a better position to handle stress and strain than most other individuals. However, they will be somewhat prone to respiratory and digestive ailments. Their joints may also give them some problem and living in a dry, moderate climate will suit them better.

If they will increase their level of physical activity, they will be able to keep away most illnesses and will also increase their own energy and stamina levels.

Born on the 9th, 18th and 27th

The planetary vibrations of Mars, Venus and the Moon are responsible for creating distinctions in their personality and setting it apart from other Taureans born on different dates. This particular combination is strong and powerful. It will have far-reaching effects on their personality and life, making it an exciting and action-packed one. All the elements of thrill and adventure will be present in their life and will give it an edge over all their other counterparts.

They are gifted with a personality that has an immense amount of strength, determination and bravery invested in it. It is dependent on their background and circumstances to see whether these powerful traits are used for positive things or not. However, in all likelihood, they will have a life that will be shaped by their own personality greatly and therefore, there are strong chances that they will use their talents and potential for the good of humanity.

They have a flair for managing people and situations. Administration will come naturally to them and they will do well in emergencies and crises. They are high on ambition and have great hopes and aspirations. They are driven by a deep desire to do well and succeed at all costs. Building wealth and acquiring a name for themselves will be some of their strongest wishes. The best part is that they will have such strong willpower that anything they want will be theirs, provided they put in the effort and hard work for it.

The influence of Mars endows them with a fiery temper and they often, lose it with people who try their patience too much. They should try and keep a rein on their anger and not let it cloud their usually accurate judgement and thinking. Their perceptive skills are astute and sharp and enable them to think and act in a rational yet sensitive manner.

It will be wrong of us to assume that they are cold-hearted, ambitious persons. They have a sensitive side and are influenced by feelings and emotions. However, they do not let them rule their thinking completely. They try, as far as possible, to maintain a practical, realistic approach to life. Their relationships have warmth and closeness in them; yet, they will not let them become a hindrance in their path to success.

Since they will have a straightforward and candid demeanor, there could be people who will not appreciate this frankness and hence will take a dislike to them. Nevertheless, they are not bothered by the opinions of others and continue to support what they feel is right. They are not afraid to voice their views and opinions with strength and courage. They are willing to face hurdles and overcome them in order to reach their goals. One thing that is for certain is that once they make up their mind, there is nothing that could stop them.

They have an inexplicable attraction for members of the opposite sex and will often have many close friends from that group. However, they are relatively sensible when making a decision about marriage and try and ensure that they settle down with a partner who suits their temperament and personality; someone who will be able to accept and understand their ambitions and strength of mind and character.

They are sharp and are able to see through plans and strategies. They do not merely live in the present but also believe in planning for the future. Also, their love for thrill and risk-taking motivates them to try out everything that is new and interesting. They are fond of travelling and spending a great deal of time outdoors in fresh air and with nature.

Finance

Their determination and diligence is responsible for helping them to accumulate wealth and building up their reserves for the future. They should keep a close eye on expenditure and try to balance it out with income. Their people management skills and their flair for administration will enable them to earn a comfortable living and if they develop the art of diplomacy, they will be able to do well in nearly all professional and business fields.

Even though, they may have to face opposition, hurdles and enmity, they are able to overcome all of these and reach their path in a successful and prosperous manner.

Health

As far as health is concerned, they are blessed with an energetic and strong physique which will be able to take on a great deal of stress and strain. They have the ability to endure long hours of hard work and still be able to take on more. They need to guard themselves against injuries to various body parts, such as the facial bones, jaws, arms and legs, and also stay away from fire and explosive substances.

Other than that, they will have a healthy and fulfilling life, as they will spend quite a bit of time outdoors and if they keep a check on their diet and rest routine, they will have everything taken care of.

GEMINI

(22ND MAY TO 21ST JUNE)

Gemini in General

Gemini, symbolised by the Twins, is a sign that is famous for its duality of temperament. Over here, we will explore this aspect in detail and understand its real nature, as well as get to know more about Geminis born on different dates. The sign begins on the 21st of May; however, it gains complete power and influence only around the 28th of May. From this date, it retains its potency till the 20th of June, from which date onwards, it starts to lose its influence to the incoming sign. The period of seven days preceding and following these dates is known as the 'cusp'.

They are affected by the influence of the Sun and the planet Mercury. Therefore, it is not surprising that they will be extremely mercurial in their behaviour and disposition. Their intelligence is razor sharp and their temperament is mysterious, complicated and an enigma to most people. They are also fickle and hence, will be inclined to change their ideas, feelings and even themselves, at the drop of a hat.

Mercury is known as the 'planet that rules the mind', therefore, it essentially endows the individual with a sharp mind. However, what is important is how that intelligence is applied and utilised. There are strong chances that Geminis will have a keen interest in literature, music, science, arts and similar lines. In this case, the individual will be focused and will achieve excellence and success in all endeavours.

Gemini has for long been considered one of the most complex signs to understand. Geminis are gifted individuals and are bestowed with sharp, adaptable brains. They tend to be quick witted and are so sophisticated in their ideas that they can outrun almost any one, mentally. Sometimes, they even surprise themselves with their intellect and astuteness.

The duality of the Gemini is something that even they themselves do not really grasp or understand. Perhaps, because they really are not convinced that they have a dual nature. They, on the contrary, have a firm belief that they are steadfast and loyal at any point of time. However, for them, the point of time is what really changes. There is no doubt about the fact, that Geminis can be extremely charismatic and warm individuals, who will often be the life and soul of any social gathering. They will charm people with their conversational skills and will be able to mingle with everyone, irrespective of all differences.

However, one should always remember that it is very difficult to bind a Gemini down and hold him to his promises. The only way or time when they will stick to their word is when they will feel that it is right to and not when anyone else will want them to. In this regard, they are often perceived to be somewhat selfish. Yet this will not be true, since they will very frequently be generous and giving souls.

They are humorous and sometimes cynical or even sarcastic. They have the ability to understand anything instantly and figure out the most complicated of puzzles. Any riddle that life may throw at them, they will be able to deal with. This will be their strength and their chief characteristic. It is rare to come across a Gemini who lacks in mental quickness and sharpness.

Geminis are persistent and focused on their goals. They know exactly what they want from life and how will they go about achieving that. Once they set their mind to something, they will not rest till the time they are able to accomplish and realise their dreams and aspirations. They have charming personalities and anyone who comes in contact with them will be struck by their graciousness and their suave nature. It is not surprising that they often become role models for their subordinates and even their peers. Irrespective of what social background they are born in, Gemini, through sheer willpower will be able to cultivate in themselves with the social graces and sophistication of the elite.

Considering their personal traits as well as their inherent intelligence, Geminis often make great diplomats, scientists, doctors, inventors and even businessmen. They know how to conduct themselves in society and win over people with their tact and charisma. Also, they have an in-depth idea of how to make the most out of investments and innovations. It is important that they be involved in professions where both their mind and their personality are catered to, otherwise they will become extremely dissatisfied and disillusioned.

They are loving and generous when in the company of friends, however, they have a tendency to forget people once they are out of sight. They are compassionate and sympathetic to those in distress and will help out selflessly. Yet, they will not remember important things simply because they don't want to. The irony of the situation is that the Gemini will never do something deliberately. There is not a single malicious bone in their body, yet they are perceived to be thoughtless by those close to them.

Geminis will always want to explore and see new destinations and places. Meeting people from foreign lands and learning about new cultures fascinate them and if they are rich and have the time, they will most definitely travel and see the world. Travelling will widen their perspective and enrich their knowledge. It will also act as a salve for their excitable and impatient nerves. They have a special fondness for anything that is fast and rapid. This includes means of transportation as well.

Their desire for change and newness will also be reflected in their thoughts and views on life. These too, will evolve and undergo many variations during the course of their life. They could endorse one thing at one time and a diametrically opposite view at yet another instance. This is yet another feature that leads to them being perceived as dual or 'two-faced'.

They are also extremely moody. There will be times when they will be extremely happy and these times will be followed by periods of intense gloom and sadness. Even in matters of love and romance, they are equally fickle. If they change their opinion or sentiments about someone, they will wipe that person out of their lives, forever. Not only that, their dual personality will allow them to love one person deeply and at the same time, adore another. They will, in all likelihood, manage to justify this to themselves and even to others.

As far as career aspirations and ambitions are concerned, they will at times give up everything just because they lose interest in it. For them, it is more important to be intellectually stimulated than successful. Not that they will compromise success in the long run. They will be so intelligent and talented, that they will normally choose professions which will continue to interest them for a long, long time.

Repetitiveness tires them mentally. They always want to do something exciting and thrilling that will keep their gray cells ticking and busy. Risks, adventures, anything that will break the dullness of everyday life appeals to these enigmatic creatures.

Considering the fact that they will be efficient, charismatic and intelligent, it is not surprising that they will often be the centre of attention in their professional and personal circles. They will be resourceful, enthusiastic and creative. If they work on strengthening their willpower and resolution, they will be able to achieve success and prosperity in next to no time. Once they are sure about what they want, life will be a cakewalk for them.

Finance

Just as the Gemini personality is difficult to understand, so are their financial conditions. Depending on what they apply their mind to, Geminis can achieve both fame and financial prosperity.

In either case, they will be able to earn a great deal of money and if they have the inclination, they will even be good at saving a fair amount for their retirement. They will be able to build a reasonable fortune for themselves and at the same time, will have enough to enjoy the luxuries and comforts of life. However, this will be possible only when they apply their minds and exercise their determination. If they adopt a laidback attitude, chances are that they will fritter away whatever resources they have.

Since Geminis have the tendency to be somewhat self-critical, they need to be on guard against excessive risk-taking and investing in get-rich-quick schemes. However, they also have times when they will tire mentally and this will lead to a break in the efforts that the Gemini will make to earn and make money. This could lead to some uncertainty of finances.

It is vital that Geminis learn to save from an early age and continue to do so, even in times when they seem to have an excess of money. It will be this habit that will stand them in good stead during lean times.

Health

For Geminis, the influence of Mercury will bring about certain peculiar features in their health and disposition. They will be more prone to mood swings and this will affect their state of health. When happy and cheerful, they will be in the best of health and when sad, they will suffer from mysterious and vague illnesses.

Since they live by their nerves, most of the time they will often tire themselves out and become exhausted. That is the reason they will need to take frequent breaks and rejuvenate themselves. If they don't do that, chances are that they will suffer from hypertension, depression and other such stress-related disorders. They should ensure that they get plenty of fresh air, sleep, and wholesome food. Simple things like these will keep them healthy and strong enough to face the world and its challenges.

GEMINI

Born on 1st, 10th, 19th and 28th

Geminians born on the above-mentioned dates will imply that they will be influenced by the planetary effects of Uranus, Mercury and the Sun. This combination of influences will enhance quite a few characteristics and give them a distinctiveness that will set them apart from their other counterparts.

Perceptive and compassionate, they have a soft and gentle heart that will be touched by acts of kindness. However, they will also be somewhat susceptible to flattery and if not handled firmly, this vulnerability can make them weak. They have a strong creative streak and will often, rely on their gifted imagination for ideas and thoughts.

They are not the kind who will sit idle and indulge themselves. They will, on the other hand, be highly energetic and will always want to be on the move. Intelligent and insightful, they have the extra edge that is needed to deal with any kind of crisis. They will not collapse when faced with difficult times; rather, they will pull in all their strength and battle things out.

Goal-driven and focused, they want to achieve all that is possible and once they decide to apply their mind, there is nothing that can stop them. They are also independent and will prefer to work on their own, since that will allow them to experiment and do things the way they want to. They do not appreciate anyone telling them how to do things. In that case, they would much rather withdraw and start something independently.

Since they have an abundance of energy and vitality, chances are that they may be engaged in more than one career at a time. They could be in a job that pays for their living and they could pursue something that nurtures their creativity and lets them be independent of interference.

Their inherent duality will be quite marked and this will make them a complex and complicated individual. Though they will be an avid reader and a good conversationalist, people close to them will find it difficult to understand them and they will often, feel misinterpreted and neglected. They are quite impatient and will not like to stay at one place for long. This is what will compel them to travel every now and then. If they are able to afford it, they will often, spend a large portion of their time in exploring and seeing the world. Their intelligence and knowledge make them adept at arguing and reasoning. They sometimes have an inclination for scientific topics and issues. Even if they engage in a profession that requires no scientific knowledge, they will continue to nurture this interest through reading and study.

Their inherently tender nature will want that they have a content and peaceful domestic life. However, there will be some unforeseen problems that might make this difficult. Nevertheless, if they are willing to adjust and change certain habits, they will surely be able to have a happy and well-balanced marital life.

Their personality is charismatic and they will often, enjoy the company of a wide and varied section of people. Their diverse range of interests makes it possible for them to interact with everyone and be at the centre of any group activity. For their peace of mind, it is important that they be involved in something that is mentally stimulating and keeps them occupied for long. Anything that is boring or monotonous will tire them out and will not allow them to evolve intellectually. Irrespective of the number of people they interact with, their thoughts and ideas will always be uniquely their own.

Considering the fact that they have such a versatile personality and are also quite independent, it will be difficult for others to know them completely. They will never be an open book. On the contrary, their innermost thoughts and feelings will never be known to anyone except themselves. This does not mean that they are willfully hiding things, just that their personality will be so dynamic that it will be impossible for them to remain the same all the time.

Finance

Number one Geminians have very little to worry about when it comes to money matters. They will be intelligent and insightful about finances and will always ensure that they have a reasonable amount saved up to tide them over lean times. They will also be quite lucky when investing in stocks, shares and the real estate market.

Their love for adventure will motivate them to speculate and take risks which will more often than not, pay off and bring them reasonable profits. They should trust their instincts and invest their money accordingly. As long as they are engaged in a profession that they enjoy and are stimulated by, they will be able to earn a lot and build their fortune.

Health

For health concerns, Geminians born on the above-mentioned dates should take plenty of breaks to rejuvenate themselves and recharge their batteries. They will often be somewhat underweight; however, will have a lot of energy that will keep them going for a long time. They will often, be neglectful of their need to rest and hence, will have to be forced into it.

As such, they will not have too many illnesses to worry about. However, they should be careful of what they eat as they will be prone to indigestion and acidity. Most importantly, they should meditate and go for walks to soothe and calm their overwrought nerves which will constantly be working. The upper respiratory system will also need some attention.

Born on 2nd, 11th, 20th and 29th

If a person is a Gemini born on any of the above-mentioned dates, he will be influenced by the vibes from the planets Neptune, Mercury and the Moon. This particular combination of influences will cast an effect on his personality and bring out features of calmness and creativity.

Liberal and thoughtful, Gemini open to unconventional and novel ideas. They have no hesitation in changing their opinions and views in the light of new evidence and facts. They have a strong sense of empathy for others and often, try to help them out in whatever way possible.

Their inherently peace-loving personality does not enjoy arguing and fighting with others. As a result, they often act as mediator. They have a great deal of tact and discretion and this enables them to smoothen out most troubles and problems with ease and finesse. This particular gift of theirs makes them a great success in professional lines such as diplomacy or even senior management roles.

Amiable and intelligent, they are able to relate to most people with ease and have the art of making them feel comfortable and wanted. Friends often, turn to them for sympathy and love. Their creativity stirs in them a strong desire to be involved in reading, writing and travelling. They want to know more about the world and history and travel will nurture that interest. They often, change their place of living and work since staying in the same place bores them and makes them restless.

Their mind is like a sponge and is always ready to receive more knowledge and learning. They do not like to restrict themselves to any one area of expertise and therefore, they are multi-faceted and quite versatile. Professionally, they do well in most fields. However, it is important that whatever they choose should interest them and stimulate their intellect. Anything that is routine and monotonous will not hold their attention for long and they will soon crave for something different and unusual. Business will also be a good idea for them. They will be best suited in a creative line that will make full use of their imagination and idealism.

They are a thoughtful and benevolent persons, who often think of others before themselves. It will always be on their mind to help others and give something back to society and mankind.

Finance

Geminians born on any of the above-mentioned dates will have very little regard for money, per se. They would much rather be involved in something that intrigues them rather than be part of a routine, humdrum life that will pay them well. They only want enough to live well and not crave too much for the luxuries of life. They are optimistic and have many dreams and aspirations. Fortunately for them, most of their dreams will be realised and they will be able to achieve success and prosperity in life.

Health

Geminians born on the above-mentioned dates are influenced by a powerful combination of planets and this endows them with a disposition that, though delicate, will be capable of dealing with most illnesses. They will need to watch their diet and ensure that they do not burden their digestive system with too much. A good amount of rest and relaxation will take care of their mental health. They should also avoid thinking too much about day-to-day problems of life since it will only stress them out and bring on other disorders.

Born on the 3rd, 12th, 21st and 30th

For Geminians born on the above-mentioned dates, the influence of the planet Jupiter along with Mercury will be critical. This combination of the two will be responsible for endowing you with certain distinguishing traits that will set them apart from your counterparts born on different dates.

They have a strong sense of ambition that ensures that they give their best to whatever they do and once they decide to achieve something, they will never rest till they achieve it. They are also their best critic and they themselves will put their work to long hours of examination. Their constant endeavour is to better themselves and for this purpose they will often push themselves to the very limit.

Their administrative and managerial skills are excellent and they are most comfortable handling large groups of people and taking care of emergencies and crises. That is the reason why they will be quite successful at a senior position in any governmental or private organisation. They have a strong sense of creativity and can come up with some ingenuous and unique ideas. The best part is that these ideas will often, lead to sources of income for them and bring them success and fame.

There are strong chances that if they have the time and the money, they will travel and soak in the sights and sounds of far off and exotic destinations. They will engage in this activity more out of interest than anything else. They do not want to learn anything as such, rather they want to have a nice time and simply unwind and relax when away from home.

Their inherent personality is a warm and congenial one. Therefore, they find it easy to relate to people from various walks of life and even though they may not realise it, they will often be authoritative and controlling. However, they will do this in a very non-threatening manner; therefore, people will not mind this and will enjoy their company and conversation.

They are gifted and intelligent. As a result, they will be able to study a variety of subjects and also be able to discuss them with style and eloquence. They want to move things quickly and anything that is slow and monotonous is boring for them. This will be true for travelling, and even in day-to-day things. They also have a strong inclination for scientific and mechanical subjects and coupled with their creativity, they can be quite successful as a writer or even an inventor.

They are sensitive to those around them and are able to pick up vibes from others. This enables them to modify themselves accordingly, thereby displaying their highly versatile personality. Although they are independent and have their own unique traits, they are also able to adapt to changing situations and people.

Finance

As far as money matters are concerned, they have the gift of being able to earn a lot of money by exploiting their potential to the fullest. They will have enough money to live a comfortable and even lavish life. However, there is the possibility that they will always have a desire to get more. This streak of materialism could be either strong or subdued; however, it will always be present at some level.

This should not imply that they will be miserly and stingy. On the contrary, they are quite large-hearted and willingly share all that they have with friends, family and all forms of charities. While this will be indeed, a noble trait, they should also keep a sufficient amount aside for themselves. Considering that they are always willing to help others, there will also be many people who will stand by them during the times when they will face problems. Therefore, on the whole, they will not have many worries on the financial front.

Health

For Number three Geminians, health could be a slight concern. Although, they have a strong disposition, they often tire themselves out mentally. The exhaustion will be more on the mental front than the physical. Therefore, the ailments that they will complain of will be stress-related, such as hypertension, headaches, and the like. The respiratory system will also be somewhat delicate and will need attention and care. Eyes should not be subjected to long hours of computer or television viewing and on the whole, Geminians born on the above-mentioned dates, should take sufficient breaks and not push themselves to the limit.

Born on the 4th, 13th, 22nd and 31st

The planetary influences of Uranus, Mercury and the Sun will be vital for Geminians born on the above-mentioned dates. These planets will come together and create a personality that will have many of the general Geminian traits, yet will be different and also will experience many unusual and unconventional happenings.

The primary traits and characteristics of their general personality have been described in the earlier pages, describing Geminian. On these pages, we will consider the uniqueness of the individuals born on the above-mentioned dates.

They are highly independent and have a distinctiveness that will set them apart from most others. They have unusual preferences and this draws them towards people who will be strange in many ways and will appeal to their own unconventional personality. It will be this trait that will bring about some of the major changes in their life.

It is their desire to study the unknown and as a result, they may have an interest in astrology, occult and related sciences. They may either explore these out of mere curiosity or they may even take them up seriously. They are very intuitive and therefore, they should learn to trust their instincts and take them seriously. Moreover, they are also innovative and imaginative. All these traits help them greatly in their professional endeavours and enable them to succeed and prosper in everything that they do.

Their creativity is profound and they may use it to express their interest in the mysterious and unknown. They could either take up writing or even discoursing on these topics. They are expressive and articulate and therefore, will be quite popular. Sometimes, though people may perceive them as eccentric, they will enjoy their company.

Since they are totaliy their own persons, they will resent any kind of interference and therefore, they may even sever ties from relatives or at least distance themselves from them to a large extent. They always want to live life on their own terms and ensure that they get their individuality and independence at all costs. Their self-respect will be most important to them. This should not imply that they will be selfish and egotistic; rather, they will only want to be given their space. They are generous and loving, but they will not want others to infringe upon them and force their decisions on them.

As far as marriage and romance is concerned, they need a partner who will understand them completely and respect their need for space and independence. Once they find the right person, they will enjoy a happy and peaceful home life. Their unconventional temperament will be reflected in their views on religion, society, politics and such topics.

Finance

Their most distinctive trait will be their unconventionality and this trait will find its way even in their financial matters. They will see money come and go in their life at various stages. There will, in all likelihood, be an element of uncertainty as far as money is concerned. However, they will not have a very tough time financially. They should maximise their own potential, trust their instincts and also engage in fields that interest them, since all this will ensure that they will always have a reasonable amount of money to support them and their family.

They will enjoy speculating and putting their money into various schemes and plans. There will be chances that they will make a profit, provided they research the scheme carefully before putting their money into it. Also, the most suitable industries for them will be those related to real estate, electronics, cinemas and anything that is creative.

Health

Here again, they will often have to face unusual conditions. While they will not seem very strong, they have a great deal of energy that will keep them going. Also, they are somewhat sensitive to medicines and will not want to take too many of them. As a result, they will often not be convinced by traditional doctors and will try out their own treatments. They will not suffer from many of the usual illnesses. On the other hand, they will suffer from strange and unusual infections and illnesses but nothing will be too serious. As long as they keep a positive attitude and do not let things get them down, they will be healthy and will be able to deal with life in a balanced and successful manner.

Born on the 5th, 14th and 23rd

Mercury is the planet that influences all Geminians born on the above-mentioned dates. Since it is the only planet that casts its effect on them, there are strong chances that they will have the most mercurial traits. Also, Mercury will be in its own sign, therefore, the effects will be more pronounced.

They are gifted with an extremely intelligent, imaginative and quick mind. They do not enjoy being caught in anything that is slow and boring. It is not a surprise, therefore, that they are somewhat impatient and restless and continually want change and newness in their life and surroundings. They will travel extensively and will also experience some career and job changes. If they are unable to bring about changes in their professional life, they will at least try to bring some in their personal life, by either moving home or changing something in their self.

Adventure, thrill and risk will give them great pleasure and they will always be ready to take on something new and fascinating. They will never think about the danger or the uncertainty involved. They will be too caught up in the moment and will relish every single bit of it.

They enjoy being on their own at times, and although social and amiable, they often seek quiet time to reflect and think. Moreover, their strong streak of independence drives them to be unique. Only a few people will be able to adjust to their personality. Even though they will have a wide circle of friends, they will have only a few who will be close to them. Even in matters of marriage, it is important that they have a partner who understands them completely and is willing to make adjustments for their sake.

In order for them to be close to someone, physical distance will play an important role. If someone is not in sight, they will forget about them. This will not be wilful; rather, they just can't help not focusing on people who aren't around them. The Geminean trait of duality will be more heightened in them due to the strong and single-handed influence of Mercury on their personality. They could be engaged in two diametrically opposite professions or they could even fall in love with two people at the same time. In any case, there will be a strong element of duality that will show its presence in their life every now and then.

Finance

It will be their inherent intelligence and sharpness that will make them succeed on the financial front. They will be able to earn great profits and accumulate a lot of wealth, based on the sound decisions that they take. They are fond of splurging on luxuries when they have the money. Not only that, they will also be quite generous and charitable. As a result, they will often give away large chunks of their wealth without even realising it.

They will have a temperament that will be mercurial in the real sense of the word. That means that they are able to change and adapt to any situation and group of people. Hence, even when they do not have a lot of money, they will be able to deal with it and be capable of working hard in order to get back to their earlier status. They are not the kind who will get depressed and demotivated. If they stay focused and not go overboard with spending, they will do very well and make a name for themselves in whichever field they are engaged in.

Health

For Number five Geminians, health will be something that they themselves will be responsible for. They are gifted with a naturally strong disposition. However, they will tend to tire themselves out mentally and therefore, bring on physical ailments as well. Their inherently restless temperament will often, prompt them to make frequent changes and always be on the move. This will cause a lot of stress and there could be times when their mind will want something while their body will simply want rest.

Since they do not like to live a life of routine, they will often have irregular eating and sleeping habits. This will have an effect on their body and will bring about hypertension, headaches, coughs, colds as well as joint aches and pains. If they follow a routine life with plenty of rest and good food, they will be able to lead a relatively healthy and disease-free life.

Born on the 6th, 15th and 24th

It will be the influence of Mercury in conjunction with Venus that will bring about a positive effect on their personality. They will be endowed with the destiny of being in the public eye and attaining a good amount of fame and fortune.

They will go through life with a great deal of luck and this will be responsible for making them prosperous and popular. Right from an early age, they will have the gift of being charismatic, attracting people towards them. They will have a certain aura that will make them the centre of attraction wherever they go.

For them, life will bring a host of opportunities and they will be able to use most of these to their advantage. That is one of the reasons why they will never be short of money. On the other hand, they will have the ability and efficiency to make money through many sources. They are also very creative. This could either be traditional or unconventional; however, it will be present and will play a decisive role in determining their career. They will do well as a writer, artist, interior decorator or musician.

They will also have good oratory skills and chances are, they will be able to make a mark as a teacher, preacher or lecturer or in any field where they get the chance to exploit their presentation skills to the fullest. Everything in their personality will play a role in determining their social and economic standing. They will have the ability to carve a niche for themselves in any section of society and form a wide and diverse section of friends for themselves.

Intelligent, warm and witty, they have the knack of rising to the top and dealing with emergencies and tough situations with a cool and calm head. That is the reason why everyone will turn to them for advice and guidance. They are also highly independent and will not like to be forced into anything. They make their own decisions and are accountable for their own life. They have a strong drive to excel and a deep faith in their abilities. These two features will be primarily responsible for motivating them and helping them to rise higher in the socio-economic ladder.

Even though they will experience many happy moments in their life, there will be times when they will want to escape into a world of their own and enjoy moments of solitude. There will also be instances when they will feel overwhelmed by feelings of sadness and loss. However, once they are engrossed in something, these feelings will disappear and they will once again be their usual cheerful self, active, energetic and ready to take on the world.

As far as their love life is concerned, they will be able to exert their charisma on the opposite sex. They will be drawn towards them and they may have a large number of admirers and affairs. However, they will take their time in deciding upon their partner and finally settling down. They will need someone who will be able to adjust to their unique personality and take their duality in stride. They could be quite an enigma for most people and it will take someone who is just as intelligent and adaptable as they are, to truly understand them and live with them.

On the whole, they will be persons who will be inherently fortunate but who will also need to work hard in order to make full use of the opportunities that life presents them with.

Finance

In matters of finance, they will be quite fortunate and will have many gifts presented to them at the most unexpected times. They may also receive money through unforeseen sources. They are wise and judicious and hence, will ensure that they always have a reasonable amount saved for their lean days. If they engage in a profession that suits their personality and utilise their potential, they will be able to make a great deal of money and accumulate wealth. Even if they are in business, they will rely on their intelligence and independence to make the right decisions. In matters of investment, they should take the advice of reliable counsel and place their money accordingly.

Health

Number six Gemineans will be fairly healthy and will not suffer from the usual gamut of illnesses. However, they will need to pay attention to their nerves and ensure that they do not place too much pressure on them. That will stress them out and make them prone to depression, moodiness, hypertension and such ailments. The one part of their body that they will need to take care of will be the respiratory system since they might be prone to coughs, hay-fever, asthma and the like. On the whole though, as long as they get a good amount of rest and peace, they will be healthy and fit.

Born on the 7th, 16th and 25th

The Moon, Neptune and Mercury will come together and influence them, if they were born on any of the above-mentioned dates. These planets will make them more approachable to the views and opinions of others. However, they will display their duality by masking this side by an authoritative temperament.

They will have a nature that will be deeply stimulated by spirituality and idealism. They will be sophisticated and creative in everything that they do. Irrespective of their social background, they have the ability to bring a touch of class and elegance to every aspect of their personality. They are sensitive and perceptive to people and situations and will have a heightened sense of intuition. In fact, they will most often, be correct in their assessment of people, events and situations.

Although they are not ambitious in the conventional sense of the word, they have a strong motivation to talk to others and convince them about their point of view. At the same time, they will be willing to listen to them and understand their approach as well. This is yet another aspect of their dual personality.

They enjoy solitude and peace and will often undertake journeys on their own to calming and tranquil surroundings such as the sea, lakes and mountains. They should, however, be careful of mishaps caused by water or in air. This desire for peace will also be reflected in their fondness for nature and natural things. They enjoy making collections of unique and offbeat items from nature. They may even take up its study and become an authority on it.

Since they are interested by what other people think or say, there are possibilities that they might take an avid interest in studying alternative science or sociology. They will also be eloquent and expressive when discussing these topics with others. However, the dual aspect of this is that they may not wish to discuss these topics and even conceal their interest in them from other people.

As far as domestic and married life is concerned, their highly independent and unconventional approach to life may cause some strain with their immediate family. When considering marriage, it is essential that they find someone who will be able to match their wave length and give them a feeling of space as well as security.

Although they are intelligent and wise, they have a certain naiveté that will make them vulnerable to cheats. Therefore, it is important that they always think before investing their money and do not fall prey to these people. Take the advice of people whom they trust and save a decent amount for their future.

On the whole, they are interesting company and once people get used to the duality of their temperament, they will be someone they will look forward to meeting.

Finance

Since their planetary influences make them highly open to others, there are chances that they will often listen to the advice of people when investing their hard-earned money. Rely on people who are experts and do not blindly follow anyone. They should trust their instincts since they will not let them down. They could come into money through unforeseen sources. However, they will be able to earn their living by using their talents and gifts.

Health

Their unconventional nature will make them prone to equally unconventional ailments. It will be difficult for a doctor to diagnose what could be bothering them. However, there is no doubt about the fact that when they are not mentally healthy, they will not feel well. For them, their mind should be at peace in order for the body to function properly. Depression and sadness will often, engulf them and at these times, they will not be able to function properly. Hence, they should try and surround themselves with positive people and cheerful surroundings as much as possible. These will have an uplifting effect on their mood and their overall well-being.

Born on the 8th, 17th and 26th

For Geminians born on the above-mentioned dates, the influence of the planets Saturn and Mercury will be vital. This powerful combination will bring about a heightened sense of independence and distinctiveness in their personality.

Although they will be diligent and devoted to their work, the hand of fate will play a strong role in their life and in determining their success. They are intelligent and gifted with a talent for logic and reasoning. As a result, they will be quite successful in fields of science, mathematics, engineering and other areas where they will need to apply their mind. Routine and boring jobs will be tiresome for them and will not make full use of their potential.

There are chances that they will feel stifled by the restrictions that society or even their family may place on them. If they are able to break free, they will be able to scale to great heights and be a well-known name. Even if they decide to live within the limitations of society, they will still manage to carve out a niche for themselves.

They are selective about their friends. However, once they meet like-minded people, they are warm and loving. They also have a compassionate side to their personality but they often try and conceal it for fear of appearing weak. Nevertheless, people who know them well will understand and accept their quirks. They often, seek out time by themselves and enjoy the thoughts that run through their active and alert mind. They have some highly creative and innovative ideas that could bring them great money and success.

Profound and passionate, they devote themselves to their task with intensity and do not rest until they have excelled in it. However, it is important that they will themselves be responsible to achieve and excel. Otherwise, they could adopt a laidback approach to life. This is one more example of the dual nature of their personality. It is important that they make the right kind of acquaintances and friends or they may find themselves entangled in some unpleasant company.

They are perceptive and take note of the smaller things. Also, they have a short temper and are liable to lose it when minor irritants crop up. It is advisable for them to learn to be calm and relaxed and not let mundane worries upset them. Although they are liberal and forward thinking, there are chances that they may be surprised to find that other people are not willing to see their point of view.

There are also chances that they might develop a spiritual or idealistic approach to life and this will help them to cope with the obstacles and hurdles that might stand in their path of success and progress. For them to be happy and content, it is important that they apply a mix of idealism and realism to life. Also, ensure that they get enough time alone to reflect on life and themselves. That will help them to evolve and grow as a person.

Finance

As far as money matters are concerned, they will be intelligent and judicious. They will always ensure that there is a balance between their income and expenditure. Also, they will try and put aside money for their retirement and old age since that will give them a feeling of security. They will have more faith in their own intellect and instincts than in other people, therefore, they will not rely on a lot of people for financial advice. They will also prefer to take the slow and steady path when accumulating their wealth rather than putting their money into get-rich-quick schemes.

Health

They need to keep a check on their nerves and ensure that they do not get unduly irritated and angry by the events in their life. The should learn to take things in their stride and their health will take care of itself. Also, should try and go easy on themselves and do not demand perfection from themselves in everything. Stress will do more harm to their inherently good system than anything else. Headaches, eye problems and infections of the digestive system could bother them. However, there will be nothing that will not be cured with good rest and wholesome food.

Born on the 9th, 18th and 27th

All Gemineans born on the 9th, 18th and 27th will be influenced by vibrations from the planets Mercury and Mars. This particular combination endows them with razor-sharp intelligence and a straightforward nature.

Intelligent and inquisitive, they have an inherently curious nature and the influence of their planets will make them more perceptive about the world around them. They are intrigued by unusual things and want to learn about them. They are confident and will be able to hold their own in any group or debate. As a matter of fact, they will be blunt and to the point even in their social interactions.

While there will be a number of people who will appreciate their candidness, there will also be some who will be hurt by it and will avoid their company. Therefore, it is advisable for them to combine their straightforward nature with some discretion and softness.

Active, enthusiastic and vibrant, they are always on the go. They have an abundance of energy and will always want to be doing something or the other. Sitting idle does not suit their personality. They are especially interested in science, mathematics and anything that is mechanical. Their ideas will always be different and will often, bring them great profits and success.

Highly independent and individualistic, they often want their own way in important matters. They resent any interference and illogical customs. Therefore, there could be some trouble on the family front, especially, during their younger years. While they are independent, they are also resourceful and multi-talented. Hence, they are able to apply their mind to anything, as long as it interests them. Even when it comes to people, they want to be in the company of lively and intelligent people.

They are very positive and optimistic. There may be times in their life when they will be saddened and depressed by certain events, however, they will never let go of their inherent courage and will always be able to overcome any difficulty and hardship. Their sunny nature will help them tide through these times and they will be able to motivate others as well to do their best and not be overwhelmed by life.

There are also indications that they could be spontaneous and natural. They often, draw people towards them by their intelligence and innocent nature. They give the appearance of one who is wise and at the same time have a certain vulnerability about them. This is another highlight of their dual personality. Their sense of humour is also unique to them.

There are strong chances that the opposite sex will be attracted towards them and they may fall in love more than once. However, once they find the right partner, they will be a loyal lover.

Finance

As far as financial matters are concerned, they are somewhat reckless and rush into deals without giving them sufficient thought. However, there is another side to their personality, which is, that they could be both reckless and wise at the same time. They may give the impression of being impulsive but will have actually given sufficient thought to how they wish to earn and invest their money.

They are intelligent enough to judge the goodness of an idea and that will help them to make the right decisions and make profits in business and investments. If in business, they will do better on their own than in a partnership. Irrespective of whether they are in business or in a profession, they should always keep money aside and save for the future.

Health

They have a good and healthy constitution; however, they will tend to push it to the limit by overwork and unhealthy habits. They should be very careful when travelling, since they could meet with accidents and get injured on the arms, legs and hips. They should also learn to balance periods of hectic work with complete rest. That will give their body the much-needed rest it deserves and they will be able to recharge themselves and become more alert and active than ever before.

CANCER

(22ND JUNE TO 22ND JULY)

Cancer in General

Cancer—the Crab. A sign that is sensitive, persistent and immensely surprising. It is the sign that begins on the 21st of June. However, over here, it is preceded by the previous sign and the first seven days are considered the cusp of that sign, therefore, the sign of Cancer starts building in power only after the 28th of June. Thereafter, it keeps increasing in strength till the 20th of July, following which it loses strength to the cusp of the incoming sign, which is Leo. There is an interesting legend behind the origin of the name Cancer. It was so named because in ancient times, the Sun at this part of the year seemed to move back and forth like the movement of the crab. Hence, the name Cancer.

Cancerians are hardworking and conscientious in everything they do, however, everything will not come easily to them. They will be most successful when engaged in something that is interesting to them and gives them a chance to explore their creativity.

Typically, Cancerians are known for moving back and forth just like the crab. They will often take up something either personally or professionally, and at a critical stage they will often move back. This will not only surprise everyone around them but also themselves. Therefore, it is only natural that the life of a Cancerian will have plenty of ups and downs.

As far as money matters are concerned, they will be somewhat susceptible to speculation and will often, either spend their money or invest it recklessly. It is important they curb both these tendencies and learn to save something for their future.

Cancerians are known to have quite a sense of humour; however, it is important that they be in the right mood. This brings us to yet another aspect of the Cancerian personality-their moodiness. They will be up one moment and down the very next. That is how temperamental they can get. However, when happy and upbeat, a Cancerian can be lively and entertaining and can keep a bunch of people enthralled by his witty and intelligent conversation.

Even when they are not occupying the limelight, Cancerians enjoy standing in the side lines and observing others. They will often, try and learn from the people around them and their introspection will often be responsible for their evolution.

Cancerians are highly imaginative and quite easy to understand, however, they are not as simple as they seem. They will often, have a deep-rooted sense of failure and rejection, because of which they may not always let go in a relationship. They are also highly emotional and sensitive to the slightest of rebukes. Always remember that the tears of a Cancerian are never superficial. When hurt, they will go into one of their melancholic moods and emerge only when they have healed sufficiently.

Normally, it has been seen that Cancerians will often, excel at whatever they undertake and hence, make quite a name for themselves in their respective fields. Being in the public eye suits them and even if they do seem modest and unassuming, praise and recognition will make them giddy with happiness. They will often, think up lofty schemes and plans to help others. As a matter of fact, they will be quite sensitive to the feelings of other people and will often try to make a difference in whichever way they can.

When criticised, Cancerians will become silent and withdrawn and will often brood over the unfairness of life. They are known to keep their feelings bottled up within themselves and even play the martyr every now and then. They are extremely warm and loving, however, because of their undemonstrative nature, most people will be unaware of their feelings. Cancerians are known to be home birds and they will often, take a keen interest in keeping a home warm and comfortable for its occupants. They will love to play the provider and take care of you when ill or sad or for no particular reason at all.

These individuals will have gifted memories and will love to hold on to heirlooms and things which have sentimental value. You will often, find Cancerians holding on to their childhood toys and similar memoirs, practically forever. Their mental powers also include their powers of intuition and perception. Their gut instinct about things will nearly always turn out to be right. That is the reason why so many of them make good astrologers or psychics. Even if they don't take it up as a profession, they will always be intrigued by these sciences and will often do a lot of reading upon it.

Their imagination and creativity will give them a natural flair for words and pictures. As a result, they make good writers, artists, musicians, teachers and even doctors. In short, they will do well in any field which will stimulate their intelligence, creativity and give them a chance to reach out to people. They will be diligent and meticulous workers with a fine eye for detail and will believe in giving their hundred per cent to their job. However, it is important that they be constantly stimulated by what they do, else they will simply quit. Even in the rare circumstance that they decide to stick it out and see what happens, it will only be for money and it will not be for a long time.

They have strong ties to the family and will honour traditions and conventions. They will also be attached to their parents, siblings and all other relatives. However, this bond will depend on individual circumstances as well and there could be instances where they separate because of some deep hurt or problem.

Cancerians have expressive faces that will reflect all their feelings and sentiments. They may not be physically demonstrative, yet their faces will be the key to their feelings. As a matter of fact, Cancerians will be so profoundly emotional, that they will be able to transfer their feelings to you as well. They will have a deep respect for the time gone by and will learn a lot from it.

Since Cancerians naturally enjoy being around people, people also like to be with them. Therefore, it is not surprising that Cancerians often become the confidante of friends and family. They are patient and gentle listeners and try and help out as much as possible. Moreover, they will also be loyal and dependable; therefore, secrets and scandals will be quite safe with them. Just as they do not appreciate others interfering in their private matters, they will in turn, stay out of other people's affairs, unless called in to mediate.

Cancerians are also similar to the crab, in the sense that they will never ask for what they want directly. They will go back and forth and in circles. It will only be when they see someone else moving in that they will act quickly and get what they want. This will be true in relationships, jobs and everyday life. However, this should not imply that they act rashly. On the contrary, Cancerians will often think over an action and mull over it endlessly. They will act only when convinced about the rightness of the action.

Most Cancerians will be fond of travel and will have a particular liking for water. They enjoy being near the sea and watching the tide come in and go out. Any water body, for that matter, will give them a feeling of quiet happiness and calm contentment. They will be sometimes, found lost deep in thought and will be blissfully unaware of the hustle and bustle around them. In such times, it is best to leave them alone. They will come out of it and be just as happy and lighthearted as before.

Cancerians have a special kind of strength. This will come from the Cancerian's inherent ability to deal with all forms of stress and turmoil. Primarily because they will, themselves, be responsible for bringing on most of the stress. Cancerians are known to have strange and inexplicable fears about financial or emotional losses. Also, they have the tendency to brood and become melancholic about minor upsets. Even with regards to illnesses, Cancerians will mostly blow them out of proportion and actually magnify the illness to great proportions. This does not mean that they lie. They actually believe that they are very ill. Despite all this, the Cancerian will be able to maintain his sanity and go through life with happiness and peace.

In short, a Cancerian will be so interesting and intriguing that once he gets caught up in his life, it will be impossible for him to get out.

Finance

In financial matters, the effects of Neptune and the Moon will be felt greatly in a variety of ways. They will bring about many unforeseen changes in the life of the Cancerian and this will have a direct bearing on his financial state and well being. As a rule, Cancerians should be wary of putting their money into get-rich-quick schemes. Speculation and trading in stocks and shares should also be done under the guidance and advice of a wise and trusted source. Wherever there is an element of doubt, the Cancerian should be careful and vigilant.

Since there is an aspect of eccentricity in the sign of Cancer, chances are that money too will come in through strange sources for these mysterious creatures. They will often, profit from the most surprising sources and investments.

When doing business, it is important that the Cancerian be absolutely sure about his partner and the nature of business. Even when investing in a business and not being directly involved in it, a Cancerian should try and stick to companies which provide for the general public rather than elitist groups. These industries will surely bring success and prosperity to him.

Inquisitive and creative, Cancerians will often make good inventors and scientists. They could also earn their fortune through industries such as shipping, oil, jewellery, and similar fields. They will also be able to maximise their creative potential in fields such as teaching, nursing, management and other areas where they will have some amount of responsibility and autonomy.

Health

The health of Cancerians is fairly good and there will be not much cause for worry. However, their mental health is more important than the physical one. If they feel that they are healthy, they will remain so. However, a Cancerian can actually think himself sick and then become sick. This is the power of their mind. The influence of the Moon on this sign is significant and it might make their overall constitution somewhat sensitive and fragile. Again, it will be a condition that could be remedied by sheer willpower and determination. If the Cancerian wants, he will be able to become the strongest person around just by willing himself to do so. It is important and vital that they remain positive and optimistic in order to keep their emotional and physical health stable.

Anxiety and stress will have a negative impact on their already sensitive souls. Therefore, it is important that they learn early on how to manage stress and have a positive self-image. These tools will enable them to recover from any illness. They will be prone to hypertension, rheumatism and disorders of the glands and blood. Allergies and stress-related disorders will also be a common occurrence.

CANCER

Born on 1st, 10th, 19th and 28th

Cancerians who are born on any of the above-mentioned dates will be ruled by the influences of the planets Neptune and Uranus as well as the Sun and the Moon. This, as can be clearly seen, is a powerful and influential combination of planetary vibes which will bring out certain distinctive characteristics in the individual. These planets will be responsible for filling their life and career with many variations. It will also be due to their influence that they will be extremely affected by the environment around them and their mood will be dependent upon the conditions that surround you.

Number one Cancerians are extremely attached to their homes, families and countries. They will be diligent and dutiful, with a strong loyalty towards their origins. If they are one of them, they have a sensitive heart that is filled with love and affection for all their close ones. They are fond of seeking out moments of quiet and peace so as to give rest to your nerves. They are not the kind to jump into the limelight. However, there are strong chances that they will be fortunate enough to become famous in whatever they undertake.

Their sensitivity and emotional temperament will be responsible for giving them the role of a parent. They are fond of nourishing and mothering people and as a result, for friends and family, they will often be a shoulder to cry on. They are supportive and gentle, giving comfort and being patient all the while.

Innocent yet wise, they can sometimes be a contradiction to themselves. They have a wide-eyed, accepting approach to life and are constantly learning and acquiring knowledge about the world. At the same time, they are wise and intelligent in several matters, especially finance and money. Although they are charitable and want to help out others, they always try and make their future secure and safe. They are judicious when spending, even stingy to an extent. For you, it is important to have some money stashed away for rainy days.

In matters of religion and faith, they are spiritual. However, they are not the kind to make a big deal out of it. For them, their faith is personal and they keep it that way. They have a strong value system, depending upon the family that they were brought up in and they try and instil the same in their children.

Inherently they are the quiet sort and this reflects in nearly everything they do. Even if they are thrust into the public eye by some act of fate, they try and underplay it. This should not imply that they do not like praise and recognition; it is just that they are not comfortable with ostentatious behaviour. They like to be acknowledged for the work that they do, but they want it to be subtle and understated.

As a worker, they are conscientious and meticulous. They want to give their best to everything. Therefore, it is not surprising that they often achieve excellence in their respective field. They also do well when involved in professions relating to social work, humanitarian activities and other profiles where people are involved.

They also have a strong mothering instinct and will want to take care of all those people who are dear to them. They are very comfortable looking after people and being a support system in themselves. What is important is that even they should give themselves more support and be good to themselves so that they can become stronger each day. Giving too much of themselves to others is good as long as they give something to themselves, too.

Finance

In matters of finance and money, we can divide Cancerians born on the above-mentioned dates into two types. There will be one category that will be very sobre and serious about life and money. They will be thoughtful and prudent when working and saving money. They will enjoy the occasional vacation, however, their priorities will be right and they will ensure that they have enough for their retirement.

Then, there is the other category who will simply believe in living life as it is. They will be restless and impatient and will want constant change in their lives. As a result, they will not be able to stay for long at any place of business or work. Hence, the income will not be much and savings will be even less. Most of their money, even if inherited, will be spent in their travels and other interests.

It is strange how both these types can be found in Cancerians born on the 1st, 10th, 19th, and 28th. However, they do exist and this is part of the uniqueness of Cancer and the influence of its planets on these individuals.

Health

As far as health is concerned, they seem physically fragile. However, they have an inner strength that will often surprise a lot of people. For them, positive and uplifting emotions will be more important than all medicines and treatments. They might be prone to digestive problems. However, they will be able to treat themselves by a dose of optimism and positive thinking, better than any doctor will, and go on to enjoy a life that is happy and healthy.

Born on the 2nd, 11th, 20th and 29th

All Cancerians born on the 2nd, 11th, 20th and 29th will be affected by the influence from the Moon, the Sun and the planets Neptune and Uranus. These planets will have a unique influence on Number two Cancerians which will be quite distinct from their influence on other Numbers.

For Cancerians born on the above-mentioned dates, the planets will be influential in bringing about a heightened sense of creativity and imagination. If they are one of them, they are extremely gifted when dreaming and planning. What's more, they will not just dream things; they will actually make these dreams come true. This is the real gift and this is what will make them prosper and succeed. They are able to visualise themselves and their aims and then are able to put in the hard work and toil that is needed in order to make it happen. There is no doubt, therefore, that they will have an ideal combination of will and skill to realise their dreams and aspirations.

Their creativity is reflected in their fondness and aptitude for drama and theatre. Everything they do has life and energy in it.

Even if they maintain a low and quiet profile, they are able to stand out in a crowd and draw attention to their aesthetic and creative abilities. They also have a strong inclination towards the arts. Therefore, they will be fond of drawing, reading, books, poetry, music, painting and the like.

Romantic and passionate, they are passionate and intense about their relationships and are extremely emotional. They devote their heart and soul into their relationships and will also be sensitive to the feelings of other people. The influence of the planets on their Number will also be responsible for making them more straightforward than other Cancerians. They will be quite candid and will often state what they feel in no uncertain terms.

Routine bores them and they will be the kind who will crave excitement and change. As a result, they will often travel to distant and exotic lands to try and absorb as much as possible. They also have a strong attachment to the past and try to collect many antiques, artifacts and curios.

Water will have a strong place in their life and they will often try and make their home next to a water body. Even if they are not able to afford a home near the sea, they will try and have one with a swimming pool at least, so strong is their attachment to water. They enjoy going to the beach, and swimming may well be their favourite exercise.

As they have a fertile imagination and abundant creativity, they are able to draw out their own destiny and be successful in whatever they do. They should remember to go easy on themselves and also develop a bit of tact, so as to make life and living easier for themselves.

Finance

Finance, money, wealth—all of them will be exposed to uncertainty and speculation in their case. They are quite impulsive and will often want to invest in schemes that promise returns in short times, thus increasing the element of risk in their investment portfolio. Always remember that it is better to be safe than to be sorry. Therefore, they should learn to go slow and take the longer route when putting their hard earned money to work for them.

As far as possible, they should stay away from unnecessary speculation and risk. They should avoid gambling with their money and keep it invested in safe schemes. It is also important that they keep some amount aside for times when income is low or when they retire. The influence of their planets will be responsible for bringing them success in ventures related to oil and shipping, therefore, they could invest their money in these industries. Whatever they do, they should always take the advice of someone who will have their best interests at heart and who will know how to make the most of their money in a safe and secure fashion.

Health

Health for them will be something that will be greatly influenced by their state of mind, more than anything else. They could be in the worst of conditions, but if they are happy, they will be healthy. Also, their health will either be very good or very poor. There will hardly be any middle ground. The influence of the Moon will be the strongest in this sign and they will therefore be extremely sensitive to the environment. They will be able to pick up the faintest form of negative energy and will react to it strongly. Similarly, when surrounded by positive vibes, they will react to them by being in the pink of health.

They will be most prone to vague aches and pains in various parts of the body. Also, they might have some gastric problems, such as ulcers, primarily due to their extremely emotional temperament.

For them, it will be extremely beneficial to have a regular diet and exercise routine and a regular dose of positive thinking to keep going.

Born on 3rd, 12th, 21st and 30th

For Cancerians born on the above-mentioned dates, the influence of the planets Neptune and Jupiter along with the Moon is significant. This combination of planetary influences will be responsible for endowing them with a self-reliant and brave spirit. They will not be afraid of voicing their thoughts and ideas and will do so with spontaneity and candidness.

If they were born on any of the above-mentioned dates, they will have a personality that will be a brief study in contradiction. They will have a strong streak of independence, yet they will have equally strong ties to family and friends. They will want to be on their own but there will also be the fervent desire to be with their loved ones.

They are not only benevolent at the same time frugal. There will be instances where they will either give generously for a cause or splurge on themselves, but then, there will also be times when they will not want to spend a single penny and will hoard all the cash they have.

Sociable and easy-going, they enjoy the company of a diverse section of people. They relate easily to those who are from different walks of life and sections of society. They will probably have to handle positions of authority and this is where their people management skills will come to the fore. They are efficient and responsible and will do well in both business and professional endeavours.

There are chances that they will initially have to work hard and struggle in order to realise their dreams. However, once they have made their mark and carved out a niche for themselves, they will be able to rise with ease. They will, undoubtedly, make a name for themselves and their diligence and determination will surely pay off.

They have an emotional temperament and are easily moved by a sad story. However, they are not weak persons, per se. As a matter of fact, they have a great amount of strength and when required, will be able to draw on it and become a pillar of support for themselves and others. There may be some hurdles in their personal life as well, nevertheless, they will be able to overcome these and use them as learning experiences. They always attempt to maintain ties with the family and their relatives. They will play an integral role in their life and the shaping of their personality.

They will be fond of travelling and will often undertake journeys to distant lands. They will be intrigued by unfamiliar cultures and will enjoy learning about them. Not only that, travel will give them an opportunity to widen their horizon and be a more aware individual. Even if they do not travel too much, they will still have an eventful and adventurous life.

They may have a somewhat laidback approach at times, however, when involved with a subject of their interest, they can be intensely devoted and passionate. They are able to excel at many things, but the important part is that they be interested in them. If they do not like them or find them boring, nothing or no one can make them do it.

They will be interesting companion and will often be witty. If their life has many positive experiences, they will develop a good sense of humour. If not, this humour might turn into sarcasm or cynicism. Therefore, for them, it is important that they look at life in a positive light and take each day as it comes. Happiness and contentment have a significant role to play in their state of well-being and these will in turn be influenced by how they perceive events and happenings in their life.

Finance

They are quite fortunate as far as money is concerned and hence, will not have to worry much about it. They will be able to earn a good income. Most importantly, once they will be able to strike a balance between spending and earning, they will not have any problems with finance. Most of the investments that they make will turn out well and bring them profits.

Health

They have a strong and cheerful disposition. Health will not be a concern and they will be one of those lucky people who will feel as good as they look. They will also have a reasonable dedication to their diet and exercise routine and will try and keep a check on any unhealthy habits. This aspect, however, may depend upon their initial years and family values.

They enjoy being out of the house and therefore, will take in a lot of sunshine and fresh air. These will do them a lot of good for their immune system. The one thing that they should work on maintaining is a balance between work and relaxation. Too much of work will put undue stress on their system. Therefore, they should take good care of themselves and strike a balance.

Born on 4th, 13th, 22nd and 31st

Cancerians born on the above-mentioned dates are ruled by the influence of the planets Uranus, Neptune as well as the Sun and the Moon. If they are one of them, they will find that the planets exercise their influence and endow them with a personality that is distinct, yet blends in with the general characteristics of Cancerians.

Inventive and innovative, they will always want to be in their own class and they will manage that with the help of their inherently independent temperament. They will not want to be grouped with everybody and will sometimes be regarded as a trailblazer of sorts. Their ideas, thoughts and opinions will be highly distinctive and even border on being strange.

Emotional and perceptive, they are very sensitive and will react strongly to all feelings and sentiments. The smallest of things will hurt them or anger them and it is essential that they learn to be emotionally secure from an early age. That will enable them to be a balanced and confident human being. Due to their emotionally highly-strung temperament, they might often face problems with family and friends. Arguments, conflicts and disputes could bother them and trouble their peace of mind. For someone of their disposition, maintaining peace and harmony will be critical for their mental, emotional and physical health.

Their strong perception of people and situations will be of great help when entering into partnerships, relationships or marriage. They will often, be right about their opinion on a particular person or situation. It will be beneficial for them to try and hone this gift further and use it wisely.

Intelligent and intense, they will be able to carve out a niche for themselves by making full use of their skills and abilities. They will be passionate about pursuing their interests and will excel in them by giving them adequate time and attention. There could be times when they will not be sure about what they really want to do, however, with time and awareness they will have a firm idea and then there will be nothing to stop them. Despite the fact that you are an emotional person, they will be strong and determined when pursuing their goals. They may seem to move away at times, but that will be only to reassess and rework their strategy and plans. They will move back into the game once they've made the necessary changes and they will be just as dogged and insistent.

There is little doubt that they will be successful. They might face difficulties and obstacles on their way; however, they will use them as stepping stones and treat them as opportunities for learning. Even if they allow themselves to be disillusioned at times, they will soon introspect and be able to pull themselves up and be positive. Life may seem hard with all its challenges, but the fruits of their struggle will surely be sweet.

They should always retain their strength of character and rely on their instincts when making a decision, and there is no way that they could go wrong. They will be somewhat choosy when making friends, however, when they are a friend to someone, they will be loyal, sentimental and supportive. They will always be ready to encourage someone and be there for them when needed. It is only natural that they expect the same from them. However, a word of advice is never to have too many expectations from someone. Always be ready to give people their space and they will respect them more for that.

Their chief traits of an exceptional mental ability and their sensitivity will set them apart from an early age and if they have the right environment and guidance, they will be able to use these features and maximise their potential, thereby, giving themselves an edge over the rest.

Finance

If born on the 4th, 13th, 22nd or 31st, they will not have too many financial worries. The important thing is that they will not be able to trust many people with their money. They will be finicky and wary when forming relationships. Also, they will form very strong preferences for and against someone. Therefore, if in business, it will be wiser for them to go solo rather than enter a partnership.

They will make money from various offbeat and unconventional sources. Inheritances, legacies, gifts and such will add to their bank balance and help them accumulate wealth.

Health

Overall, they will be a strong and healthy person; however, on the occasions when they will fall ill, it will be due to some vague and abstruse reason. There may also be a situation when they will be considered a hypochondriac and not taken seriously. However, this will not be entirely true since they will be convinced that they are really ill and more often than not, they will be. The fact of the matter is that for they, most illness will be mental and psychological. If there is something that is bothering them, it will manifest itself as an illness and they will feel unwell. That is why they will need to become emotionally stronger and surround themselves laughter, positivism and good friends.

Keep a strict eye on their and always have clean wholesome food, since they might have a sensitive stomach and be susceptible to food poisoning.

Born on 5th, 14th and 23rd

According to the laws of astrology and zodiacs, Cancerians born on the above-mentioned dates will be influenced by the planets Mercury and Neptune, along with the Moon. This particular planetary combination will endow the individual with emotion and spiritualism, among other things.

If a person is born on any of the dates given above, then they will be a compassionate and gentle soul with a sensitive heart that will be moved by a sad story or poem. They will always try to make things better for people around them and will go to great extents to bring comfort to those who are distressed and unhappy.

They will also be easily influenced and will be affected by people and the environment. Appreciation, encouragement and all forms of validation will form an integral part of their life and these will be great motivators for them. This particular trait may make them susceptible to flattery and sycophancy, if they are not aware of it. It is important that they learn to distinguish between genuine praise and insincere talk.

It is quite possible that during their initial years, they will not be sure of themselves and may lack confidence in their potential. However, with the passage of time and maturity, they will evolve and develop a deep and stable sense of self-reliance and courage in themselves. Thereafter, it will not be a tough task for them to deal with life and its multitude of challenges.

They have a profoundly spiritualistic nature and will often turn to religion and spiritualism for strength and relief. They will be curious about other faiths but will not be a fanatic. Rather, they will have the grace to accept and embrace the goodness in all faiths.

Intelligent and sharp, they are able to grasp concepts and ideas with quickness and clarity. Moreover, they will have a strong ambition to excel and be the best in whatever they do. Therefore, they might also have a tendency to be dominating and controlling. Reading, mind games, and anything that will stimulate the brain will be their favourite pastime. Once they figure something out, they will want to move on to more interesting activities. Change and variation will be an integral part of their life.

It will be this desire for change and newness that will compel them to travel and see different lands and countries. They might even be tempted to settle in a country other than their native one. Not only that, the longing for a change of scenery will often extend to their professional life and they may go in for some frequent changes in their career.

They will be quite lucky with money and might come into it by means of an inheritance, legacy, lottery and such unexpected sources. However, it will be solely dependent on them whether or not they will be able to keep it. They will need to strike a balance between spending and earning. There will be times when they will be overcome with a desire to spend and splurge. There will also be times when they will simply want to save. The secret is to not go overboard with either pattern.

They will also have a tendency of wanting to ensure that all their plans and schemes are realised. This can be a difficult expectation to deal with and not everybody will want to function in so rigid a manner. Therefore, it will be beneficial for them to learn to relax and take things easy. Remember, a laid-back attitude is not a bad one. It will make life simpler and in this day and age, simplicity is the key to happiness and contentment.

Although, during their initial years of adolescence and adulthood, they may not have a great deal of determination and decisiveness, as they mature they will acquire these traits and soon they will be an integral part of their character. They will most likely be the kind who believe in constant learning and self-development. Therefore, they will indulge in a lot of introspection and will try and improve themselves. Once they have the determination and confidence in their self, they will be able to accomplish anything they want; especially, since they have the intelligence to go with it.

They will not be brutally blunt; rather, they will be diplomatic and tactful, since they want to protect the sentiments of other people. While this is a helpful habit professionally, in their personal life, they should try to suppress their real feelings. That will only end up hurting them and making their life difficult. Therefore, what they could do is try to speak their mind in a polite manner. Their tact and discreetness will make them quite successful in a political environment, should they choose to enter it.

They will also be extremely adaptable and will not have a problem interacting with people from cultures other than their own. As a result, they will be able to develop a multi-faceted personality and will have a wider perspective of the world around them. Even when they disagree with someone, they will tend to go along with it rather than be vocal and argue about it. While this is good, when they want to maintain the peace, they should try not to do it at the cost of their self-esteem.

Overall, they will be a perceptive, insightful and intelligent soul who will experience a lot of change in life and character. Every step will take them closer to their ultimate goal of self-realisation and contentment. They will surely be able to reach the pinnacle of success through their diligence, dedication and determination.

Finance

Money, for them, will not be a problem. Most Number five Cancerians make a good amount of money when working on their own. Being in a job or a partnership business will not always turn out to be their best option. They should try and make it on their own before turning to other alternatives. They will be gifted with an extremely sharp and keen mind; however, they will be so multi-talented and resourceful, that they will often get bored doing the same thing over and over again. A routine job, therefore, will not keep them interested for long and they will crave for something that is more flexible, stimulating and creative. Once they are able to figure out what is it they really want, they will be able to do really well and gain good profits from it.

Health

They will be gifted with an amazing ability to recover from illness, irrespective of how serious it may be. Moreover, they will also be affected by their thoughts. Therefore, they should try and think positive thoughts and illness will not be a worry for them. However, they should try and take things easy. Stress and nervous disorders could be a concern and may have long-term effects. Their legs and feet will be sensitive and therefore, they should take adequate care of them.

Essentially, for good health, all that they need is plenty of good food, sleep and exercise. Occasional vacations will help them to rejuvenate themselves and recharge their batteries.

Born on 6th, 15th, and 24th

If a person is a Cancerian born on any of the above-mentioned dates, they will be influenced by the vibes of the planets Neptune, Venus and the Moon. This particular combination which has the role of Venus will fill their life with plenty of romance and love, aside from making it an out of the ordinary type of life.

Gentle and sympathetic, they will be thoughtful about others and will try and give as much of their time, money and patience as is possible. They will also be involved in charitable causes and will in their own unique way, try and make a difference to society. They will be emotional and highly influenced by their friends and family. They will have a strong hold on them and they will often look to them for guidance and assistance.

They will have a certain charm and as a result, people will be drawn to them and be intrigued by them. This will enable them to build a strong social network and work their way up the ladder. Their drive to succeed and excel will also be a strong force in facilitating their growth and prosperity.

As far as marriage and domestic life is concerned, they will have to work hard in order to adjust and keep the peace. It is important that they learn to love their partner and make some amount of compromises in order to maintain the balance and harmony in their house.

Although, they have a keen curiosity for all things that are supernatural and spiritual, they are not blindly superstitious. They will have a healthy respect for the supernatural and the spiritual and will believe in fate and destiny, yet they will also have a strong self-respect in themselves and will want to make the most of what they have. They will work hard and give their best to everything.

They will have a sensitivity that will be hidden by a tough exterior. There will be times when they will laugh in order to hide their sadness. They will win people over with their dry humour and it will be quite easy for every one to relate with them, since they will be open and sensitive to them as well. Their warm and loving nature will bring them closer to others and though they may seem tough, they will actually be quite gentle inside.

Finance

They will be quite lucky as far as money and wealth are concerned. There are strong chances that they will come into money through marriage or inheritance. They will also try their hand at speculation and may invest in some property of their own. It is important that they take the advice of someone who is experienced, especially as they have quite an impressionable nature.

On the whole, they will not have to worry too much about finances. They will be intelligent when handling money and will ensure that they maintain a good balance between their income and expenditure.

Health

They will be blessed with a strong constitution and a good amount of energy and enthusiasm. As a result, they will be able to avoid most illnesses and when they are ill, they will have good recuperative powers. What they need to be on guard against will be too much work and stress. That is what will affect their nerves and make them prone to stress related disorders such as hypertension, allergies, glandular problems, etc. Therefore, the should remember to take a break every once in a while and go easy on themselves. Pushing themselves to the limit will only have a negative effect. They are lucky to have an inherently strong constitution, which will be able to bear the brunt of overwork to a large extent. It will be this strength and energy that will enable them to tide them over any illness. Be sure to follow a diet of nutritious food, regular exercise and sleep routines. It will never be too late to make amends and bring changes in their lifestyle.

Born on the 7th, 16th and 25th

For all those Cancerians born on the above mentioned dates, the influence of the planet Neptune and the Moon is extremely vital. Both of them will combine to endow them with a profoundly religious temperament and an abundance of creativity.

If they are born on any of the dates above, they will have a tendency to have unique and unconventional interests. Even as a child, they will be different and will often have their own identity from a young age. If given the right environment, they will be able to develop determination and self-control, which will enable them to be highly successful as an adult. Their confidence in their abilities will increase with age and they will be able to realise most of their aspirations and dreams.

They will be creative and imaginative. As a result, their emotional nature will also be finely developed and they will be intuitive and perceptive. If they take an interest in such matters, they might develop significant powers of occult and psychic behaviour. However, this will largely be dependent on their background and their inclination towards these arts. Nevertheless, their inherent ability to 'sense' situations and people will be of help to them in many areas of life.

There will also be a certain subtle, yet definite sophistication in their personality and preferences. Irrespective of their background, they will have dreams to be someone special and famous. They will carry themselves with class and dignity and everything that they do will only serve to take them closer to their real dream and goal of being someone others will look up to.

They will also have strong religious or spiritual tendencies. So deep will be their reverence, that they might even take it up on a professional level. They will be filled with a desire to help others and guide them towards righteousness and a higher level. They will also be involved with charities and voluntary organisations in their attempt to give something back to society.

While they will want to be known and famous, they will not want to be in the limelight at all times. This is one of the contradictory traits of their personality. They will achieve success and prosperity; however, they will retain their spiritualistic attitude towards life and humankind. This attitude will also help them to overcome difficult times and if they haven't started thinking positively, now is the time for them to look at obstacles as opportunities and bring greater contentment and happiness into their life.

Travelling will bring them great joy and they will particularly enjoy travelling by sea or by air. So deep will be their love for travelling, that they will often, spend a significant portion of their time and money on it. New cultures, foreign customs and a whole different world will appeal to their instinct and impulse to learn more about the world.

They will also be tied strongly to home and family. However, for someone of their disposition, it will be beneficial to marry late in life, since by that time, they would have figured out what they want from life and also from their partner. It is important that they should be willing to adjust and be adaptable to their partner, in order to make the marriage stronger and more stable.

Finance

Cancerians born on the 7th, 16th and 25th will have strange and unconventional experiences with regards to money and finance. They will often, gain great profits from the most unexpected sources and similarly, there could also be the possibility that they may lose some of that wealth through unforeseen circumstances. In any case, money matters for them will never be as traditional as they are for most people. They may also come into money through inheritance and legacies. However, these, too, may have some conditions attached to them.

The best advice for them will be to develop a strong sense of confidence and belief in themself. That will enable them to take some risks and follow their dreams. This will also help them to build their own wealth and be more secure financially. Relying on others will always be uncertain. They are gifted with talents and abilities that will propel them towards success. The key is to tap into them and be persistent and determined. Nothing will stop them once they have started believing in themselves. Money matters will be resolved and there will not be too many hitches with their investments.

Health

Their physical health will be affected largely by their mental health. Therefore, they will be as good as they feel. Negative thoughts, low self-esteem and pessimism will be dísastrous for them. It is important that they develop a positive and confident approach towards life and its aspects, in order to remain healthy and fit.

Although they may not be physically strong, they have mental toughness. Once they decide on something, they will ensure that they see it through. That is why they should develop a strong faith in their abilities and potential and there will be nothing that will stand in their way. If they continue to be anxious and stressed out, they will be prone to ulcers, headaches, colds and other stress-related disorders. These will cease their hold on them, once they change their attitude.

Born on 8th, 17th and 26th

Cancerians born on the dates given above will be ruled by the influence of the planets Neptune, Saturn and the Moon. This trilogy of planets will have definite and distinctive effects on the personality of the individual and will enhance certain characteristics while reducing others.

If they were born on any of the dates given above, they will have a strong and sombre mind. They will not be inclined towards frivolous behaviour and trivialities. They will treat life with seriousness and will be firm and strong-willed in everything that they do. There will also be chances that they will be more mature and responsible than their other counterparts, at an early age. They will have a logical and intelligent way of dealing with the various aspects of life and will not fritter away their time in useless activities and mindless chatter. They will be focused on what they want and how they are going to achieve it.

This should, however, not imply that they will be dull and boring. On the other hand, it simply means that they will want to spend their time and life in a more worthwhile fashion and will at the same time, be cheerful and upbeat about it.

There are strong indications that till the time they reach middle age, they will be bound by the ties of family and obligations towards others. As a result, they may feel stifled and suffocated. However, they will carry out all their responsibilities and simply wait for the right time. They will have complete faith in themselves and their fate. As a result, they will be able to bear long periods of stress and toil, since they know that ultimately they will reach their goal.

Although they are intense and passionate emotionally, they do not have the art of being expressive. Therefore, there are chances that they might not tell people how they really feel and will often subdue their feelings and sentiments. This might become an issue in matters of love and romance. If they are unable to express themselves, they might not be able to tell their partner how they feel. However, this will vary depending on family background and childhood experiences.

They will often, have to bear the burden of others and lend a helping hand more often than they will want to. However, they will do all this with a smile and will not complain, since it will not be in their nature to do so. There are chances that they may not receive the gratitude that they deserve for being helpful and compassionate. This will hurt them and they may withdraw into a shell. It is important that they realise their self-worth and go through life with their inherently strong sense of determination and persistence. They should be resolute and nothing will be able to obstruct their progress and success.

Although, they may face many constraints and limitations during their initial years, once they develop and build their sense of independence and strength of mind, they will have little to worry about. They will overcome obstacles with courage and strength and ultimately reach their goals and aspirations.

As far as their career aspirations are concerned, they will have one of the two options that normally face Cancerians born on the above-mentioned dates. They could be really lucky and get to pursue their dreams and hone their talents into their career. In this case, they will enjoy what they do and take great pride and pleasure in their job. In the other case, they may be compelled to take up a particular professional line due to family or economic factors. Even in this case, they will be successful and will make money, however, they may not get the chance to explore their inherent potential and make the most of it. Nevertheless, they will be successful and prosperous, provided they devote themselves to their work and maintain they sense of integrity.

Fundamentally, it has been seen that most Cancerians born on these dates will have to struggle in their initial years. However, once they find their footing, they will be firm and persistent and will rest only when they reach their goals. Not only that, they will often, set their sights higher than most people and will drive themselves to achieve that high goal.

In matters of religion and faith, again, Number eight Cancerians can be of two types. They will either be fervent and ardent devotees or they will be atheists. They will not follow a middle path when it comes to religion.

Since they are the sort who will enjoy taking on responsibility and leading a life that is serious and logical, they will do well in positions of authority either in the government or in the private sector. Leadership roles will suit them and they will carry out their duties with seriousness and propriety. If engaged in business, they will do well in fields such as oil, mining, real estate and similar lines.

Finance

For Cancerians born on the 8th, 17th and 26th, money will not be too much of a problem. They will have an innate sense of determination and this will ensure that they build up their wealth and retain it. Since they will have a mature outlook to life, they will not indulge in unnecessary risk-taking and will prefer to stick to the more conventional and safer modes of investments.

Health

They will have a strong constitution and will be able to lead a healthy and fit life. However, as they will be somewhat serious in their outlook, they may need to see life in a lighter vein every now and then. That will help them to be more cheerful and keep most illnesses at bay. They will be prone to disorders of the digestive system, especially acidity and may also face some problems with the joints and bones. They should follow a routine of healthy food and regular exercise, as well as spend some time with people who make them laugh and smile. This simple regime will keep them in health.

Born on the 9th, 18th and 27th

For Cancerians born on the 9th, 18th and 27th, the influence of the planets Mars, Neptune and the Moon becomes critical and significant. This combination of planetary influences will bring about certain unique changes in the individual's inherent personality. These will make them rebellious and straightforward and also place certain hurdles in their path to success.

They will have a strong and definite defiant streak. They will not tolerate any illogical restriction and restraint. They will often want to be their own person and will not pay any attention to the dictates of others. They will be highly unconventional and self-reliant; however, they will also be prone to being short-tempered and irritable. They will not be extremely patient, especially when they have something on their mind.

They will have a blunt and candid way of talking and more often than not, will hurt people with the way they put things across. It will be advisable for them to develop softness and discretion in their speech. This will serve in the best of their interests, professionally and personally.

There is the possibility that their path to success will be filled with many ups and downs, therefore, it is essential that they be tough and strong-willed so that they can deal with failure and be able to get back on their feet in no time at all. A lot of changes in their life will also be brought about by their own love for adventure and risk. They will want to experience everything that life has to offer and will embrace it with open arms. Fear and uncertainty will have no place in their personality and once they find their true calling, they will be relentless in its pursuit.

Everything they do will bear their stamp of innovation and entrepreneurship. Even if they are working for someone else, their work will have its own unique identity and they will give their hundred per cent to it. They will not want to settle for anything but the best and this will reflect most clearly in their work.

Since they will have a highly independent attitude, there is the possibility that they may not have too many close relations and friends. They will want to be with people whom they genuinely love and respect and will not want to waste time on hypocrites and selfish people. Their spirit for adventure will often lead them into unexpected situations and mishaps. It will be a wise decision for them to invest in good insurance and protect themselves from financial uncertainty.

Their life will be interesting and filled with many twists and turns. They will not be content leading a regular, systematic existence. Excitement and thrills will fill them with a longing to be a part of the wider world and it is with this spirit that they will travel to far-off places and learn more about life and people. It will help them if they become more oriented towards living with others rather than fighting them. Once they get used to the idea of being part of a team, they will be a capable and trustworthy team member.

On the whole, they will have a cheerful and bubbly personality. Combined with their strength, they will be efficient and capable of dealing with any situation that comes their way. Crises and deadlines will bring out the best in them. They will quite enjoy being pushed to the limit so that they can exploit their potential to the maximum. There is no doubt, that they will be confident of becoming someone to reckon with and this belief will empower them to realise their dreams and goals.

Finance

Money matters for Number nine Cancerians will not be worrisome. There will be times when there will be a surplus of cash and money; however, these might be followed by some lean times. However, they will have the strength to be able to withstand the tough times and enjoy the good ones. It is important that if entering their own business, they do sufficient study and research in order to make profits. Risky ventures and get-rich-quick schemes do not suit them and they will only end up losing money in them. They should always remember that when they do have the money, they should save a large portion of it for their future. Extravagance and splurging on luxuries will be their weak point and they will need to guard against this.

Since they will have plenty of unique and innovative ideas for business ventures, there are many chances that they will be quite successful as an entrepreneur and will be comfortably well off at nearly every stage in life.

Health

For Number nine Cancerians, health will not be a huge concern. They will be gifted with an abundance of energy and strength and hence, they will be able to bounce back from any illness or disease. As far as ailments are concerned, they will have to take special care of their eyes, legs and feet. Also, be especially vigilant when travelling to avoid unforeseen mishaps and accidents.

LEO

(23RD JULY TO 23RD AUGUST)

Leo in General

Leo—a sign symbolised by the Lion, is indeed, a sign that has strong and kingly qualities. It is a sign that begins on the 21st of July. However, it is preceded by the cusp of the previous sign that is, Cancer and therefore, assumes complete power somewhere around the 28th of July and then retains it right till 20th of August, where it begins to lose strength to the cusp of the incoming sign, that is, Virgo. Here, we will study the fundamental traits of Leo and find out what distinguishes this sign from all the rest.

Ambitious and purposeful, they are always focused on rising above the benchmark and being way ahead of everyone else. So strong is their desire to excel and be the best that irrespective of their background, they will be able to succeed and reach where they want to. Their willpower, determination and efficiency will give them all the power they need in order to be the best.

They will also be inspired by and drawn towards people who are equally strong and have achieved something in life. Their friends and acquaintances will be those individuals who have enough self-respect and focus in their lives. Even if someone makes a mistake but is honest and sincerely apologetic about it, the Leo person will willingly forgive and forget.

One of the most distinguishing and prominent characteristics of Leos is their big-hearted and charitable spirits. They will be compassionate and will be absolutely willing to share their lives and possessions with everyone else. Family, friends and even acquaintances will have an important place in their life. However, despite the fact that they will be warm and loving, they will also be self-reliant and independent and will not want others to run their lives for them.

Goal-driven and tenacious, they will not rest till they achieve what they set their mind to. They will work hard and with sincerity and overcome all that stands in their path. They will have to deal with people who are jealous of them and conditions that make realisation impossible, yet they will continue working and moving closer towards what they want. It is not surprising, therefore, that they will be able to attain their aims and objectives, sooner or later.

Leos have an innate tendency of stimulating and driving others to do well and rise to great heights as well. As a result, they will often be natural leaders and will win the admiration and love of their subordinates, peers and superiors. They will have a strong, charismatic personality and will always be able to attract people towards themselves and their beliefs.

Normally, these individuals will have immense tolerance and will be able to take a lot of pain and pressure. However, if someone hurts them deeply, they will become real lions and will become so courageous that they will even amaze themselves. They will have an immense amount of strength and perseverance, and as a result, will not want to face defeat in anything. Success is what they will want and that is what they will eventually accomplish.

Frank and spontaneous, they will be warm and loving individuals who will exude this warmth all over and make people feel comfortable and at home without much effort. They will also be natural and liberal in their temperament. This will not mean that they will not have any opponents or envious people. Their popularity and spontaneity will sometimes, hurt others who will be jealous of them and try to ruin them.

Leos will not be affected by what people think of them. Also, they will handle their enemies with their characteristic class and charisma. Most importantly, they will not let their progress be hampered by jealous and conniving people. In any case, they will not appreciate any kind of sly, cunning behaviour. As friends, Leos will be extremely loyal and devoted. They will stand up for and support their friends, no matter what. What is important to them is that their loyalty should be reciprocated.

They will also be magnanimous in everything that they do. Everything about them will have a touch of subtle royalty. Their walk, way of speaking, interacting with people, dress, everything will reflect their classiness and sophistication. Even if not wealthy, Leos will be able to look graceful and behave with certain nobility. They will also love to do things on a grand scale. Parties, events, celebrations, will all be a large affair with lots of friends, family, food and fun.

Leos will have an unwavering belief in the goodness of humanity. As a result, they will sometimes, be disappointed by friends and relatives. This sadness might also lead to separations and heartbreaks for the strong yet sensitive Leos. Leos will also be gifted with great management skills and will be extremely efficient at handling teams and getting good results from them.

As a matter of fact, they will, invariably, be glad to accept most tasks and take on more than they can handle.

Since, Leos will be innate leaders, they will need to work on controlling their tendency to dominate and control others. Also, they will often want to have things done their way and this might hurt people and rub them the wrong way. Being stubborn and obstinate, they will work hard on wanting people to be the way they want them to. This is one of the traits that they will need to reduce or curb, in order to be more efficient with people and friends.

Leos will also have a strong sense of pride and vanity. They will enjoy being in the limelight and basking in the appreciation of others. However, more often than not, they will have worked hard for it and earned it. Since, they will want to be high up in the social or professional ladder, Leos will often be inspired by people who are already up there. They will, consciously or otherwise, emulate them and be motivated by them. This will increase their knowledge and make them more aware human beings.

Leos will do well in most fields. Politics, management, acting, are just some of the fields where they will excel. What will be important to them doing well will be their interest in what they are doing. If they are stimulated by what they do, they will devote themselves to the task and excel at it. Mundane and monotonous activities will not interest them and they will not want to simply settle for something less than the best.

Finance

Leos will have quite a bit of luck with regard to money and wealth. If engaged in any business, they will do quite well and make a good deal of profit. Similarly, if engaged professionally, they will be quite successful and will climb up the corporate ladder quickly and profitably. Their hard work, enthusiasm, energy and integrity will be responsible for bringing success and profits to them. Wise investment of the money earned and a balance between spending and earning will all prove beneficial for them. Spending is something that they will need to curb, since they will be quite fond of luxury and will try and splurge on it as much as possible.

They are also generous and will often, support charities and organisations involved in relief and support work. They are intelligent and diligent and hence, there is little doubt that they will make quite a fortune for themselves.

Health

Leos will be influenced by the warm rays of the Sun and hence, will be blessed with a robust constitution. They will be filled with energy and will glow with life and strength. Even when ill, they will recover with quickness and be back on their feet in next to no time.

They are fond of good food and will therefore, have to guard themselves against stomach disorders. Also, their tendency to take on too much will make them susceptible to hypertension and stress-related disorders. Other than that, they will be healthy and will hardly ever suffer from any major illness. They should ensure that they get plenty of sunshine, fresh air and nourishing food. These will keep them in the pink of health.

Some form of exercise is also important for them, otherwise the joints could give trouble and rheumatism or arthritis might affect them at some stage in life. Exercise will also help to prevent any cardiac or gastric disorders.

In view of the fact that Leos are sensitive to their surroundings, they should stay in happy and positive environs, because excessive sadness, boredom or melancholy will have a negative influence on their temperament and physical health and well-being.

Leo

Born on 1st, 10th, 19th and 28th

If a person is a Leo born on 1st, 10th, 19th or 28th, he will be influenced by the planetary vibes of the Sun and Uranus. This particular planetary alliance will gift them with a sharp mind and a strong sense of diligence and determination.

Leos will have fiery ambition and will be focused on realising their dreams and aspirations. They will be positive and cheerful, filled with warmth and radiating energy in everything that they do. Their personality will be such that people will be drawn towards them and will aspire to be like them. They will ensure that they deliver what they promise and this diligence of theirs will never go unnoticed. Hardworking and loyal, they will have a wide circle of friends and success in nearly all their endeavours.

Their sense of purpose will be so strong, that even if they encounter failure, they will take it in their stride and work around it. They will not let setbacks overwhelm them; rather, they will try and see the best in every situation. They are innovative and independent. Their views and opinions will most decidedly be their own and they will use their words to motivate and inspire others. They will be especially intense and strong-willed in deciding who they like and who they do not. As far as love and romance are concerned, they need a partner who will let them be their own person and at the same time be someone they look up to. If they find the right person, they will plunge head-long into marriage and be passionate about it.

They will be fond of being in the limelight and hence, appreciation and awards will make them very happy and give them a sense of satisfaction. They like to be recognised for the work that they do. If this doesn't happen, they could become morose and disappointed. They also have a fiery temper and will quite often lose it at someone or something. However, they will also be pacified quite easily and will forgive, as long as they are convinced that the erring person is genuinely sorry.

They have a warm and generous approach and will be moved by people who are less fortunate. They will constantly try and make things better in their own way and this will bring great deal of peace to them. They will be a faithful and dependable friend and will fight for a worthy cause without any fear. Their courage and strength will emerge in full form when faced with a crisis. Truly, they are not the kind to buckle down under pressure; rather, they will make the most of a situation and will surely overcome all odds.

If there is something that they are passionate about, they will not be affected by anything or anyone. Their opponents, circumstances and resources will not be allowed to stand in the way of their progress. They will be like a strong wind and will blow away any obstacle, however large it may be.

They will do well in nearly anything they attempt. However, dramatics, politics and humanitarian activities will bring out the best in them. They will be a natural leader or actor and will have the ability to move the masses by their words or actions. If as a child they have been instilled with the right values, they will be a valuable asset and will live a life of integrity and humaneness. It is not surprising, therefore, that they will be a source of inspiration for many. They, too, will be inspired by strong and ambitious people who have achieved a lot in their own lives and they will follow their example in their own existence.

They are also emotional and close to people they value. They will be loving and caring and will enjoy entertaining friends and loved ones. Their fondness for good food and luxury will make their parties popular and they will quite often, be the centre of attraction due to their sense of humour and warm approach.

Finance

As far as financial matters are concerned, they will be luckier than most others. The main reason behind this will be their positive attitude and that they will treat all hardships as mere stages in the path to prosperity. Even if they had to struggle during their initial years, they will see that only as a temporary phase. Their hard work, diligence and determination will pay off and they will enjoy the life they always wanted, sooner or later. Money will not be everything for them. However, they will value it and realise its importance. That is why they will be willing to work hard for it. More than money, though, they will enjoy fame and popularity. If they are acknowledged for the work that they do, they will be a happy soul.

Their professional life will be made up of two phases. The first one will be the phase of hard work and toil. The second phase will be the one where they will lie back and savour the fruits of all that hard work. They will also be wise when investing their money and at the same time, will enjoy spending it as well. Comfort and luxury will appeal to them and once they reach the stage when they can afford it, they will go all out to splurge.

Health

Since their innate temperament will be a cheerful and optimistic one, they will not suffer from many illnesses. They will not be predisposed to melancholy and brooding. As long as they are busy and active, they will be as fit as a fiddle. During childhood and adolescence, they may suffer from the usual minor ailments; however, as an adult they will be relatively disease free. What is important is that they should surround themselves with interesting work and a circle of close friends and relatives. Take an interest in physical activity to keep the body agile and maintain a balance in their food habits.

Born on 2nd, 11th, 20th and 29th

Leos born on the 2nd, 11th, 20th and 29th will be ruled by the planetary influences of the Sun, the Moon and Neptune. This combination of influences is a fortunate and beneficial one. It will enhance certain positive features in the individual, such as his intellect, charisma and optimism.

In case they were born on either one of the dates given above, they will have a strong and remarkable personality. People will be able to trust them easily since they will believe in keeping promises and living with integrity. They will have a flair for words and will use them with finesse to make their point and even charm members of the opposite sex.

Romantic and optimistic, they will be attractive and charming in everything that they do. They will have a knack of being the centre of attention and will bask in the glow of love and affection. Their self-confidence will also be a major reason people will be able to depend on them and they will always try and ensure that they do not let anyone down.

One of the features that will be softened due to the influence of their ruling planets will be their blunt and candid speech. They will, in comparison to their other counterparts, be quite discreet and subtle. They will know what, where and how to say things. This will increase their popularity and will also make them quite successful if they decide to get into politics.

Professionally, they will do well in any field which will make good use of their tact, management skills and diligence. It will also be important that they are engaged in a job that allows them to think creatively and be of some vital use. Mundane and dreary routine jobs will bore them and stifle their energy and enthusiasm. They will have quite a strong influence over people and combined with their other skills, this will make them quite a dynamic personality. Therefore, they will do well in fields such as teaching, training, law, preaching, and social work as well as in a managerial profile in any business organisation.

Liberal and generous, they will be a warm and trustworthy friend. They will be the kind who will support friends and fight for them without batting an eyelid. Their home will be the gathering spot for their social circle and they will enjoy entertaining and socialising. Their warmth and affectionate nature will be so endearing that hardly anyone will be able to remain angry with them for long. As a result, they will not have many enemies. Even if someone does not agree to their opinions or views, they will not hold it against them and will let them be.

For someone like them, who sets high standards for themselves, it will be important that people around them also give their best to everything. It will hurt them to see anyone they know not maximising their potential and shying away from being the best they can be. In this sense, they might be perceived as dominating and controlling. However, their intention will be to help and improve. They might get carried away and become harsh, yet they will only want to ensure that their friends or team members are giving their one hundred per cent.

They will be fond of observing the world around them and this will enhance their skills of perception and intuition. However, they will not be judgmental and biased. All they wish to do is to widen their horizon and learn more about relating to others. This skill of theirs will be helpful if engaged in any social or humanitarian work. They will be able to reach out to people in distress or trouble and make them feel calm and worthy. Not only that, they will also have an approachable air because of which others will feel comfortable and secure in their company. Relatives and friends may often confide in them and seek their advice, since they are not only good at counselling, but they are also patient listeners.

They are not afraid of working hard in order to get what they deserve. If not born into wealth, they will work their way up the socio-economic ladder and reach the goal that they set for themselves. Diligent and determined, they will not let minor failures disillusion them and they will be enthusiastic and positive about achieving their targets. The most important thing is that they will have complete belief in themselves and their abilities. This is what will motivate them and keep them going, even in difficult times.

Finance

From a financial standpoint, they will be quite lucky. Earning money will come easily to them and even if they are not born into a rich family, they will be able to accumulate quite a bit of wealth for themselves. However, there are chances that they may not value it greatly. They will give away money to charities and people in need, without even thinking about it. Even if friends and relatives borrow money, they will not bother asking back for it. This could result in them not having enough for themselves. It will be advisable if they curb their generosity a bit and also remember to save something for themselves. This, however, will not be the case if they have grown up in a family where money was valued right from the beginning. In that case, they will have a healthy respect for it but will not let it become the most important thing in their life.

They will earn by virtue of their gifts and abilities. Their eloquence, comfort with people, management skills, flair for dramatics and the arts will all be responsible for ensuring a decent flow of money. They will also do well and earn a good salary if working with an organisation at a position that suits their intelligence and capabilities.

Health

For them, health will be a priority. They should ensure that they get enough rest, exercise, sleep and nourishing food. Spend time outdoors and absorb the beneficial rays of the sun which will fill them with positive energy and strength. They will also need to protect their throat and lungs which could be somewhat sensitive and prone to infections. As long as they have something stimulating to occupy them and keep them engaged, they will not have many worries and will be happy and content.

Born on 3rd, 12th, 21st and 30th

In case persons are Leo born on any of the above dates, then they will be influenced by the planetary vibes of the Sun along with Uranus and Jupiter. This particular alliance of planets will bring about certain distinctive qualities in their already dynamic personality and will surely give them an edge above the rest.

They will be gifted with an enhanced sense of ambition and motivation. They will always be goal-driven and filled with an immense amount of energy to achieve and realise their dreams. They will not be the kind who will settle for anything but the best. For them, life will always be a fast-paced journey and the destination will be success and prosperity.

They will be extremely devoted to the task at hand and will always and under all conditions, give their one hundred per cent to everything they do. Their meticulous attention to detail will set them apart from the crowd and it will only be a matter of time before they are recognised and appreciated. For them, appreciation will be valuable and they will cherish it. Working and not getting credit for it will not be something that they will enjoy and chances are if in a thankless job, they will soon quit and look for better opportunities.

They will be loving and jovial, because of which their circle of friends will be large. They will enjoy socialising and meeting new and interesting people. They will also have the gift of making others feel important and needed. However, they will need to guard themselves against the desire to be the focus of attention all the time. Should learn to share the limelight and they will have even more friends with them.

They are a born leader and have a wonderful knack of making the masses listen to them. Their way with words will be their greatest asset and so will be their human touch. They will do extremely well in a position of power and authority. They will have a deep sense of integrity and will never misuse the power that they are entrusted with. However, since they will want everybody to be at their best, they could drive them too hard and be perceived as a dictator. If they curb this tendency to dominate and control, they will be a great role model for everyone around them.

The influence of their ruling planets will give them the ability to be successful in fields of law, politics and government organisations. They will do exceedingly well when involved with the public or the major section of society. Doing humanitarian work and social service will bring out the best in them and will appeal to their sensitive and benevolent side.

Not only are they generous, they are also warm and affectionate and enjoy taking an interest in their home and domestic life. As far as their love life and marriage are concerned, they will need to ensure that they marry someone who will respect their independence and individuality as well as be supportive and encouraging of them. If they make a few adjustments and try being less controlling, they will have a successful marriage. They are fond of children and will be very good with them. They will be able to maintain a sense of discipline and at the same time, balance it out with light-hearted fun and enjoyment. Life will be cheerful and sunny with them, and their sense of humour will often lighten up many faces and hearts.

There will always be a certain gracefulness about them. Even if they do not belong to a royal family, their carriage and demeanor will be noble and stately. They will also have high aims and will not be daunted by any hurdle, circumstance or condition. They are confident and if they focus and work hard, they will surely achieve everything. Their strength of character and determination of purpose will ensure that success is theirs, eventually.

Their desire to be the best and reach the pinnacle of success will be fiery and will motivate them to deliver their best. It is not surprising therefore, that once they set their heart on something, they will not rest till they have it. This strong ambition will be their strength and their weakness. They may tend to push themselves too hard and take on too much, so much so that they may simply buckle under the pressure. Always maintain a healthy balance and be sensible about what they can and cannot do. There is nothing wrong with being laid back and relaxed for a while.

As they enjoy praise and adulation, it is advisable that they remain on their guard against flattery. They should always trust their instincts and be impartial and clear when dealing with people. Keep in mind these suggestions and there will be nothing to stop them from leading a life that is successful, happy and healthy.

Finance

They will be quite sensible about money and investments. As a result, they will make wise decisions when multiplying their income and will be able to build up quite a bit of wealth. They will also be quite intuitive to the ways of the world and will have a flair for predicting the trends of the market. Therefore, investing in stocks and shares will be quite beneficial for them. However, always remember to take the advice of someone who is knowledgeable and reliable about these things.

They will not believe in simply saving all that they earn. Rather, they will use it to surround themselves with luxuries and comforts. They might also have the tendency to splurge and be extravagant. Moreover, they could also put their money into an upcoming and large business. Whatever they do, always ensure that they keep a sum aside for rainy days and that they rely on the counsel of dependable people.

Health

In matters of health and fitness, they will be quite fortunate and will not have many worries. However, they will be fond of rich food and drink and if not kept in control, this fondness could make them susceptible to obesity, hypertension and even cardiac problems. They should balance out their diet with exercise and healthy food and this will not be a concern. Too much of stress is also not beneficial to their health. They should alternate periods of hectic activity with periods of rest and relaxation. This will help their body to recover from all the wear and tear and make them stronger for future endeavours.

Born on 4th, 13th, 22nd and 31st

Leos who are Number four people are influenced by the planetary rays of the Sun and Uranus. This combination will make them more independent and individualistic than their other counterparts born on other dates. We will go ahead and study more of their unique characteristics in the following pages.

They will be completely their own person in thought and word and deed. Everything that they will be and do and say will be influenced by their own ideas and learning. They will not be the sort who will be dependent and submissive. Self-reliant and liberated, they dislike irrational restrictions and regulations. They will be their best when allowed to be free and natural.

The traditional and mundane will not interest them. As a result, from an early age, they will try and find out new and different ways of doing things. They will enjoy novelty, innovation and change. Thinking out of the box appeals to them and they will constantly be working on being different from the crowd. There are strong chances that they will be a trailblazer in everything that they undertake and life will never be boring and routine with them around.

Since they value their independence, they will find it very difficult to be bound by the ties of family and kinship. As a matter of fact, being bound and expected to behave in a certain manner will irritate them and they will try and break away from it as soon as possible. They will respect everyone's privacy and will want the same from them. If they do not get it, chances are that they will want to be on their own and lead their own life.

Exploring new places and meeting new people will be activities that they will enjoy simply because they give them the chance to learn, absorb and most importantly, will not be boring. They thrive on adventure, excitement and newness. Therefore, for them, life should be constant innovation and change. Moreover, as they will be somewhat offbeat, others might find it difficult to keep pace with them and therefore, most of their plans could involve only a limited circle of friends.

As far as romance and love is concerned, they should try and develop more understanding and serenity within themselves. This will go a long way in cementing their bond with their loved one and giving the relationship stability and endurance. Otherwise, partners may find it difficult to keep adjusting with them and giving into their desires all the time. Once they find the right person and meet him or her halfway, they will be a loving and compassionate soul who will want the relationship to become permanent and lasting.

While they will not have too many close friends, they might have some enemies or rather, people whose sentiments have been hurt by their rather straightforward and unusual views on religion, god and similar subjects. Therefore, it will help to be more discreet about such things.

They are a strong person and will be able to take many things in stride. Also, since their life will be quite eventful, their inherent strength will help them in overcoming challenges in their path and standing up to those who oppose them. Moreover, due to their unconventional temperament, their friends will be few and they will need to rely on their independence and courage to be able to face the world on their own. However, the friends they have will be loyal to them and they will be devoted to them as well. It is important that you have a positive and affirmative attitude which keeps them motivated and focused throughout.

Finance

They will be just as different and independent with finance as they will be with everything else. While it may seem that they may not have much value for money, they will be enamoured by the authority that it will give them. It is important that they trust their own instincts when deciding on how to invest or even earn their money. With their strong independent streak, a partnership will not be very successful, unless they meet someone who will understand them completely.

Their intuition and sharp business acumen will be helpful when they invest their money and they could also use this knowledge and talent to help others. Therefore, being in professions such as banking, will be one of the areas where they will be successful and prosperous. On the whole, they will work more for mental satisfaction; however, the money that they earn will be a definite plus point.

Health

Number four Leos are blessed with a strong constitution. However, this will be largely dependent on their internal state and their surroundings. It is important that they live in a cheerful and positive environment and that they are occupied and busy with something. Otherwise, they could become sad and irritable which will give rise to several psychosomatic ailments. Other than that, they are not susceptible to the regular gamut of sickness and disease. They should ensure that they get plenty of sunshine and exercise to make their bones strong since they could be somewhat brittle and give them slight concern every now and then.

Born on 5th, 14th and 23rd

Leos born on the dates given above will be affected by the vibes from the planets Uranus and Mercury along with the Sun. This combination of planetary influences will bestow the individual with a sharp intellect and a distinctive identity. These individuals will also have most of the general qualities of Leos, however, some will be more pronounced than others. This is what will set Number five Leos apart from the rest.

The influence of Mercury on Number five Leos will have both positive and negative aspects. Let us first consider the positive aspects. Mercury will endow the individual with intelligence and rationale. If they are born on any of the dates given above, they will be fortunate as they will have the uncanny and useful art of reasoning and logic. They will be able to take sound decisions and most of them will serve a purpose in deciding their prosperity. On the other hand, they might also become too rash and reckless. There may be some things that they will simply plunge into and not give sufficient thought to. Mercury will also be responsible for making them somewhat short on patience. They will become irritable if things take too long and this could hamper their progress and affect your state of mind.

It will be the vibes that they receive from Mercury that will fill them with a strong sense of ambition and motivation. They will be constantly in the pursuit of goals and dreams. This pursuit will give their life focus and meaning. It is not surprising, therefore, that most Number five Leos will have a comfortable life and will often seem to have everything going for them.

Their inherent confidence and poise will be remarkable. They will also have warmth that will make others feel wanted and cared for. Even if they do not like someone, they will not make that person feel unwanted or unloved. And yet, they will not be hypocritical. So strong is their charisma. This facet of their personality will primarily be due to the alliance of the Sun with Mercury. This influence also gifts them with a sharp sense of business and finance. As a result, they will be able to make the right financial decisions and will often build a decent bank balance for their future.

They will certainly not have a boring and mundane life. It will be filled with twists and turns and will keep them on their toes at all times. Change, new situations, new people and new jobs will be a constant feature of their existence. This will be the result of Uranus and Mercury. They will also be fond of travelling and absorbing new cultures and modes of living.

Passionate and intense, they will devote themselves to their aims and interests. Friends and family will also be an integral part of their life. They will be sociable and have a good sense of humour. Combined with their sensitivity and caring attitude, they will be a loyal and dependable friend. People will be charmed by them, mostly in the first instance, and they will go on to prove their value.

They will have the tendency to bottle up their feelings for fear of hurting others. While this can be good, at the same time, it is essential that they look after themselves as well and do not put too much stress on their own nerves. Talking to trusted friends and relatives will help. Also, they could try being tactful and at the same time, express their sentiments and emotions.

Although they are hardworking and determined, they enjoy working for short-term goals rather than long-term ones. This is mainly because they enjoy change and newness. Anything that goes on for too long will bore them and they will cease to take an interest in it. Even if they continue, their passion for it will decrease and they will not be able to deliver their best. They will be the kind who will be fired with the thrill of working on something challenging and absorbing, something that has not been tried before. It is not surprising therefore, that they will do well in fields where there is constant change and innovation. Science, experiments, law, medicine, and even management will be some of the fields where they will do well.

They are quite strong in their views and opinions. Since they have a strong sense of reason and logic, it is not easy to argue with them. They have a way with words, which when combined with their ability to reason, make them a sure winner. Also, they will be fluid in their movement and there will be a certain grace in their carriage. This will make them quite good at dancing, gymnastics and sports.

The element of change and novelty will also follow them in matters of love and romance. They will probably have a few love affairs before they finally decide to settle down. For someone to pin them down, they will have to be quite a bundle of mystery and intrigue. It is important that they interest them; otherwise, they will get bored and decide to move on. Once they find the right partner, they will be a faithful, loving and fun person to live with. They might have a slightly possessive attitude; however, it will not be stifling and they will be willing to make some amount of adjustments.

They will be quite independent in their thoughts and actions. They will do what is right by them and there will not be many people whom they will listen to. Their identity will be their own and they will ensure that it is distinct from everyone else. They will not like to be tied down to tradition and conventions. Different and original will be their chief trademarks.

Finance

They will be blessed with sharp business acumen. Therefore, they will make wise and profitable decisions when investing their own money as well as the money of other people. Their ability to adjust to any condition or circumstance will make it easy for them to have a diverse range of business interests and gain from many sources. What they will need to be on the look out for are selfish and self-centered people who will try and use them and their intellect for undesirable and illegal purposes. As long as they trust their sound judgement and choose the right partners and friends, they will continue to succeed and prosper.

Health

Living a life filled with a lot of change and pressure can put stress on their nerves and entire system, thereby tiring them out and draining their energy. It is important for them to have adequate rest and peace in their life. Taking a holiday every now and then will do well for their nerves and will also suit their personality. They should eat their meals at regular intervals and eat wholesome food since they will be somewhat susceptible to indigestion, acidity and gastric problems.

When ill, they will want to recover really quickly. They will also try and combat stress and pressure with artificial stimulants like alcohol, drugs, nicotine, etc. It is important that they do not succumb to these as they will lead them only to ruin and misery. What is important is to balance out periods of hectic activity with complete relaxation. That will work best for someone like them.

Born on 6th, 15th and 24th

Number six Leos are influenced by the vibes from the planets Venus and Uranus along with the Sun. This alliance of planetary vibes results in making the native more loving, attractive, independent and vibrant than the rest.

Let us start by considering the influence of Venus on Leos born on the above-mentioned dates. If they are one of them, they will be warmer and more caring. Also, it will be their loving temperament that will be largely responsible for their prosperity and success. They will be highly compassionate and sensitive. Also, they have a strong sense of benevolence and will often go out of their way to help the weak and needy. This characteristic of theirs is appealing to people and they will normally have a wide circle of friends.

They will be quite passionate when in love and will make their partner feel extremely special and wanted. They could also become too possessive at times. This does not imply that all they are interested in is love and romance. They will also be devoted to their goals in life and working toward ensuring a better future.

Their personality will be such that they will make friends with ease and will also enjoy being in the company of those who will appreciate and acknowledge them. Again, this should not imply that they like flattery. However, they like sincere praise and appreciation. Socialising, as a matter of fact, will be one of their prime interests. They love to attend and have parties. Gatherings will bring out the best in them and they will be known for bringing life to a party. Their cheerfulness and warmth will be charming and contagious. It will envelop everyone and spread a feeling of happiness. It is not surprising, therefore, that they will have a wide circle of friends, acquaintances and associates.

They also have strong bonds with their home and family. They will know their priorities and will ensure that all aspects of their life are well looked after. They have good organisational skills and this will help them to deal well with the day-to-day problems of life and work.

They will be successful in theatre, arts, literature, music and similar lines. They will also do well in the more conventional forms of occupation such as teaching, management, banking and business. What is essential is that they are interested in the line of work and that they are recognised for the efforts they make. That will be enough motivation for them and they will continue to give their best to what they do.

One of their interesting habits will be to observe others and learn from them. They will often, be found staring at people and trying to figure out the story of their life. The best part is that they will not be judgmental. Yet, they will have an interest in them. They often like to be with young people and this keeps them young at heart. They will not let age cramp their style and if something intrigues them, they will go right ahead and do it, irrespective of their age.

Due to the presence of Uranus in their Number and sign, they are often drawn towards different and unusual people. This accounts for their own unconventional views and opinions. There is also the possibility that they may not be understood properly by others and this may result in some hurt and sadness in their life. Their good intentions and ideas may be misconstrued leading to difficulties in their life. However, they will be resilient and will be able to come out of all hardships with strength and optimism.

They will be one of those people who will not be able to see any flaws in their friends and family. Once they make friends, they will be able to stand up for them and support them in everything they do. However, it will be wise for them to sometimes, pay attention to what others say as well, since it will enable them to make the right choices and not get involved with undesirable elements.

They will be fond of luxury and extravagance because of which they may often end up spending more than what they can afford. Also, they will be generous to a fault and will love to give expensive gifts and presents to dear ones. On the whole though, they will have a fortunate and happy life filled with plenty of success and prosperity. There will be some ups and downs, but nothing that will hurt them for long.

Finance

Considering the influence of their planets and the diligence of their temperament, they will be able to earn quite a bit for themselves. Even if born into wealth, they will be able to multiply it and increase it. However, they will need to curb their desire to splurge and overspend. They will make most of their money through investing wisely and also by cashing in on their inherent talents and gifts.

As long as they maintain a balance between earning and spending, they will be able to have a comfortable amount for their later years. They will also be generous and contribute to charities. This again will be a good habit, provided they keep something for themselves as well.

Health

Unlike most people, they will be quite lucky in matters of health and fitness. They will enjoy a life of health and happiness. Minor ailments may crop up every now and then; however, serious illnesses will not be a part of their life. Despite this, they should take adequate care and exercise regularly to keep their limbs agile and their heart in good condition. As long as they eat well and have adequate rest and exercise, they will have a strong and healthy disposition.

Born on 7th, 16th and 25th

Leos born on the above-mentioned dates will be affected by the vibes from the planets Neptune and Uranus along with the Moon and the Sun. This is indeed, a powerful combination and will surely have certain significant influences on the personality of the individual.

This particular combination will bring a lot of uniqueness and freshness in their already independent way of thinking and acting. They will not conform to the usual modes of behaviour and will often be known for their own unique ways and ideas. The presence of Neptune in their sign will be responsible for endowing them with a strong ambition. This ambition will be unconventional as well, since they will not wish to exert authority over others but will want excellence from themselves. They will be relentless in pushing themselves to the limit and getting the best out of themselves each time.

They will have a fondness for music and the arts. Everything such as literature, poetry, drama, and cinema will interest them and they will endeavour to soak up as much of it as possible. Moreover, they will also have an interest in astrology, occult and similar sciences. These will intrigue them mainly because they will be different and offbeat and hence, will be a mystery to them.

Sensitive and graceful, they have an air of elegance. Even when wearing the most casual clothes, they will look dignified and sophisticated. While they may or may not have strong religious beliefs, they will be a generous and loving person. They will try and give as much as possible to humankind and will expect very little in return. Their sincerity, warmth and compassion will make them a successful social worker or humanitarian.

Romance and love will bring both happiness and sadness to their life. There may be some romances that may not go well, while there may be others which will light up their existence. What is important is that may will have a serenity which will not allow them to become disillusioned and depressed by those who hurt them. They will simply move ahead and, when they find the right person, will make a very happy home.

Their life will be interesting and filled with experiences that will be out of the ordinary and will add immensely to their knowledge on life and living. They enjoy and welcome change. They will seek out change by travelling to far-off destinations and doing things that are new to them. It is important, however, that they do not become too reckless or impulsive since that will put unnecessary pressure on their nerves.

As a professional, they will do well in any field as long as they are interested in it. They will be multi-faceted and hence, have an aptitude for anything. Moreover, they will be able to adjust and adapt to changing situations which will make it easier for them to try out a diversity of options before finding the one that is best suited to them and their temperament.

Perceptive and emotional, they have a finely developed sense of intuition where they are able to make the right judgement about people and situations. So strong is their instinct and perception that they will have an innate flair for mysticism, occult or anything that is futuristic and imaginative. They are extremely sensitive to other people and their sentiments and feelings. Therefore, they always make an attempt to be tactful and discreet as much as possible.

Overall, though, Number seven Leos will have a life that will be interesting and inspiring. They will be motivated themselves and will be able to bring out the best in others as well. They work hard at being humane and compassionate. It will be a life that will be eventful yet tranquil.

Finance

Money for them will be a contradiction of sorts. They will not value money immensely however, they will need to earn it in order to survive and exist. Therefore, there are chances that they may need to work and take up jobs which don't really interest them just because of the need for money. In case they are involved in business, they will do well as long as they make wise investments and trust their instincts and not rush into anything recklessly.

Health

For them, health will be more mental than physical. If they feel good, they will be healthy and if they do not feel good, then they will be sick. Therefore, it is important that you remain positive and surround themselves with cheerful and optimistic company since that will keep them upbeat and healthy. Even if they don't look strong, they will have internal strength that will enable them to handle anything that comes their way. They will be very particular about their food and exercise. Also, they will not suffer from the usual routine of illnesses. If they do fall ill, it will be psychological illness. However, their strength to recover will also come from within them.

Born on 8th, 17th and 26th

Leos born on the 8th, 17th and 26th are influenced by the vibes from the planets Uranus and Saturn along with the Sun. This alliance of planetary influences is remarkable and strange, therefore, resulting in certain changes and traits in the individual as compared to other Leos.

The Number eight Leos, will, by virtue of their planetary influences, be given the chance to achieve a lot in life and make a name for themselves. However, this will largely be determined by their own perception of their strengths and abilities. If they have a positive attitude towards themselves, there will be little that will challenge their progress and success.

They will have a charitable and compassionate temperament and will gain much satisfaction out of bringing happiness to others. Unfortunately, they may not receive the acknowledgement and appreciation that they rightly deserve. Moreover, they will be endowed with a personality that will be unique, in the sense that it will be made up of several contradictory traits and features. We will look at this aspect of their personality in some detail.

They are ambitious and focused on what they want from life. However, there will also be in them, a strong streak of stubbornness due to which they will often refuse to budge from their stand, even if it will eventually benefit them. Similarly, they will want to succeed and prosper; however, they will work best on their own and will not want to adjust to the ideas of others. This could result in a delay in their progress. All things said and done, they will be a force to reckon with and will sooner or later realise all their dreams and aspirations. The secret lies in perseverance. If they keep working at it, they will surely reach the top.

In matters of faith and belief, they are not moderate. They will either be a complete non-believer, discarding all such ideas with contempt, or they will be a staunch devotee, bordering on being a fanatic. This, too, will be a facet of their multi-dimensional personality. They will never be boring and will constantly be questioning and observing. This will make them a fascinating company and when in the mood, they will be able to keep groups of people enthralled with their conversation and wit.

Passionate and profound, they will be highly engrossed in reaching their goals, achieving happiness and being someone in the larger society. While there are chances that they will be quite materialistic in their early life, the latter half of their life will see their most benevolent side. So, while they may accumulate and build wealth in the beginning; later on, they will give it away and be satisfied by the feeling of peace and contentment. Whatever the case may be, there is no doubt that their life will be an interesting and intriguing one. It will be filled with unusual occurrences and coincidences that will bring equally unusual results.

As far as home and married life is concerned, they will be quite happy and content. However, it is important that they marry someone who will be willing to accept them the way they are. Therefore, it is advisable that they be completely honest with their partner. Also, it will help if they are less stubborn and try to see the goodness in the other person's point of view. Other than that, they will have a warm home and a loving family which will bring them more joy than sadness.

Since they enjoy being on their own, there are chances that they will not have a wide circle of friends. However, they will have a few close friends and these people will share some similarity with them, in terms of personality, occupation and interests. They will also enjoy out of the ordinary things and may seem peculiar to the rest of the world. What is important is that they will be a loyal friend and once they decide to trust someone, they will be as solid as a rock. Therefore, they will also expect this from the people who are close and dear to them.

They will be highly influenced by the state of their mind and their feelings will often be reflected on their face. They will not be the sort to hide behind a mask. Rather, they will be expressive and vocal. Therefore, it is important that they always remain as positive and cheerful as possible. It will be good for their physical and mental health.

Independent and idealistic, they will have to face the world and support what you believe in. They have the courage to be strong on their own. They should just reach within their self and find the answer to all their questions.

Finance

It is essential that they exercise great prudence when investing their money as they will not find it very easy to depend on others for guidance and advice. They should not invest too much money without having given enough thought to the investment. They should research all their options and only then, invest.

Since they are highly individualistic, it is important that if they have a business, it should be run solely by them. They will accumulate their wealth through land, family businesses and jewellery.

Health

In matters of health, they will have a fair amount of luck. They will either be blessed with an abundance of physical energy and strength or they will have great mental powers. In either case, it is important that they do not tire themselves out and give themselves enough time for peace and calm. Too much stress either on the body or on the nerves will make them ill and irritable. Therefore, they should take good care of their body and their soul; nourish them with good food and peaceful surroundings.

If and when they do fall ill, it will be due to vague and mysterious reasons. However, it is important that no matter how serious the illness is, they should always keep a positive attitude. By doing this, they will be increasing and quickening their recovery. Aches and pains, as well as disorders of the digestive system will be some common complaints that they may have. Their legs and muscles will also need frequent exercise in order to prevent any leg injuries and ailments.

Born on the 9th, 18th and 27th

Number nine Leos are ruled by the vibes from the planets Mars, Uranus and the Sun. This particular alliance of planetary influences brings about an abundance of energy and spontaneity in the individual. We will study more features unique to the Leos born on 9th, 18th and 27th.

They will be answerable only to themselves and will be a rebel against all rules and regulations which do not have a foundation in logic. For them, reason and logic will be extremely essential and critical to all theories and values. This will also be responsible for their strong sense of justice and fair play. They will never be underhanded or devious. Whatever they want, they will be straightforward and upfront about it.

They will also be a true lion, in the sense that there will hardly be anyone who will be able to lay down the law for them. They will make and break their own laws and will not tolerate being dominated by anyone. Rather, they will be quite a trend setter and trailblazer and will want to try out different things, regardless of the risk involved. Needless to say, their life will be quite an adventure and they will often be associated with various unusual activities. Anything that appeals to them will be pursued and tried.

This should not imply that they are reckless and irresponsible. On the contrary, they are meticulous and hard working and will devote long hours to the realisation of their dreams, aspirations or merely the task assigned to them. They will not settle for second best in anything, therefore, there is the chance that they will put too much pressure on themselves to excel at whatever it is that they are doing. They are innovative and creative and will constantly try to better themselves and others. This will help them to evolve and grow as a person and as a professional. They should just keep in mind that sometimes, flaws, too, have their advantage. So, they should go easy on themselves and others, as well.

Their inherently responsible and intelligent temperament will make them quite natural at handling positions of authority. Therefore, they will do well in government offices, army and other public offices. Also, administration and people management will help them to deliver their best.

Life for them will never be routine and mundane. It will be interesting and more like a roller-coaster ride where they will have a good number of ups and downs. They will always find a way to bring change and innovation into their life. Being stuck in a rut is not their way and it will be their constant endeavour to have something engrossing to keep them busy and active. Idleness does not suit them and they will be at their best when doing something that suits their personality and stimulates them.

Due to their highly independent and strong-willed temperament, there will be people who will often get hurt and bitter by their success and prosperity. Also, their blunt and candid way of talking will sometimes hurt egos and sentiments. Therefore, it will not be surprising that they have quite a few adversaries. However, this number will be balanced out by the number of friends that they have owing to their benevolent and caring attitude. Once they are sure of a person, they will be a trustworthy and reliable friend. As a matter of fact, their benevolence will be so deep-rooted that even if an enemy is in trouble, they will be willing to help him or her out.

In matters of romance and the heart, they will be often drawn to unconventional partners and intrigues that will fascinate and thrill them. However, when they settle down, it will be with someone who will be able to match their wavelength and let them be the independent soul that they are.

Since their life will always have something or the other going on, they will need to stay on guard against mishaps and accidents. Also, they should not push themselves too hard and should take enough periods of rest. This will keep their nerves calm and tranquil. They will be fond of playing sports and this will be one of the ways of keeping fit and healthy.

They will be quite a people's person, despite their preference for isolation. As a result, they will often make friends with people who are in important positions and places. This will also be responsible for some of their success and prosperity.

Finance

As far as their initial years are concerned, they will need to work hard and diligently in order make a name for themselves and earn a living. However, with time, they will develop their instinct for money and business and that is when they will accumulate most of their wealth. There are strong chances that they will be able to make good profits from sound investments in land, business and gold. Stocks and shares should be invested in but only after sound advice and sufficient research.

Health

Fundamentally, Number nine Leos have a strong and healthy build. However, they will tend to put undue stress on themselves and this will result in an increase in body temperature and occasional infections of the blood. Due to a highly adventurous life, they might be prone to accidents and mishaps, every now and then.

VIRGO

(24TH AUGUST TO 23RD SEPTEMBER)

Virgo in General

Virgo—the Virgin. The symbol of this sign tells us a lot about the personality of the individuals born under it. They will represent the virginal qualities of tranquillity, balance and quiet intelligence. This sign begins on the 21st of August and continues till the 20th of September. Initially, all Virgos start with a temperament that is chaste and righteous. However, as far as their later personality is concerned, a lot will depend on how life treats them and how they figure out the world. They are highly malleable and will often fit themselves into any mould, as long as it seems right to them.

Virgos are people who will be known for their ability to succeed, despite odds. Gifted with unusual intelligence and capabilities, they will be able to bring to life nearly all their dreams and aspirations. They will have a strong ability to retain all information that they lay their hands upon and will be careful about who they trust and depend on. They will have the tendency to be somewhat critical of things around them and will look at everything minutely. Perfection is something that they value, both in themselves and in others. This will make them capable judges and critics.

Creative and aesthetic, they will have a natural flair for fashion and interiors and will often keep beautiful and warm homes. They will also be neat and organised and will want 'a place for everything and everything in its place.' Noisy crowds, messy areas and general disarray will affect them greatly and they will feel quite uncomfortable in such surroundings. Although, they will not be the type who will come up with earthshaking ideas, they will be able to work and implement them. One of the most distinctive traits of a Virgo is his or her ability to persevere and ensure that a task reaches completion.

They have a flair for arguing and reasoning. Also, they will be the kind who will have a respect for authority and will tend to listen rather than defy. Therefore, they will make good lawyers, scientists, teachers and even business people. They will bring a sense of stability, determination and endurance to everything they do. Therefore, success will never be too far away for them.

Reading this, one should not start imagining the Virgo to be boring and dull company. On the contrary, Virgos often have a unique sense of humour and can make you laugh at the oddest of things. They will also have a special charm that will draw you towards them. Good, patient listeners, they will always be ready to provide a supportive shoulder to you and will be sensitive to your thoughts and feelings.

They are extremely sensitive to surroundings and will also be influenced by sounds, colours, smells and tastes. Anything that jars any of the senses will be rejected and replaced by something that soothes and calms. Although they may seem lost and dreamy to you, they will be highly realistic and practical. They will look at life in the real sense of the word and will behave accordingly. It is difficult to impose upon a Virgo or take advantage of him. They will want their way in most situations, however, at the same time, will be open to reason and logic. The irony is that Virgos will never see themselves as being critical or judgmental.

Yet another contradictory aspect of the Virgo personality will be that while they are respectful of authority and power, they will not blindly follow discipline. That is probably the reason one may find some Virgos being reprimanded for indiscipline more than once. If something makes sense to them, they will be willing to follow it, however, if it doesn't, they will not be afraid of breaking it to suit their purpose.

Since they are practical and grounded in reality, they will often have a strong materialistic streak—one that will motivate them to work harder in order to obtain the pleasures of life. However, this should not imply that they will be show-offs and boastful. Rather, they will be just the opposite and will be quite judicious about spending. Wastefulness will certainly not be a part of their temperament. They will also be equally practical and realistic about the fact that they will need money in the future and hence, will save a decent sum as well. Not only will they be grounded in reality but they will also be quite perceptive and will be able to pick up vibes and will be able to form quick and accurate opinions about people.

Their tendency to be judgemental will also be offset by the fact that they will be equally critical of themselves and will demand high standards from their own performance. They will try to keep improving themselves in some way or the other. It is important for us to understand that the Virgo will perceive improvement as per his own eyes; therefore, what may be positive for him may not be the same for us. They also at times, have the tendency to be short-tempered and touchy about trivial matters.

However, they will not be the kind to get into loud and noisy fights. They would rather settle things quietly than create a big fuss.

They will have a fondness for beauty and will often try to reflect it in some way or the other. It could be in their homes, their personality or even their appearance. They will have their aims clear in their head and they will be willing to put in hours of work in order to achieve it. It has been generally seen that their efforts will not go to waste and they will succeed but it will take time and patience.

Love and romance will awaken in them a profound passion and they will be devoted and caring lovers. While they do not believe in public displays of affection, they will be quite possessive. They will also have strong preferences and opinions and it will be very difficult for others to try and change the way they see the world. The only way they will change their views and attitudes will be if they themselves feel the need to change.

Finance

Most Virgos will be lucky in financial matters. They will be intelligent and will have sharp business acumen. This will be coupled with a judicious spending nature and an independent thought pattern. They will not be pushed around easily and will nearly always go with what they feel is right. It has generally been seen that Virgos tend to profit from investing in land, gold and similar fields.

Health

Health for Virgos will not be too much of a matter of concern, which will be surprising, especially since they tend to put too much stress on their nerves and pressurise themselves into performing perfectly. Aside from minor ailments, they will need to take special care of their digestive system and nervous system. However, nothing will be too serious and will be taken care of by following a regular exercise and diet routine. Also, they will need plenty of sleep and relaxation in order to recharge their batteries and be ready to face the world.

Virgo

Born on 1st, 10th, 19th and 28th

Born on the above-mentioned dates, you will be influenced by the planets Uranus and Mercury along with the Sun. This particular combination of planetary vibrations will make them more intellectual and perceptive than usual. They will have an enhanced level of gathering and grasping information. This will be the primary influence of the planets. However, there will be other changes as well, which we will learn about in the following pages.

They will be a reflective and pensive individual. They will weigh and analyse the minutest of things and this will add to their knowledge. Hard work and toil will be second nature to them. They will not tire of devoting themselves to the task at hand and will not rest till they accomplish whatever may be their goal. They will be fairly ambitious and will especially, want to obtain most of the luxuries of life. However, they will have to work hard in order to reach the top of the ladder and there are chances that during their early years, they will have to face some hardships and obstacles, especially if not born into a rich family. Nonetheless, they will not let their circumstances get them down and will be prepared to put in the required efforts.

Aesthetic and talented, they will have a flair for language and will enjoy appreciating beautiful things in a variety of forms. Considering the fact that they will be intelligent and multi-faceted, they will need some time to decide what they are best suited for, professionally. However, once they do find their area of expertise, they will be quite successful and fortunate.

Although they have most things in their favour, they will need to work on curbing their inherent restlessness and impatience with life and also with people. Being more patient and accepting will do them a lot of good and will also bring them peace of mind and contentment. As far as possible, they should try and enhance their strengths and work on building concentration and belief in themselves. Once they have these in place, there will be little that they will not be able to achieve. Also, if they become more tolerant of people, they will enjoy the company and loyalty of a circle of friends and acquaintances. Even though they will be the kind who will enjoy being on their own, they will still at times, crave for the company of others.

They also have a strong dislike for brashness and inane behaviour. Pointless humour and vulgarity will not find favour with their meticulous and organised nature. They will appreciate those who have the ability to relate to others and are gentle and compassionate. On their own part, they will have an academic interest in medicines and their properties. Knowing what cures what will be something that will intrigue them and they will often have a well-stocked medicine cabinet.

Although they are benevolent and considerate about others, they will also be high on self-esteem and will know exactly where to draw the line. Saying 'No' firmly and gently will never be difficult for them. They will have the ability to do so without offending the sentiments of the other person. Moreover, since they will sincerely be a generous soul, whenever they refuse someone, people will not be able to hold it against them.

Their intelligence and wisdom will be coupled with a profound compassion and a strong sense of realism. All these traits will play a significant role in shaping their career and their social life. They will surely prosper and profit from their endeavours. Most importantly, while they may get dissatisfied easily, they will not get disillusioned that quickly. They will be willing to try till they reach their goals. And, that will serve you in good stead.

Finance

They diligence and devotion to their goals, as well as their inherent intelligence will enable people to trust you and therefore, they will be able to obtain good jobs, positions and pay packets. Even in business, they will be able to make profits and do fairly well. They will be wise about spending and investing and therefore, they will always be able to live the life that they want to.

Health

Considering what I have told earlier about being interested in medicines, they will be blessed with good health and will rarely, if ever, need to use those medicines. At the same time, it is important that they get a lot of sunshine and fresh air in order to keep their health in optimum condition. Mostly, they will be prone to ulcers caused due to overwork and anxiety. Therefore, try and relax and take things easy rather than pushing themselves into a corner every now and then.

Born on 2nd, 11th, 20th and 29th

Neptune, Mercury and the Moon will come together to influence Virgos born on the dates given above. This particular combination will bring about certain changes in the individual's personality, thereby, setting him apart from other Virgos born on different dates. The presence of Mercury, itself, indicates that change will be an integral part of their life and they will learn to deal with it, early on.

Intelligent and gifted with a creative and productive imagination, they will have everything that is needed in order to succeed and prosper in today's world. However, they will be somewhat mercurial and fickle. As a result, they will want variation and newness every now and then. This will make it difficult for them to stick to something for long, unlike most Virgos. This should not imply that they will not be hardworking and conscientious. On the contrary, they will be highly dedicated; it is just that they will lose interest rapidly.

They will have a simple and unassuming outlook. Even if rich, they will not be a show off. Rather, they will believe in building wealth and spending sensibly. Splurging and wastefulness will not be part of their temperament. They will also have a balanced approach towards relationships, which implies that while they will be empathetic and approachable, they will also be firm in setting limitations for friends and will not like to be imposed upon.

Emotional, yet not expressive, they will be sensitive and will be affected by the surroundings and the people around them. It will be primarily due to this emotional temperament that they could be prone to moods of melancholy and sadness, at times. Even though they may have everything going for them, there could be instances when they will feel lonely and neglected. This could even make them somewhat irritable and eccentric.

They will have a mind that will be always open to learning and acquiring new information. As a result, they will soak up all the information that they see around them and will be able to not only retain it, but also apply it in the appropriate situations.

Nearly always their perception and intuition will be sharp and accurate, further strengthening the power of their mind.

In matters of the heart, they will be quite picky when finding the right person to settle down with. It is important that they find someone who will be able to understand their quirks and have patience with their sense of independence and privacy. However, they will be a gentle and devoted lover with a quiet passion and a strong sense of possessiveness.

They will have a strong desire to experience change and as a result, they will often travel to different places. Travelling for them will be both an educative and entertaining activity. They will enjoy the experience, since they will be able to learn more about different cultures and at the same time, it will offer them a break from monotony. Along with travel, they will also have an inclination for nature and beauty. They may or may not have the talent to garden or grow plants; however, they will take great pleasure in enjoying the aesthetics and tranquillity of nature.

Due to the presence of the Moon among the planets that influence them, they will be subject to moodiness and temperamental behaviour depending upon the cycles of the moon. During these times, they should try and take time out and relax and not push themselves too hard.

Finance

There is a strong possibility that they will have a pronounced materialistic streak and will therefore, like to earn a great deal of money. Whether or not they have this inclination, they will be able to use their intellect and their talents to earn a decent living and have a comfortable life. They will not be the kind to splurge and go overboard with luxuries; however, they will enjoy them. At the same time, they will ensure that their future is well provided for.

Their skills and abilities will make them successful in fields of business, literature, teaching, administration and even as a journalist.

Health

While they will have a good, hearty constitution, they will need to keep a strict eye on their food, since they could be prone to food poisoning. Also, stress and moodiness could affect their digestive and nervous systems. Other than that and the usual colds and coughs, they will lead a healthy and relatively easy, going life.

Born on 3rd, 12th, 21st and 30th

Number three Virgos are influenced and ruled by the vibrations of the planets Mercury and Jupiter. Both these planets will exercise their influence on the individual and bring about distinctive changes that will make their personality somewhat different from other Virgos born on different dates.

They will have an ambitious and striving temperament. They will not be easily content and will often have a strong desire to rise higher and above their standing in life. In order to achieve this, they will often place a lot of pressure on themselves and push themselves to the limit. They will frequently have a clear idea of where they want to go in life and there will be nothing that will stand in their way. While they will not be loud and will refrain from broadcasting their dreams and aspirations, there will be no doubt that they will want to achieve a great deal from life. Their actions will speak louder than their words.

They will have a quiet yet firm manner and will enjoy exerting authority over others. However, they will also be intelligent enough to realise that domination alone will not help in the achievement of goals and targets. Therefore, while they send the message across, they also try to be understanding and compassionate towards others. Their inherent personality is gentle and loving; as a result, people feel secure in their company. Also, their strong faith in themselves and self-assurance will inspire confidence in others. If they can curb their tendency to be critical and controlling, they will make a good leader.

Their personality will have some conflicting traits in it as well. For instance, while they will be big-hearted and liberal, they will also have the inclination to accumulate wealth and save stringently. Their benevolent spirit will be seen in their desire to support the less fortunate and if they have the resources, they will surely go out of their way to be of help and support. Again, although they may seem naïve at times, yet they will be wary of people and will not place their trust in them easily and quickly. They will conduct their business in a cautious manner and will not appreciate nosiness and interference. They will also be quite choosy as far as friends and acquaintances are concerned and will not be quick to form relationships. They will first evaluate and see if the person is trustworthy and dependable and only then will they go ahead and forge a bond with him or her.

As far as marriage is concerned, they will be most well suited with someone who will let them be the stronger one, the dominant one. If they marry someone who is equally or more dominating than them, they may have some amount of conflicts during the initial years. In order to maintain domestic harmony and peace, it will be advisable for them to learn to compromise and adjust. This will go a long way in helping them, in their your personal and professional life.

They will have lofty dreams and aspirations, however, they will also be well grounded and will have a fair idea of what can be achieved and what cannot. Irrespective of this realism, once they decide on something, they will not rest till they have reached that goal. They will be analytical and will be intrigued by science and such complicated matters. The planets that influence their Number will make them most suitable in a position where they have responsibility and independence. Also, it should be a job that they are interested in.

Order and administration will be second nature to them and they will be quite successful in resolving chaos and acting as a mediator. While they have the ability to judge others, in all likelihood, they, themselves will not be able to see anything wrong in their own personality. One should try and understand this in some depth. It is not that they will not be self-critical. It is just that others will not be able to point out something that is incorrect or wrong with them. They will introspect and then decide if they need to work on something or not.

Considering the fact that they will be devoted to their goal and will try and make the most of life's opportunities, they will be quite successful. However, they should try and become more accommodating on the personal front, since that will bring the warmth and love of human relationships in their life and enrich it further. They will be prosperous and progressive and undoubtedly will rise above the status in which they were born. While materially they will gain, they should try and achieve the same success on an emotional and personal level as well. That will complete the picture and make them a well-rounded and content individual.

Finance

They will be fortunate in financial matters and will not have to worry too much about them. Since they will be a hard working and dedicated individual with an inherent inclination towards saving, they will always have enough for the uncertain future.

they will be multi-faceted and will be able to use your many talents to increase and supplement their income. They will also be perceptive and aware and hence, will try and make the most of every situation, from a financial standpoint.

Health

Their desire to excel and succeed will be so strong and profound that they will often overlook matters of health. That will make them prone to digestive ailments, diabetes and other stress-related illnesses. The best cure for them will be a good holiday and plenty of sleep. That, alone, will be able to take care of most of their complaints and will also refresh and rejuvenate them.

Born on 4th, 13th, 22nd and 31st

For Virgos born on the 4th, 13th, 22nd and 31st, the planets Uranus and Mercury, along with the Sun will come together to change and influence their personality, distinguishing it from that of other Virgos born on other dates.

They will be creative and self-reliant. Due to the presence of Uranus, they will have some unusual characteristics and habits that will make they seem somewhat quirky. Their thoughts and ideas will be highly imaginative and novel and will never be conventional. Being offbeat and individualistic will come naturally to them. They will view life in a way that will be different from most other people and this perspective will be unique and refreshing.

Since they will have a radically different approach to life and issues, they will find it somewhat tough to meet and befriend people who share the same viewpoints. However, if they do meet like-minded people, they will be a good company and will enjoy happy times with them. They will have an ambitious nature and their determination to succeed will be so strong, that there could be instances where the line between good and bad may get blurred. Their independent nature may also lead to arguments and conflicts with loved ones.

Despite the fact that they will be motivated and driven to succeed, they may not be considered prosperous by others, since their approach towards materialism and wealth will be very different from their own. Unlike most Virgos, they will not be driven solely by the desire to have and amass wealth. While they will enjoy the comforts of life, they will not hesitate in giving it all up for a cause that they feel is worthy. There will be quite a few times in their life when you may be misconstrued and people may be hurt or angered by them. They will try hard and resolve such conflicts; however, they will not be disillusioned or disappointed by them. They will take them in their stride and will continue to work towards their goal.

They will take their time to form relationships; however, for them most of their problems will be due to other people. They will have the knack of getting into trouble because of someone else. However, they will always manage to get out of these situations and not think much about them. Therefore, if venturing into business, it will be beneficial for them to start on their own rather than get into a partnership. They should also always rely on their own powers of judgement and make their own decisions instead of following what others do.

Their life will be one that is filled with unusual and unexpected situations. There will be plenty of changes and ups and downs that will keep them on their toes and will make things interesting. One thing is for sure, they will lead an eventful life and whether these changes have positive or negative outcomes, they will always derive some learning from them and have the ability to move on. They will be intelligent, yet not in the traditional way. They will need to find what interests them and then there will be no holding them back. Novelty and innovation will greatly appeal to them and they will always come up with some idea or the other. Their hard work could make these ideas productive. However, it remains to be seen whether they will be accepted by society or not.

As far as marriage is concerned, they will have to find someone who will be able to adjust to their unusual habits and will be open to accepting their ideas and opinions. They will also need someone who will love them for who they are and will not try to change or transform them. If they will feel the need to change something, they will do it themselves but they will not like to be told by other people, even if it is by someone they love and care for.

Finance

Their diligence and dedication will pay off and they will be able to make money, even if it comes late in life. However, they will need to be very careful, since there could be people who might try to cheat them out of it. Therefore, they should try and invest most of their money in safe schemes and not be too adventurous and unconventional about it. They will be able to earn most of their wealth through their own independent means and if not born in a rich family, they will strike out on their own and carve a niche for themselves.

Health

Number four Virgos will be more influenced by their minds than by anything else. Even in illness, they will be able to cure themselves, if they think positively and are determined to get better. Although they have a strong and robust disposition, they could be prone to some vague and strange illnesses that will prove to be a dilemma even for doctors. Yet, they will have the ability and the power to be able to cure themselves and bounce back with renewed energy and stamina.

Born on 5th, 14th and 23rd

For Virgos born on the above-mentioned dates, the influence of the planet Mercury will be most significant and will have a profound effect on the personality of the individual. The presence of Mercury in this Number will have far-reaching effects since it will be present in its own house and hence, will make the personality more distinctive and unique.

Due to the strong presence of Mercury, their personality will be highly changeable and flexible. They will, unlike most Virgos, be open to adapting and adjusting to others and will do so with grace and ease. They will also be open to ideas and opinions of others, however, will be independent and individualistic in their actions. While they may consider the advice of others, what they do will ultimately depend on their own thoughts and discretion.

It will be their adaptability and openness that will enable them to fit into any career or social circle. They are intelligent and multi-faceted and as a result, have the potential to succeed and prosper in nearly every field. The sole criteria, however, will be that it should interest and fascinate them. Anything that is boring and routine will not be their cup of tea.

Being the perceptive individual that they are, they will be able to pick up vibes and will also be quite good and accurate in their judgement of others. Not only that, they will also have a knack of predicting things, every now and then. Therefore, they should trust their gut feeling and go with it. Listening to others and taking their advice is good, however, they should also exercise their own initiative.

They will have a high level of confidence and belief in their abilities and potential. This will enable them to take on anything and accomplish it. Obstacles and hardships will also be dealt with and overcome with determination. They will be focused and goal-oriented. Also, they will be sociable and fun-loving, with a generous spirit and a discreet nature. All these qualities will undoubtedly make them a popular person, reliable friend and a dedicated worker.

On the relationship front, they will enjoy gatherings and solitude alike. The best part is that they will be able to balance both with perfection and therefore, will liven up parties and conversations with their intellect and wit. Moreover, their adjusting and accommodating temperament will bring people closer to them and they will be able to adjust to any company anywhere. This will also help them when travelling, which is something they will be immensely fond of. On the one hand, travelling will help them to visit new and different locations and therefore, be a break from routine; on the other hand, it will also be a learning experience and for them, that will be important and entertaining. Marriage will be something they will enjoy and considering that they are open to another's opinions and willing to adjust, they will make a loving and caring partner.

The most important thing is that they should retain your strengths and not let them become their weaknesses. While it will be nice to be sociable, they should not let people take them for granted. Similarly, while they listen to others, they should also use their intelligence and not become a 'yes-man'. If they crave for attention and love, they might try and become popular at any cost. However, if they are relatively secure and self-confident, they will be able to lead a satisfied and fulfilling life.

Professionally, they will do well in nearly every field, since they are able to fit into any circle and will have an aptitude for pretty much everything. However, since they are particularly creative and inventive, they will do well in literary, mechanical, defense, education and similar areas. It is critical though, that they realise the significance of persistence and keep up their efforts even if faced with difficult times or a slight monotony in the job. They will also do well in business and will be able to make good profits and gains. Aside from the material standpoint, they will also enjoy fame and popularity since they will be a dependable peer and a good leader.

Finance

Virgos born on dates which come to the Number five are fortunate since they have a highly 'mercurial' nature and are able to adjust to any situation and circumstance. Therefore, even from a financial perspective, they will do well and will have the ability to accumulate wealth. With diligence and dedication, they will be able to rise high and as a result of their sound commonsense, will save a good amount set aside for their future. All they will need to focus on is making the most of what they have and ensuring that they put aside enough for the future. Everything else will fall into place automatically. they will not have to worry too much about finances and leading a comfortable life.

Health

They will be blessed with a sound disposition and will have immense energy and stamina. However, they will need to take care of their nerves and not put too much stress on their system. Otherwise, their usually resilient immunity could weaken and make them susceptible to infections and ailments. They will also need plenty of sleep and time in the sun to relax and refresh themselves. Generally, though, they could be prone to insomnia, facial twitching or stammering and mysterious aches and pains.

Born on the 6th, 15th and 24th

A Virgo born on any of the above-mentioned dates, will be significantly influenced by the vibes of the planet Venus and this singular influence will bring about remarkable changes in their personality. They will be highly compassionate and intensely emotional about people and relationships. We will examine their personality in greater detail in the following pages.

It will be the influence of Venus on their birth date that will endow them with a warm and humane temperament. They will be passionate and profoundly influenced by emotions of love and affection. So strong will this influence be that there will be times when they will be torn between two or more admirers and will not know who to depend on and commit to.

Most of their life and personality will be shaped during their childhood and adolescence. There are two categories that they may fall into. On the one hand, they could be deeply spiritual and chaste in their outlook and views, with a strong attachment to the home, kith and kin. On the other hand, they could have a liberated and independent approach, where they will want to lead an energetic and adventurous life. Depending upon how they are influenced during their early years, they will adopt either one of the two paths.

Active and enthusiastic, they will have a fondness for animals and the outdoors. They could have a flair for gardening and even if they don't take this up actively, they will certainly enjoy spending quiet time in the presence of beautiful flowers and fragrances. They have a desire to stay fit and at the same time, indulge in good food and drink.

The influence of Venus will make them creative and aesthetic. They will enjoy literature, music, arts, and the like. They may take them up professionally or merely as a hobby. However, they will definitely be influenced by them. They will also be devoted to the tasks at hand, and therefore, they will be quite successful in whatever professional line they may take up.

Venus will also endow them with an attractiveness that will be unique and alluring. they have a warmth that will make others feel comfortable and needed. It is this personality that is alluring and will give them a circle of friends that they will cherish and enjoy. They will be empathetic and will be someone they will love to laugh and cry with. However, they will also need to be on their own at times and will, equally enjoy the times of solitude and peace.

Being so emotional and sensitive could make them somewhat vulnerable. As a result, they should try and work on being more objective and approach situations with strength and realism. They will be inherently practical, just that the influence of Venus will blur the line between idealism and realism. They will do well in life and will be happy and content with all that they have. Yet, they will not be complacent and will strive for excellence in their own unique way.

Finance

Financially, their life will be quite unusual. While they will be successful in their professional undertakings, they will also be lucky enough to receive help and gifts from people, both known and unknown. Even when they are short on cash, there will nearly always be someone or the other who will help them out.

They will be quite prudent in spending and although, their Venusian tendency might make them splurge on luxuries every now and then, they will balance it out by saving rigorously at other times.

Health

Like I wrote earlier, they will have a sound disposition and will be fond of exercise; however, they will have a tendency to over indulge in good food. This could create some problems with their digestive system. Also, they might be prone to respiratory infections and some injuries as well. They will also be adventurous and therefore, they will need to take caution when out in the rough outdoors.

Born on the 7th, 16th, and 25th

The influence of Neptune, Mercury and the Moon will be significant for Virgos born on the dates given above. Those born on any of these dates, will be fortunate, for they will have three influential planetary bodies shaping their personality and giving them an exclusivity that will place them in a niche of their own.

Inherently sophisticated, with elegance that will set them apart, irrespective of their socio-economic standing, they will always create an impression of having a high amount of self-confidence and poise. They are also quite creative and have a vivid imagination that will be able to dream up ideas which will be unconventional yet productive.

Everything that they do will have a touch of class in it. Their appearance, overall personality and even their profession will have gracefulness in it. Even if they are not born in a family with nobility and money, they will be able to cultivate elegance in their life. They will persevere and overcome odds and oppositions in order to establish their position in society.

They are optimistic and inclined towards philosophy and mysticism. Yet, there will also be a side of their personality that will be somewhat cynical of such things and will not want to believe in them completely. Intellectual and artistic, they will be offbeat and yet, will conform to traditions with ease. They will often take the unconventional path and at the same time, remain rooted in customs and norms. They will not be rebellious without a cause. On the contrary, they will believe in standing up for something that they truly have faith in.

Logic and reasoning will be their forte. They will try and see things from different perspectives and then form their own opinions. The best part of their personality is that they do not believe in forcing their views on other people. They will be liberal in that respect and will believe in freedom of thought and expression. Non-interfering and individualistic, they will not like others to give out uninvited advice and opinions.

It will be their ability to analyse that will lead to an interest in science, research, and general study. They may or may not be a scholar, in the literal sense of the word. However, they will always be on the path of learning and absorbing new information. Life itself, will be their education and every day they will learn something that will help to make them a better and stronger person.

While they have a fondness for comfort and luxury, they may have to work hard during the initial years of their life, especially if not born into wealth. Once they are established in their career, they will be able to lead a comfortable and happy life, filled with the pleasures that they desire. Yet, surprisingly, they will not be highly extravagant. They will be balanced and have value for money, which will ensure that them save enough for the future. Also, they will be generous and giving. Charities and support groups will get their money, time and efforts.

On the relationship front, they will form friendships with people who are more mature than them and are able to understand and accept their unconventional side. They will also admire people who have achieved a lot in their lives, since they will serve as an inspiration to them. They will be interesting company and will be able to converse on a wide range of topics. As a result, their friends too, will be from diverse walks of life. Marriage will be a happy experience and they will be a loving and devoted partner. While they may find it difficult, they will enjoy it and try and bring happiness into the relationship as much as possible. Ambition is important for them; however, they will not let it become everything for them. That will enable them to achieve and yet maintain the harmony in their personal life as well.

Finance

If there is one thing that will make them worry, it will be their finances. Not that they will have a lot to be really anxious about; however, they will tend to think that they are lacking, in some way or the other. They should learn to relax and trust their instincts in investing and multiplying their wealth. They will be able to earn a good amount and lead a comfortable life. They will do well in both business and career, due to their industrious nature and rational outlook.

Health

Health will be more a case of mind rather than body. They will be influenced by their thoughts and if they think they are ill, their body will become affected accordingly. That does not imply that they will be a hypochondriac. They will sometimes be really unwell. Also, they will become tense and anxious easily. Therefore, it is important that they learn to relax and think positively at all times. They will be prone to ailments of the digestive and nervous system. Remember to take a holiday whenever possible and recuperate from the stress and strain of everyday life. That will keep them in the best of health.

Born on the 8th, 17th and 26th

Number eight Virgos are influenced by the vibrations of the planets Saturn and Mercury. Those born on any of the above-mentioned dates will be affected by the radiations from these planets and this will further impact their personality, life and disposition.

They will be quite mature and responsible in their outlook and will prefer solitude to socialising. They will, as a matter of fact, enjoy their own company more than that of others. Also, some of their ideas and thoughts may be unconventional and hence, will not meet with social approval. There are chances, that in their personality, due to the influences of the planets, the tendency to criticise and be cynical will be enhanced. They will expect and demand perfection from nearly everyone and since, they will often not receive it, they will feel sad and disappointed.

Although, they are self-reliant and determined, they would have had a hard life till around the age of thirty-five or so. They might have to battle odds and rebel against unnecessary limitations in order to develop and build their own identity. In the event that they are born into a family where such limitations do not exist, they will naturally evolve into a mature, confident person. They will have the perseverance that is needed in order to succeed and will not be afraid of hurdles and failure. They will be willing to learn and will absorb all the information that will intrigue them and be of use to them.

Intelligent and distinctive, they will bring their special touch to everything that they do. They will have a profound interest in literature, music, arts, theatre and will often succeed in these lines. They will be diligent and will devote long hours and considerable effort to the achievement of their goals. However, at times, they may not get due recognition for their efforts and this could disillusion them. However, with their kind of personality, they will not let this get them down and they will soon be back on track and putting in the same effort as earlier.

While they are not stingy, they will also not be extravagant. They will be one of those who will be able to maintain a fine balance between earning and spending. This prudent attitude will be reflected in many other aspects of their life. They will not be the kind who will rush into things and then regret them later. They will, in all likelihood, give a lot of thought to their actions.

They enjoy the little things in life and will not have a strong materialistic bent of mind. They will take pleasure in walking and reflecting on life and themselves. Introspection will be something that they will frequently indulge in and self-improvement will be a constant quest with them. It will be their desire for perfection that will motivate them to develop the same in themselves. While this is a good habit and will enable them to evolve, they should also try and understand and accept their limitations as well. That will make them more realistic and not set them up for disappointment. They will lead a life that will be marked by growth and learning.

While they will have a marked preference for solitude, they will also have a few friends and acquaintances that will bring happiness to their life. They will make friends with caution and will not place their trust in everybody easily and freely. Once they are sure about the person though, they will be a loving and compassionate soul and a good listener as well.

Finance

Like I said earlier, they will have learnt the art of balancing expenses with income and therefore, be able to lead a life that is relatively free of financial worries and strain. They will however, at times be too careful and therefore, will not be able to take advantage of the speculative market. They will benefit from the guidance of a trusted financial advisor and once they invest their money wisely, they will be able to earn good profits on it. Also, their carefulness will prompt them to save for their future and this will ensure that their retirement years are as comfortable as possible.

Health

Number eight Virgos will be blessed with a strength that is more mental than physical. Although they may not have a body that is strong, their mind will be agile and sharp enough to take on anything. Also, they will have stamina to endure hardships and overcome obstacles with ease. If they lead a life which does not have too much of exercise, they will be prone to digestion problems, allergies, colds, lowered immunity and such. Therefore, it is advisable for them to exercise regularly and follow a regular routine in order to lead a life that is healthy and relatively disease-free.

Born on the 9th, 18th and 27th

It will be the influence of the planets Mars and Mercury that will affect the personalities and the lives of Virgos born on the above mentioned dates. They will be affected by these two planets in a variety of ways. Since both the planets are compatible, the influence will be positive and will fill them with traits such as an increased zeal for life, enthusiasm and decisiveness. There will also be traits that will set them apart and give them an edge over

others. For instance, they will be quite tactful and discreet in their behaviour and conversation.

They will be gifted with a mind and a body that will be sharp and active. They will not be the kind to sit idle and waste their time. Even when relaxing, their mind will constantly be working and ideas and thoughts will move in and out of their head. Also, they will have a fondness for adventure; therefore, they will often be engaged in sports and activities that will quench this particular need.

Not only will their mind be dexterous, they will also have capable hands and will be quite efficient in fields such as surgery, engineering, construction, writing, scientific experiments and such professions. Their ideas and thoughts will be unique and one-of-a kind, therefore, they will at times, be subject to criticism and disapproval. Nevertheless, they will not let this affect them. Their conviction in themselves will be so strong and unwavering, that they will be able to withstand tough times and troubles with endurance and faith.

Their confidence and motivation will be inspiring and will often place them in the spotlight. They will do well as a teacher or a leader where the public will be able to make the most of their qualities and strengths. They will be willing to share their skills and talents with others and this will further enhance their popularity. They will also have the discretion that is needed to prosper and will often keep their plans and thoughts to themselves. At the same time, they will also be straightforward when the occasion demands it and will not hesitate in being honest and open about their opinions.

The inherent desire for perfection will be found in them as well and they will strive to accomplish excellence in every aspect of life. They will also demand high standards from those around them and will get irritated when they fail to deliver. While excellence is a positive goal, they should also learn to take it easy and not become obsessed with it. Being too harsh and cynical will only make life difficult for them and they will lose valuable friends and relatives. Therefore, they should learn to be somewhat easy going and less rigid.

Since they are blessed with a sharp and gifted mind, they will be able to come up with innovative and offbeat ideas that will enable them to create usefulness in diverse fields such as agriculture, land development, etc. They will often propagate the use of modern techniques and methods and will not hesitate in experimenting and trying out different things. To bring about change and novelty will be something that will be extremely close to their heart and irrespective of what professional field they may be in, they will always try and accomplish this.

Their desire for adventure and thrill could lead to tricky situations and they might be somewhat prone to mishaps and injuries. Therefore, they should always exercise caution when indulging in such risky behavior. As far as their social life is concerned, they will be quite popular and will balance out times of hectic socialising with times of quiet peace and solitude. They will need some time to themselves to think and contemplate about life and its various aspects. However, they will be warm and friendly and will often go out of their way to make people feel comfortable and wanted.

Success and progress will not be difficult for them since they will be hard working and diligent in everything they do. They might have to make extra efforts, yet in the end they will all pay off and they will benefit by reaching their goals and realising all their dreams.

Finance

Money and finance will be subjects that they will be comfortable with and will not have to worry too much about. Their success in life will mostly determine the amount of money they have. Also, their intelligence in investing what they earn will yield good returns and will help them to build up wealth and a secure future from a financial point of view.

Health

They will be blessed with health that is strong and enduring. Therefore, they will be able to resist the onslaught of many illnesses and infections. However, they will be, to some extent, prone to injuries and accidents caused due to carelessness. It is important that they exercise caution and do not rush into adventurous activities without thought.

LIBRA

(24TH SEPTEMBER TO 23RD OCTOBER)

Libra in General

Balance and equilibrium is what the Libra person is constantly in quest of. The sign of Libra is represented by the pair of scales, and like the scales, the Libra is perpetually trying to find balance and harmony in his life. This sign begins on the 21st of September and then continues till the 20th of October. Libra is ruled by the planet Venus in its negative aspect with Saturn in its exaltation, and the Sun in its fall.

Individuals born under this sign have many characteristics that set them apart from others; however, one thing that is truly distinctive is their astute mental agility. Like the pair of scales that symbolise them, Librans will constantly evaluate and weigh all that they are about to do and say. Hence, at times, it may seem that they are indecisive and don't know their own mind. However, this is not entirely true. It is simply that the Libran individual needs to be sure about the correctness and balance of the actions and words.

It has also been observed and said that Librans are a bundle of contradictions. For instance, they will be polite, yet straightforward. They will enjoy parties yet will seek solitude. Again, this is just their inherent temperament that pushes them in different directions so that they can find that ideal balance; a place where everything will be symmetrical in order. It is this desire that motivates them to be neat and organised in everything they do. Even their clothes and overall appearance will have an element of balance and order. They will not be flamboyant, yet will be able to make a statement in a sophisticated and elegant manner. Disorder and chaos have no place in their lives and they will take on the role of peacemaker and mediator in conflicts and arguments. Harmony and order are what bring happiness to these souls and they will try and achieve them at all costs.

Reasoning and logic will be their strengths and they will often win arguments and debates, provided they have been able to convince themselves of their own stand. They will also be skilful with words and will be able to use the power of language to their advantage. Their fondness for logic and language will make them successful in fields such as writing, law, science, medicine and research.

Librans are also perceptive and responsive to their environment. When in a happy and positive atmosphere, they are cheerful and upbeat, filled with enthusiasm and energy. On the other hand, imbalance in their surroundings will pull them down and affect them in a negative way. They will become sad and low on energy and will retreat into their shells.

The backbone of their personality will be their staunch idealism and deep sense of morality and righteousness. They will be optimistic and will retain a strong belief in all that is good and noble. Despite the fact that they are blessed with a strong intuition, they will often rely on reason and truth before arriving at any conclusion. They will have a multi-faceted personality and will be known to have many moods and sides to their persona. At times, one will wonder if the same person is being referred to; so varied will be their character. They will be expressive and emotional. However, one will not find them indulging in displays of affection in public places. They will believe in showing their love and respect for someone in ways that are mature and ruled by reason. Emotionally, they will need to work harder at maintaining the balance they desire. Librans can be vivacious and upbeat one minute and gloomy and melancholic the very next. It will require a lot of dexterity and efficiency on their part to be able to rein in their emotions and feelings and react with poise and composure.

As far as their social lives are concerned, Librans will enjoy the warmth and camaraderie of a wide and diverse section of people. They will be able to charm people with their wit, intelligence and graceful actions. When in love, they will often spend a great deal of time being analytical and evaluating their emotions. It is important for them to realise that emotions such as love and affection should not be over-analysed.

Creative and innovative, they are deeply influenced by arts, music, literature and theatre. While they may or may not take a professional interest in these fields, they will surely indulge in them as pastimes and a form of recreation. Unlike most idealistic people, Librans will not live in the past or pine for the future. Rather, they will live in the present and will not be tied down to the past. Even the future will be treated with cool reasoning and therefore, for the most part of their lives, Librans will be free of unnecessary worry and tension.

Intellectual and inquisitive, they will often, have a lot of questions about life and its various aspects. As a result, they will do well in fields of education and research. Not only that, it will be this inherent curiosity that will motivate them to find out what is best for them and for their counterparts. They will often step into the public eye as a result of their desire to bring harmony to the lives of other people.

They will have a strong sense of compassion and loyalty. Often, they will place others before themselves. However, this should not mean that they will be doormats or martyrs. They will have a healthy sense of self-esteem and at the same time, will be able to consider the needs of other people and place them above their own selves.

Despite the fact that Librans will forever be looking for harmony and equilibrium, they will often disrupt this harmony in their own lives by splurging on too much food, drink or even emotions. One can even find the same form of contradiction in their tendency to push themselves to the limit physically and then not wanting to do anything for the next couple of days. Like I said earlier, they are not indecisive; they are simply trying to find the balance. They will have a strong tendency to nurture and nourish. Hence, one will often find Librans taking care of friends, family and relatives with compassion and tenderness.

Finance

We will find that the Libran personality will have quite a few strong and dominating features which will have an impact on financial matters and issues. While they could prosper and make a lot of money, they will also find it difficult to hold onto it for too long. They will often, be caught between trying to balance out the spending and the saving aspects of their personality. It is important to understand that Librans will be conscientious and will climb the ladders of success and fame with relative ease. However, in matters of money, they will need to exercise more caution and stability than in any other aspect of life. If they are able to achieve the harmony that is needed, there is no doubt that they will be both successful and rich.

Health

Librans, inherently, have a strong inclination to take care of their physical and mental well-being. They will work hard at maintaining a level of equilibrium and hence will be able to retain their peace of mind. For those Librans who swing between extreme emotional and physical activity, it is essential that they learn to be more well adjusted and stable. Otherwise, their health will suffer on quite a few accounts and will make them prone to ailments relating to both the body and the mind.

More often than not, they will push themselves too hard in their periods of hectic activity and hence, will affect their digestive system, kidneys and immunity, in general. While they will fall ill easily, they will also be able to bounce back to good health in relatively less time than others. They should be careful and diligent about their diet and exercise routines and should not neglect any aspect of their health.

LIBRA

Born on the 1st, 10th, 19th and 28th

There will be quite a few planetary influences that will affect and mould the personality of Librans born on the above-mentioned dates. All in all, the presence of the planets Uranus, Venus, Saturn and the Sun will be crucial in shaping the character of Number one Librans and giving them the uniqueness that will set them apart from their other counterparts. At this particular time, the planet Venus will be in the Negative aspect while Saturn will be in its exaltation. The Sun will be in its 'fall' and Mars will be in its 'detriment.'

Indeed, the alliance of planets on their Number is different and will have a power of its own. This planetary combination will be responsible for endowing them with a personality that will be both diverse yet typically Libran. They will be gifted with a quick mind and talented and will be able to use their skills and abilities to carve a niche for themselves and reach the goals that they set for themselves.

They will be impartial and fair in their approach and will always try and take the right path, even if it is the more difficult one. They will have a stronger than usual tendency to play the mediator and restore the atmosphere of peace and harmony. Confrontations, violence and chaos will distress them deeply. However, they will not hesitate in taking a firm and determined stand when the occasion rightly demands it and it will be only fair to be tough. Therefore, if there are people who think that they have double standards, they will need to explain their reason behind their approach.

Due to the influence of Venus, they will have a profoundly romantic and idealistic temperament. Whether they will be expressive or not is another matter. However, they will be moved by beauty and creativity. They will be affectionate and warm towards others and will try and make them feel as secure and comfortable as possible. It is important that they also place themselves at the same level and do not get taken for granted by those who do not value their affection and sentiments.

There is a strong possibility that they will be fairly determined and goal-oriented. However, they will need to overcome hurdles and deal with obstacles on their path to success. If they persevere and believe in themselves, they will surely succeed and there will be little harm that their enemies can do to them. They will also have the tendency to be somewhat blunt and straightforward. Therefore, there could be people who will be hurt by their candidness and frank demeanor.

Professionally, they will do well in a wide variety of fields since they will be multi-faceted and talented. Their sense of fairness will make them a success in the fields of law and justice. Their humaneness and analytical skills will help them in fields of education, science and medicine. They could also try their hand at politics, since they will have a flair for the subject.

On the social front, they will have a circle of friends that will define them and be as diverse as them. They will enjoy entertaining and being in the limelight. At the same time, there will also be instances when they will retreat into themselves and be happy with their own company. Also, they will have the ability to be both, lively and vivacious, cool and collected. Their personality will attract a cross section of people and nearly everyone will feel comfortable and entertained in their company.

Their diligence and devotion to their dreams and aspirations will be critical in ensuring their realisation. They will not waver from their pursuit. However, there could be occasions when the goal itself could change. Their dedication, nevertheless, will remain the same.

They will be charming and graceful, yet they will be able to let their hair down and relax and be completely at ease with themselves. Their personality will intrigue some people and charm the rest. There are strong indications that they will be someone people will look up to and depending upon their background, they could well become a role model and source of inspiration for the masses.

Finance

Since they have a mind that is razor sharp, they will have the good fortune of cashing in on their mental talents and profiting from them. Physical labour will bring them returns, yet it will be their mind that will be the stronger contributor. They will have a goal that they will want to accomplish and it will be for this mission that they will want to build up their wealth. Materialistic comforts will not have too large a place in their life. Their Venusian influence might make them splurge a little every now and then, however, they will learn to balance things out and come back to normal, in next to no time.

Health

Fortunately for them, the planets will influence their health in a positive fashion and will give them very little to worry about. They will be in the best of health when occupied completely. Idleness and lethargy will actually ruin their health and will give them stress and anxiety. They will be the proverbial busy bee and will be happiest when engaged in something absorbing. As long as they do not neglect their diet and exercise, they will be physically and mentally fit. They should take special care of their digestive system and be careful when travelling, to avoid injuries and mishaps.

Born on the 2nd, 11th, 20th and 29th

It will be the Moon, Neptune, Saturn and Venus that will come together to influence those who were born on the above mentioned dates. Again, this is a potent combination and will surely have far-reaching effects on their basic personality and disposition. There will be quite a few traits that will be enhanced while there will be others that will be subdued.

Their true mettle and strength will be seen in times of crisis. In nearly every case, they will have the ability to rise to the occasion and deal with it in a mature and responsible fashion. However, at the same time, in everyday life they will have a tendency to be somewhat sensitive to criticism and could even let it cloud their usually astute judgement. Therefore, it will be advantageous for them to make critical decisions on their own, free of the influence of other people.

Highly motivated and perceptive, they will be able to succeed in nearly every endeavour that you undertake. They will have the ability to foresee the result of their strategy and hence, will be able to put in the desired amount of effort and time. They will also not get disillusioned by temporary set backs and obstacles in their path. They will only work around them and not let them get them down. Such will be the strength of belief that they have in themselves.

Warm and caring, they will love easily and with all their heart. Their sincerity and tenderness will appeal to the opposite sex. However, they will find it difficult to express their love and they may need to work on being more demonstrative. Also, it is important that they are absolutely sure of themselves before they commit to marriage. Since, they have the tendency to want too much in a partner; it will be wise if they give marriage sufficient thought. They will also need to guard against being overly careful and not recognising the right partner. Balance is what they will strive for and balance is what they need.

Emotionally, they could, like the pair of scales, swing between extremes. Unless they learn to rein in their emotions at an early age, they will have to make extra efforts to pull themselves out of melancholy and gloominess every now and then. On the whole, though, they will have a cheerful and positive disposition, with just occasional patches of sadness. When low and sad, they will often want to be left to themselves and they will use this time to achieve their internal equilibrium. On the other hand, when happy and upbeat, they will like to be in the midst of the people they love and this will bring them great joy and warmth. Because of their contradictory temperament, their friends and acquaintances will often feel that they don't know them completely.

Adventure and travel will be something that they will be quite fond of and will want to spend time and money exploring unusual destinations. These trips will serve as relaxation and education for them. They will also be open to the idea of settling in countries other than their native land. If they have the resources, they will surely spend a great deal of time in visiting lands that fascinate them and appeal to their sense of creativity and beauty.

It will be this fondness for creativity that will instil in them a love for poetry, painting, music and theatre. If they take a keener interest in them, they could even use them professionally. They will also have a strong sense of fashion and will take great care in dressing up well and with elegance. They will also have a fondness for beautiful things and hence, will often splurge on them. The approval and esteem of their friends and family will make a big difference to them and they will often mould their social behaviour to suit them.

This should, however, not imply that they will not have a strong sense of confidence. They will believe in themselves, yet they will be secure enough to make others happy. The bottom line is that praise will bring happiness to them. Therefore, it will all be worth it. They will be independent and will not want to bow down to conventions and norms without knowing the reason behind them. At the same time, they will not be completely unconventional. They will have pretty much mastered the art of tight rope walking and will be able to balance out quite a few aspects of their life with ease.

Finance

It is important that they develop a strong approach towards people who try and take them for granted. Otherwise, they will have to face losses in financial matters. They will not be terribly interested in large-scale businesses and enterprises, and will want to be engaged in activities that involve the mind more than the body. Their imagination and creativity will be intense and they will be able to make good profits out of them. However, it is important that they be wise to the ways of the world and do not let anyone outsmart them.

There are quite a few chances that they will travel to foreign lands and will be able to make a name for themselves. This will however, be dependent on factors such as their family and their background. If rooted deeply to their family, they will not want to take such a big step. However, even then, they will make a reasonable amount of money and lead a life that is comfortable and secure.

Health

They will be gifted with a mind that is sharp and alert. However, they may at times, feel that their body does not have the same amount of strength. They will be imaginative and will constantly be thinking of something or the other. Lack of activity could make them susceptible to back and spinal problems. Also, they will be prone to colds and coughs and will need to take special care of their respiratory system.

Born on the 3rd, 12th, 21st and 30th

The combination of Jupiter, Venus and Saturn will be responsible for influencing and bringing about the changes in their character that will set them apart from Librans born on other dates. Since they have the good fortune of Jupiter being one of their planets, they will be high on ambition, determination and steadfastness. There will be other features as well, which we will discuss in the following pages.

They will be able to advance and grow at a good pace, professionally and personally. There will hardly be anything that they will not be able to achieve. They will have high aspirations and they will not be happy to occupy a position that is lower in the social order. To rise above their present situation is something that will greatly motivate them. they will be mature and responsible. Therefore, positions that require trust and integrity will suit their personality and they will be able to do justice to them as well.

Straightforward and diligent, they will at all times, endeavour to follow what seems right to them. Fairness and objectivity will characterise their judgement and hence, they will often be referred to as a mediator. People will trust them and they will often do their best to retain their trust. They are benevolent and thoughtful. Helping the needy and less fortunate will be something they will take great joy in. Their time and money will in all likelihood, be available to all those who truly deserve it. However, it is important that they are cautious and are not taken for granted.

They will often, like to counsel others and provide guidance and advice. Since they are an intelligent and sincere person, their advice will mostly be respected. While they will generally be a kindhearted and considerate soul, they will not have much regard or patience for individuals who waste their time and money. They will take quite a severe stand with them.

On the social front, they will be able to mingle easily with a wide variety of people. Making friends and acquaintances will be an art with them. They will have the charm and the gracefulness that will attract others, especially people in prominent positions. Moreover, there are strong chances that even they will be well known in their area of expertise; therefore, socialising with the rich and the famous will be fairly simple for them.

They will believe in discipline and order, both in their professional and personal life. However, as a superior, they will respect the lives of their employees and will not be a dictator.

The planetary influences indicate that they will enjoy a happy and satisfying marriage. Their home will be warm and secure and they will be blessed with children who will love and respect them. This will complete their world, since professionally they will be successful and socially, they will enjoy the company of popular and intelligent people.

There will be people who will be envious of them and therefore, will try and create problems for them. They will however, have the strength of mind and character to be able to stand up to these people and overcome all hurdles. They will not let such things deter them from pursuing their goals and dreams.

They will be high on enthusiasm and will often want those around them to be equally involved and dedicated. When they do not see the enthusiasm they desire, they could be quite critical and demanding. However, they will also be wise enough to realise that not all people are equal and hence, will learn to compromise. They will, like the pair of scales, be balanced and will always try and ensure that their actions and thoughts are in keeping with what is acceptable. Dominating over others is not something that they will take great joy in. They would rather practise equality and treat everybody with the same respect and consideration.

Finance

Their good fortune will extend to financial matters as well. Since they will, in general, be a hard working and sincere worker, making money will not be a difficult task for them. Also, their prudence and sense of balance will ensure that they save enough to enjoy a future that is comfortable and secure. They will profit from investing in most businesses and industries. There is also the chance that they will gain from legacies and inheritances.

Health

There are chances that they will be somewhat prone to illnesses during their early years. Thereafter, though, they will be healthy and strong. Even if they will contract any kind of infection, they will have the ability to recover quickly. They will need to be on guard against injuries and accidents.

Born on the 4th, 13th, 22nd and 31st

There will be four powerful planets that will unite to influence them, who, were born on any of the dates given above. These planets will be the Sun, Venus, Uranus and Saturn. The exact influence of these will vary in intensity. However, there is no doubt about the fact that they will be set apart from their other Libran counterparts. For instance, the influence of Venus in its negative house will bring about unconventional experiences in the matters of love and romance.

They will probably have some unusual experiences in life due to the combined influence of Uranus and Saturn. It will be this influence that will also be responsible for them being drawn towards people who are unconventional and offbeat. They will enjoy thinking out of the box and being different from the ordinary.

Loyal and obstinate, they will know their mind and not let anyone change it for them. If they believe someone, they will trust them completely and nothing that anyone will say will alter their opinion. Moreover, they will also be quite stubborn and will often stand their ground. This could create some tensions in relationships with family members and relatives.

Their imagination and creativity will be distinctive from the rest. This will enable them to be expressive and make the most of their inherent talents. If pursued with seriousness, they will be able to earn good profits and succeed in such lines. However, it is important that they use their logic and reasoning in order to avoid being taken for granted. As far as relationships and marriage is concerned, they will need to meet the right person before they commit. They will need a partner who will understand and accept their unconventional behaviour and be willing to make adjustments. Since they are stubborn, chances are that they will not want to make many changes in themselves.

Success and prosperity will come to they only after they have put in hard work and toil. The exception to this will be if you were born into money. They will also have astute perceptive skills and will often be able to visualise exactly what they want from life. It will be this sound perception that will help them when making decisions and opinions about people and situations.

They will also have the tendency to argue and debate on just about any topic. Even if it is not a topic of concern, it will just be something that thery will feel strongly about. They will not be bothered about whether they support it or not, they will simply take the stand, when everyone else does not. Therefore, if the majority will agree, they will merely disagree and then, give sound logic for the same.

They will be fond of adventure and thrills. Risky behaviour appeals to them and they will enjoy travelling to interesting destinations. With a fondness for risk, it is important that they protect themselves from accidents and injuries.

Finance

Since they have to work hard for most things, money will not be any different. Only when they will put in time and effort will they be able to earn money and build up their wealth. They should exercise caution when investing money and even when choosing their profession, since that will determine their income. Splurging will not be something that they will indulge in, yet it is important that they should save enough for their future.

Health

The fact that they are unconventional will affect their health as well. Therefore, they will be prone to illnesses that will be just as unusual as your overall personality. However, they will be blessed with the ability to recover from illnesses and will also have a great deal of mental strength. This will help them to cope with the stresses of life and lead a life that will bring peace and harmony to them.

Born on 5th, 14th and 23rd

For those who are born on the above-mentioned dates, the influence of the planets Saturn, Venus, Mercury and the Sun will be critical. These planets come together to create a union that is intriguing and powerful. In particular, they will be responsible for endowing them with a strong mind and personality.

On these particular dates, the planet Venus is in its negative house and Saturn is in its exaltation. Therefore, life for them will be eventful and interesting. They will have many unusual experiences and will also be deeply compassionate and loving. The presence of Venus heightens the sensitivity of their nature and they will be the kind who will willingly and happily make changes and adjustments for the ones they love.

Sophisticated and elegant, they create a favourable impression on everyone. Irrespective of their background, their cultured tastes will be inherent and they will not be inclined to using rough and crude language or manners.

They will have the Libran contradictions in their temperament as well. In their special case, they will be tender, sympathetic and loving to all those who will merit their attention and care. At the same time, they will also be realistic and balanced. they will be intelligent and will have sufficient commonsense to realise if they are being taken for granted. They will be firm yet gentle and will ensure that others respect their independence and identity.

Peace-loving and tranquil, they have the art of bringing harmony to their environment. Inherently, they will have a fondness for soothing and happy atmospheres. Therefore, whenever there is a conflict or any form of chaos, they will strive to resolve it at the earliest. This should not imply that they will not know how to fight things out. It is just that their method of battle will be much different than that of others.

There are strong indications that they will have a straightforward and steadfast temperament. As a result, when there is something that they don't agree with, they will simply stand their ground and refuse to budge. They will not indulge in shouting and screaming, they will make their point in a quiet, unpretentious yet definite manner.

They have an intelligent and keen mind with the ability to grasp quickly and apply their knowledge with skill. However, there could be times when they might feel restrained by family or social obligations. They may have the feeling that due to being bound by relationships, they were unable to achieve their full potential. It is important that they do not drift towards self-pity since that will hamper their ambitions and motivation. Considering the fact that the planets have gifted them with a strong character, they will be able to deal with most set backs and move through life with a positive attitude.

Number five Librans are fortunate since they are extremely resourceful and flexible. There will hardly be anything that they are unable to learn, adopt and do. Moreover, they also have a nature that will be open to change. They are able to adjust to new people and surroundings with relative ease. However, at no point in time will they be comfortable with those individuals who are crude in their behaviour.

They do not have a strong desire for materialistic goods and luxuries. While they will want to lead a life that is comfortable and secure, they do not want to actively participate in the 'rat-race'. Their desire to have a sound and stable future will prompt them to be judicious and prudent about spending money. There may be people who will think that they save for luxuries, yet the fact of the matter is that they save for a rainy day.

Romance will have a special place in their life and with the presence of Venus, chances are that their love life will be interesting and different. They will be drawn towards people who are charming and intelligent. They will enjoy good humour and conversation. As a result, they will want someone who will keep you entertained and will also give them the warmth and security of love. They will be a caring and devoted lover and will try to make life as comfortable as possible for their family and loved ones.

Creativity will also be enhanced in their personality. While they will not be as critical as most Librans, they will still want perfection in many areas of life. They will have an interest in arts, music, literature and theatre. They will also make a good editor or critic and could even try their hand at any of their interests, professionally. Chances are with their talent and fortune that they will be quite a success.

All in all, they have a personality that will be cheerful and uplifting. You have a contagious enthusiasm for life and will motivate anyone who meets them. It will be their optimism and happy attitude that will fill them with an enviable youthfulness.

Finance

For them, money and financial issues will be subjects on which they will be able to give sound and reliable advice to friends and family. However, it will be another matter as to how much of that advice they apply to their own life. They will make a good amount of money in their professional endeavours and also by applying their intelligence. They have a flair for investing money properly so as to make the maximum profits out of it.

Since they are a benevolent and caring soul, chances are that they will often give away portions of their money to the needy and deserving. However, they will be prompted by worries about their future to save and keep aside enough for their old age. Therefore, irrespective of the amount of money that they have, their future will be happy and content.

Health

The planets will come together to endow them with a robust constitution and strong immunity. However, they will have the tendency to take on too much stress and push their nerves to the limit. This could have a negative effect on their health and well-being. They have to take special care of their digestive system and watch what they eat. Stress and hypertension could also make them prone to nervous tics and infections in the mouth.

Born on 6th, 15th and 24th

Venus and Saturn will be the planets that will play a crucial role in influencing those who were born on any of the dates given above. These two planets will come together and bring certain characteristics to their personality, which will set them apart from Librans born on other dates. The influence of Venus will be stronger than that of Saturn and it will be responsible for endowing their personality with charisma and magnetism.

They will lead a life that will be entertaining and filled with fun and enjoyment. The company of friends and the warmth of kinship will fill them with great joy and contentment. They will be sociable and will also be quite attractive to the opposite sex. Hence, love and romance will never be too far from their life.

They will take great pleasure in throwing and attending parties. Having a wide and diverse circle of friends will give them the opportunity to examine various types of behaviours and temperaments. They will also be the kind who will have many friends but only a few close ones. It will be these close friends who will truly know and understand them.

There is no doubt about the fact that they are intelligent and gifted. Their talents and potential is great. What is important is that they learn to exploit this potential in order to profit from it. Once they learn that, there will be little that will be difficult for them to accomplish. It will be as a result of this sharpness and astuteness that they will be able to rise high and build their wealth and reputation. They will be diligent as well and will not waver from their goal. They will be determined to achieve all that they want and they will not rest till you attain it.

Their innate sense of creativity and aestheticism will be heightened and they will display a sense of fashion, style and an interest in literature, arts and music. There is a strong element of uniqueness in their personality. Being a part of the crowd does not suit them. They would rather set the example and then let others follow.

Despite the fact that they enjoy entertaining and socialising, they are not foolish with money. They will be able to entertain people by the pleasure of their company more than anything else. Hence, spending huge amounts of money will not really be essential. They will not run after wealth. However, at the same time, they will have a healthy respect for money and will value it properly.

While life for them will be positive and favourable, it is important that they use discretion and diplomacy in their relationships. If they make friends with the wrong set of people, they could face a lot of trouble in their life. Therefore, at all times, they should trust their instincts and common sense.

Finance

Financial matters will be favourable for them and they will be able to earn a good amount of money from their professional undertakings. Also, investing their money in safe and secure schemes will profit them. As far as business ventures are concerned, they will not have any problems with partnerships and mergers of any kind.

Health

They are blessed with a good, healthy constitution and the ability to recover from illnesses with ease and strength. They will not be prone to many infections and ailments. However, they need to ensure that they do not over-indulge in anything, including food and drink. Throat and skin problems may bother them occasionally but there will not be anything serious.

Born on the 7th, 16th and 25th

For all Librans born on the above given dates, the effects of the planets Venus, Neptune and Saturn becomes important. These three planets bring about changes in the inherent Libran personality that distinguishes them from the other Librans born on different dates. One of the most significant changes is the fact that they are extremely keen and sharp. Their mind has the ability to pick at any information and retain it, to be used at an appropriate time.

Like other Librans, for them too the sense of balance and harmony will be important. Once they have learnt to balance out the features of their inner self, they will be able to make use of all their talents and abilities to the utmost. By balance, I mean that they should not get swayed in any one direction and neglect the other completely. Understand that if they are intelligent, they are also human and therefore, susceptible to failure.

Perfection will be something that they will be driven by and hence, will often set high standards for themselves. They will be gifted with a fertile imagination and will be able to dream lofty and noble dreams. Life will be filled with creative opportunities for them.

Since they are so intelligent, they will also be somewhat unusual and unconventional. Their opinions and views will be solely their own and they will be prone to changing them at any time. There is no doubt that they will win many friends and admirers, however, they will take their time in trusting them and relying on them.

They have a strong streak of independence and enjoy exercising their will. Determined and persevering, they will not rest until they achieve what their heart desires. There is a strong possibility that they will be one of the two types of Number seven Librans. They could be sensitive to criticism and hence, refrain from too many initiatives, or they could be reckless and spontaneous in everything that they do. Even if you are of the former sort, they will not stop dreaming about what they want from life. And, if given the opportunity, they will surely realise those dreams.

As far as relationships and marriage is concerned, they will be attractive to the opposite sex. However, they will often, not be sure of what they want from their partner. As a result, they could change their mind frequently and wait a while before finally settling down with someone who will understand their unusual personality and respect their intelligence.

Finance

It has generally been observed that Number seven Librans witness a great deal of ups and downs in their financial life. There will be times when there will be an abundance of wealth and there will also be times when they will have just enough. Their spending patterns will also change accordingly. Sometimes, they will splurge and other times, they will scrimp and save. Therefore, people around them may find their behaviour erratic and irregular. It is just that they will need to arrive at a 'balanced' situation.

Business and investments will bring them good returns and they will simply have to rely on their instincts and the advice of trusted sources. It is important that they invest enough for their retirement. This will ensure that their future is not subject to the fluctuations in their present.

Health

Health for them will be fairly good and sound. They will not have to suffer serious and chronic ailments. In the rare event that they do, they will be able to recover quickly and will be back to normal in next to no time. Food and drink should not be taken in excess. Regular exercise will help to avoid disorders related to the digestive system.

Born on the 8th, 17th and 26th

Number eight Librans will be influenced by the vibes of planets Venus and Saturn, which will work together to bring about variations that will both favour and enhance the inherent personality that they have been gifted with.

Conscientiousness will be one of their foremost traits and will be a real strength for them. They will not hesitate in putting in long hours of work and effort to bring about the results that they want and the success that they deserve. They will be dedicated to their goal. However, due to the Libran tendency to be indecisive, they might change their goal at times. Nevertheless, they will continue to pursue it with the same seriousness and determination.

There is little doubt about the fact that they will be intelligent and inclined to view life with a mature outlook. This should not imply that they will be dull and boring. On the contrary, they will be interesting company, since they will be able to converse on a variety of topics with ease and flair. They will be quite successful in fields where they will get to engage in mental activity along with physical labour. Research, writing, medicine, law and teaching will be just some of the areas where they will succeed.

Since they are wise and fond of learning, they will be able to express opinions and views that are unconventional and truly original. While there will be many people who will admire this strength, there will also be others who will oppose it and will be jealous of them. Therefore, it is advisable for them to learn tact and diplomacy since these traits will stand them in good stead and bring them greater success.

Despite the fact that they may choose unusual and offbeat professions, they will be able to make a reasonable amount of money from them. Considering the fact that they are both intelligent and hard-working, this will not be a surprise. They are a generous and compassionate person, who will take pleasure in using their money and time to help those in distress and need. Institutions and individuals will both benefit from their generosity.

The influence of Saturn will be intense and will be responsible for a great deal of progress and prosperity. They will have the capacity to rise high and reach their goals, irrespective of all the hurdles that may stand in their path. They may encounter obstacles and envy along the way, however, they will be mentally tough and will be able to deal with these impediments and at the same time, retain their balance.

For them the element of balance is more important than most other Librans. They will work hard to ensure that everything in their surroundings bears harmony and equilibrium. It will be difficult for them to function to the best of their abilities in environments of chaos and confusion. Fighting, violence and harshness will be things that they will strive hard to remove. However, they will enjoy healthy arguments and will often take the opportunity of supporting the opposite side. Given their intellect, they will most often win as well.

Leadership is another trait that will come quite naturally to them. They will enjoy being able to motivate and inspire other people. However, the good thing is that they will not be a dictator and therefore, their subordinates will respect and admire them more than ever. In the event of them being a subordinate, they will not be very happy and will wait for their chance to rise and move up the ladder.

Socially, they often swing between the two extremes of talkativeness and quietness. They will often, want to converse and mingle with others while at other times they will simply retreat into their shell and reflect on their life and self. Relationships and marriage will not be an issue of concern. They will be able to fit in and adjust to most people and therefore, their home and family will be happy and well-settled.

Finance

For them money will not be something that will drive them. They will enjoy working more for their own pleasure than for building up their wealth. Despite this, they will often, be successful and will amass a fair amount of money. It is important that they learn to maintain the balance between giving away their money and saving for the future. There is the possibility that they may donate more than what they can and therefore, the future will become uncertain. The best advice that I can give them is to invest their money wisely and then donate whatever they think is fit. Risky investments and businesses should be avoided at all costs.

Health

Since they are gifted with an extremely sharp and over-active mind, they need to work especially hard at giving it a rest and not pushing it to the limit. Stress and strain will take their toll and make them prone to illnesses of the nervous system. They will have a tendency to think too much and hence, could get depressed and melancholic every now and then. What is important is that they remain positive and get plenty of relaxation and fresh air, which will recharge and refresh their mind and body.

On the whole, they may be somewhat susceptible to constipation, respiratory ailments and headaches.

Born on the 9th, 18th and 27th

In case of those who are a Libran born on any of the above-given dates, they will be ruled by the influence of the planets Mars, Saturn and Venus. This will bring about variations in many aspects of their personality and also the events of their life. These planets will combine and mould their personality in a manner that will be unique and individual. Their life, therefore, will be changed and will take a course that will be distinct from the ones taken by Librans born on dates other than Number nine.

The influence of Mars will be dominant in their particular case. Therefore, they will be gifted with qualities such as spontaneity, courage and ambition. They will be filled with an immense amount of zeal and enthusiasm. They will not hesitate in taking any action as long as it seems right to them. While this will be an admirable trait in most situations in the modern world, there are also chances that they may hurt a few people with their candour and therefore, make some enemies. It will be in their interest to inculcate the attributes of discretion and subtlety.

Their mind will be filled with new and intriguing ideas and concepts and they will have the desire to try all of them. From an early age, they will have dexterous hands and will be quite comfortable handling complicated tasks. Gifted and ambitious, they will soon succeed in whichever profession they venture into. They are also quick on the uptake and will know how to use words to suit their purpose. Therefore, it will not be surprising if they carve a niche for themselves in the field of law and politics.

There is also the strong possibility that you may start their own business venture. Even in this case, they will be successful and will be able to overcome odds and failure with grace and strength. If in a business, a sole ownership will be more suitable than a partnership. However, even if they do have a partner, it is important that he understands them and accepts their views without much resistance. They will also do well in a position of leadership and will be able to manage people in an effective manner. People management will be closely related to their ability to develop tact.

They will have an active social life and will make many friends who will bring them joy and warmth. Since they are somewhat stubborn, they may have some problems with relatives and family members. Their personality will be such that members of the opposite sex will automatically gravitate towards them. They will be popular and will marry someone who will bring them contentment and peace. There are strong indications that their children will be just as intelligent as they are and will therefore bring them much happiness.

In short, they will be fortunate and at the same time, will play an important role in shaping their own destiny.

Finance

Prosperity will never be far from them and hence, money will not be too much of a concern. They will want to save some for the future and once they learn to curb their bluntness, they will have enough money to enjoy a life that is comfortable, secure and stable.

They will often, help out friends and family members who are in need and even if they have moved away from their family, they will always be welcome to their help, time and money. It will be this benevolence that will bring them good fortune in the times to come.

Health

In their early years, they will be somewhat fragile and prone to infections and ailments of the digestive system, liver, etc. however, after their twenty-first birthday, they will become healthier and will have enough energy to be able to deal with minor illnesses and lead a wholesome life. They will need to be on their guard against accidents and injuries. They may have some problems with their teeth, jaws and the facial bone structure.

SCORPIO

(24TH OCTOBER TO 22ND NOVEMBER)

Scorpio in General

There is so much of awe that surrounds the sign of Scorpio. It is indeed, surprising that just the word conjures up images of power and authority, strength and courage. Well, a lot of that awe is indeed, well-deserved. The sign of Scorpio is enigmatic and mysterious in a way that is truly unique.

This sign of the zodiac is symbolised by the Scorpion and begins on the 21st of October. However, since it is preceded by the previous sign, it is in the cusp for the first seven days and attains complete strength only around the 28th of October. Thereafter, it remains powerful till the 20th of November, after which it loses strength to the cusp of the incoming sign. We will understand the mysterious Scorpio personality in the next few pages and find out more about their complexities and passions.

The first thing that will strike you about Scorpios is that they will never be moderate. There are no mid-ways for them. Intense and passionate, everything they do will have a lot of fire and energy in it. The best part is that often, they will not even make a big deal about what they are doing, yet it will have an impact on all those around them. Right from the beginning, their personality will exude power and strength. They have the ability to command respect everywhere they go. They will bring a certain aura to the environment and will be able to charge things up with their quiet yet determined strength.

There is little doubt about the fact that they will be able to move masses with their words and actions. Their influence over others will be seen from an early age. They are also intelligent and will have a mind that will be able to work in both positive and negative directions. They will be able to make mischief and will also have the ability to do great good. More often than not, they have a flair with words and will be able to use them to motive and inspire people.

There is the possibility that quite a few Scorpios will have the ability to use their way with words not just to influence people, but also to hurt and sting those whom they don't like. Their tongues can be as sharp as swords and can cut through very deep.

Normally, it has been seen that Scorpios can be divided into two categories. One will be exceedingly humane and charitable while the other will be ruthlessly ambitious and driven. What is important is that they will bring their inherent fire and zeal into anything they pursue. Another noteworthy feature about them is that though they are intense and passionate, they are able to keep their calm when faced with a crisis. They will be able to deal with emergencies and difficult times with remarkable composure and independence.

Since they have minds that are razor sharp and quick, they are able to come up with innovative and unique ideas that will help them succeed and prosper. They are usually very flexible and can adapt to most situations and people with ease. As a result, they will often succeed in just about any professional sphere. They have an interest in literature, science, medicine, the armed forces and business.

Scorpios also have the ability to deal with obstacles and enemies by using their mind more than their body. In most situations, they will rely on their mind to strategise and plan every step and then, simply execute the same. Rash and reckless behaviour is normally, not associated with them. Discrete and secretive, they will keep their plans and schemes to themselves and will not place their trust in people quickly and easily. They will hence, be quite successful as diplomats and mediators.

Fiery and determined, there is nothing that a Scorpio will aim for and not achieve. They will be able to attain pretty much everything that their heart desires. One reason for this is that they will be quite realistic about their goals and will not set unreasonable goals for themselves. They will know their abilities and potential and will work hard to use them to the maximum.

Despite the fact that Scorpios are known to have a sharp tongue and a hot temper, they are also admired and loved by those who know them. The anger of the Scorpio will rise like mercury but will fall equally quickly. Once they see reason, they will be ready to forgive and move on. The critical part is to make them see reason. They will normally rely solely on their own instincts and opinion about a person or a situation.

When they form friendships, they will be loyal and devoted. They will believe in standing by their friends and giving them love, respect and attention. However, they will not make friends easily and will normally just have one or two close friends. As far as other relationships are concerned, they can be quite set in their likes and dislikes and will often, form a dislike against someone without any particular reason.

It has been observed, that most Scorpios tend to lead a dual life. In other words, they could be one person at home and a totally different person outside. Or, it could be that they are one person for themselves and another for the rest of the world. In either case, they will lead a life that will have two sides to it. Their inherent mysteriousness will motivate them to take an interest in matters of occult, astrology, and such lines. Whether they actively engage in it or not will solely depend upon their level of interest in the field.

Another distinctive feature of Scorpios is their eyes. They will have eyes that will reflect mystery, enigma and the sheer strength of their soul. Even the way they will speak will reflect their latent power. Most of this strength comes from their inner belief in themselves. They have a complete certainty about their own strengths and drawbacks. Irrespective of what everyone else around them says or feels, Scorpios will be able to move through life with a strong degree of self-esteem and individualism. They will not be affected by the criticism of others. While they will like praise, they will not let is go to their heads. Scorpios have the ability to control how they feel and what they react to. That is probably the reason, why most of them are able to deal with life with success and a cool assurance.

Most Scorpios are emotional beings, yet they have the ability to hide how they feel and keep their emotions under wraps. One can nearly never look at a Scorpio and truly understand what he or she is feeling. It is remarkable how they are able to keep their own feelings concealed, while at the same time, are capable of reading others' minds. They are fluid and agile and every action of theirs will have an innate gracefulness in it. There will be nothing erratic or irregular about their actions. One of the most endearing features of Scorpios will be their smile. While it will rarely make a full-blown appearance, when it does, you can be certain that it was a smile from the heart and not a false one. It will also be a winning and heartwarming smile that will charm its way into your life.

Even if some Scorpios have to face hardships and difficult times during their childhood, they will have the strength and the courage to battle out things and ensure that they succeed. They will have the presence of mind that is needed to move through life in a smooth manner and deal with obstacles with detachment and effectiveness. That is the reason it is not surprising that all their efforts will bear fruit and that they will be successful and prosperous. Scorpios are not afraid of toil and labour and will work hard to reach their goal. They have the ability to motivate themselves and their ambition to succeed fires them and compels them to put in their one hundred percent. They have a hidden restlessness that will cease only when they feel that they have achieved what they wanted from life. Till then, they will be constantly working, physically and mentally.

Spirited and sincere, they will not hesitate to do anything, provided it takes them closer to their goals. They are endowed with great strength and power by the planet Pluto and they will make full use of these features. They will be able to take most of life's hurdles without complaining and will, as matter of fact, have their own unique way of dealing with failures and set backs.

Although they are known to be discrete, yet they can be remarkably blunt and straightforward when asked for their honest opinion. They will not believe in sugar coating the truth and will give it you the way it is or at least the way they see it. This could hurt some people and motivate others; however, they will not change. All this should not make you form the opinion that Scorpios are heartless and lack sensitivity. It will surprise you to know that they have tender hearts and when they love someone, they do it completely and will be willing to do anything for them.

They are moved by those who are sick and afflicted and will often, go out of their way to make life better for them.

From a material standpoint, Scorpios don't have too many needs and wants. As a result, most of them will lead fairly simple lives and will not be the kinds to splurge on unnecessary items. Even if rich and well-to-do, they will have lifestyles that will be austere as compared to their counterparts. They will also have a generous streak and will often want to help out friends and family members who are less fortunate than them. They will not hesitate to lend a helping hand to people who deserve it.

Marriage will be something that they will not take to very easily. Since they tend to keep their emotions to themselves, they will not be very demonstrative about their affections and will tend to mystify their partner. It will take a person of equal intelligence and great patience to understand the Scorpio and keep him or her happy. However, the Scorpio's loyalty is legendary and they will ensure that they provide a happy and secure home for their family.

Finance

Ironically, though most Scorpios are realistic about many things, they tend to be quite optimistic and idealistic about financial matters. They will get taken in by schemes and plans that promise easy profits. Therefore, it is important that they retain and use their instincts even when dealing with money. Moreover, their tendency to be generous to anyone in need can also cause a strain on themselves. However, most of them tend to lead simple lives and therefore, a lack of money will not prove to be too much of a worry for them. Nevertheless, it is important that they learn to invest only in secure schemes and also put aside money for the future.

Health

Scorpios as children are somewhat fragile and prone to illnesses, especially, of the stomach. However, as they grow, they gain in strength. Yet, most of their strength will be mental as compared to physical. Nevertheless, they will be able to ward off most illnesses, especially, after their twenty-first birthday and will have amazingly good recuperative abilities.

On the whole, they will lead healthy and fit lives. Yet, they should not put too much strain on their nerves and should avoid overindulgence in anything. The respiratory system and the reproductive system will need special care and so will the heart, legs and back areas.

Scorpio

Born on the 1st, 10th, 19th and 28th

Scorpios, who are born on the dates mentioned above, will be impacted by the influence of the planets Mars (negative), Uranus in its exaltation and the Sun. This combination will bring about changes in their personality at the same time, will let them retain the innate mystery and aura of being a Scorpio.

The influence of the Sun on Number one Scorpios is immense and it will bring to them a strong sense of authority and power. They will exude confidence and everything they do will bear their distinctiveness. They will have the ability to inspire and motivate those around them and enable them to realise their inherent strengths and aspire for greatness. As a matter of fact, it will give them a great deal of satisfaction to see others do well and become successful.

They are imaginative and have a sharp, creative mind that will constantly be churning out ideas and thoughts. Since they are intelligent and possess the power that is needed, they will be quite successful in bringing about changes in the society and the system. If they put their mind to it, they will be quite successful in administration, politics, and similar offices.

Despite the fact that they will be inspirational and helpful, they will also have a strongly ambitious temperament and will be extremely goal-oriented. They will be driven to achieve what they want and will not rest till they reach their destination. They will not be bothered by what others tell them. Their discouragement or cynicism will not affect them in the least. However, they will also have the tendency to be critical of others and will want those working with them to be equally dedicated and diligent. Aggression will run deep in them and even if they succeed in masking it, it will surface and show itself in many subtle ways.

One should not for a moment imagine that they will be serious and boring at all times. They have a sharp sense of humour and will often see the lighter side of things. There could also be times when they will mask their sarcasm in humour and soften the sting in their words. One thing is certain, when annoyed they can sting with their words. They will, however, have a way with words and will often be able to conceal their sarcasm in dry humour. Whether written or verbal, they will be able to make their attack and hit the nail on the head using just the right kind of words. This is an art that seems to be innate in their personality.

Although they seem strong and emotionally secure, they are actually quite sensitive and will feel hurt when ignored or uncared for. They will hold a grudge and will feel better only when they've got their due or the other person is sincerely apologetic. If there is one thing that can melt away their resentment, it is a genuine, heartfelt apology.

They have high ambitions and often aspire to rise above their current position in life. Therefore, even if they were born into money, they will want to multiply it. Another notable feature of their personality is that they will want to do things on a large scale. However, they will not be the kind to rush into things, but will spend sufficient time evaluating the viability of such ventures.

Not only will they be efficient and capable in matters of business, but they will also have an aesthetic bent of mind and hence, will have some degree of interest in literature, music, arts, etc. Since they possess good powers of oration, they will make a good lecturer, politician, and in general, a good leader. They have the inclination to work and therefore, will do well in nearly any field. What matters most is that it gives them the opportunity to rise and to make a difference of some sort. Once they have decided on what they want from life, there will be nothing that will be able to stand in their way. They will be the epitome of diligence and determination and will relentlessly pursue their goals and dreams.

They will have a relatively realistic view of life and will not expect it to be a bed of roses. At the same time, they will not be a pessimist. They have hope and belief in themselves and will expect that despite the odds, they will be able to succeed and prosper. It will be this attitude that will be largely responsible for their achievements and triumphs in life.

Finance

Considering the fact that they are ambitious and hardworking, it is not surprising that they will not have money problems, as such. They may have to work hard for it; however, they will soon reach a position where they will be able to afford all the comforts and luxuries of life. Even if born into a rich family, they will spend time and effort in trying to increase the wealth and build a bigger empire. Their intelligence in investment will pay off and they will be able to ensure a secure future for themselves and their family. However, it is important that they do not get swayed by get-rich-quick schemes and also that they put their money only into safe and secure investments.

Health

Number one Scorpios are usually robust and energetic people. They will have the ability to fight most illnesses and recover quickly and completely. However, as a child, they may have health problems and a fragile constitution. The respiratory system will pose some problems and they should try and get a great deal of sunlight and fresh air in their daily life.

Born on the 2nd, 11th, 20th and 29th

It will be the influence of the planets Mars, Neptune and the Moon which will be critical for those who were born on any of the dates given above. Since the Moon is in its fall in this sign in the house of Scorpio of Mars negative, there will be many unusual and conflicting traits present in their character.

They will be independent and will be well aware of their potential, their strengths and weaknesses. Realistic and persevering, they will be ready to take quick decisions and move lithely through life. They will overcome hurdles and obstacles with relative ease and will not be dejected by failure and hindrances.

Ironically, despite the fact that they will be realistic, they will also have a tendency to be idealistic and lose themselves in the world of dreams and fantasies. They will often, build castles in the air and lose touch with the real world. That is why, even though, they may be gifted with great creativity and imagination, they will not be able to make full use of it, unless they learn to snap out of their dreams and get back to work.

Life for they will seem a constant struggle, yet even then they retain a sense of hope and will always feel that things will get better. Once they decide to work at making them better, they will surely change. However, the critical part lies in them not dreaming things away. Therefore, it is important that they strengthen the realistic aspect of their personality, while merely nurturing the idealistic one.

They will often look towards others to help them. At the same time, they will have a strong sense of pride and self-reliance and will not want to ask for help. These are the kinds of contradictory traits that I was referring to earlier. They will simply expect that others should go out of their way to be of assistance and when they aren't, they will be hurt and disappointed. As far as friendships and relationships are concerned, they will be drawn towards people who will intrigue them and will seem more mysterious than even themselves. They will be loyal and dependable as a friend and will lend a helping hand without a thought.

Both Scorpio men and women born on the dates given above are profoundly influenced by the emotion of love and it plays a significant role in their lives. They will be drawn towards the opposite sex, yet will need to work hard at building and maintaining a relationship. They may have to learn to compromise, adjust and balance things if they want a home that is warm, loving and stable.

Change will fascinate them and as a result, they will often, change their goals and aims without really achieving much.

Therefore, it is important and vital that they learn to focus on one thing at a time, complete that and then move on to another. That will enable them to achieve much more in life than otherwise. They are intelligent enough to be aware of their talents, strengths and weaknesses. They just need to be grounded enough to tap into them and realise their true calling.

Finance

They will have to be judicious about managing their money and ensure that they invest everything securely so that their future is well provided for. They will often come into money through unconventional sources and it is essential that instead of splurging or giving it away, they should keep it aside for a rainy day. They should not get taken in by what everybody tells them, trust their instincts and use their own potential to make money and build a secure and stable future for themselves and their family.

Health

They will have strength and vitality, yet at the same time, they may have a wiry, lean physique, which could give the impression of frailty. It is important that they do not put too much pressure on their nerves and learn to relax every now and then. Sleep will do them more good than any medicine. They will be somewhat prone to disorders of the reproductive system and the respiratory system. Insomnia could also give them some problems.

It will be most favourable for them to remain in positive and cheerful surroundings since they will be affected by negativity and pessimism. Melancholy and sadness will have a negative effect on their health and well-being.

Born on the 3rd, 12th, 21st, 30th

The planets Jupiter and Mars will come together to influence those who were born on the above mentioned dates. This particular alliance of planets will be extremely influential and will endow them with characteristics and features that will bring success, fame and fortune into their life. However, it is important that they should use those traits and features in ways that are positive and progressive.

They will have a great deal of self-esteem and individualism. They will be able to take on positions of responsibility and trust and will live up to the expectations of others. Ambitious and strong-minded, they will want to succeed in life and move ahead. There are indications that they might have to face hurdles and obstacles in their life during the early years. However, they will be able to overcome all of these and will become stronger and more resilient.

There will be several plans that they will have and their sharp, alert mind will forever be thinking of more. Since they have the good fortune of being gifted with talents and intellect, most of their plans will serve to bring them profits and fame. They will just need to make a great deal of effort to work those plans through. The tough times that they will face will give them the maturity that they require to survive and succeed in the world. Everything they encounter will have some purpose and meaning and will be related to making them a better and more productive individual.

It will be noticed that in most instances, while they will not be arrogant or conceited, they will have a feeling of superiority over others and this will be reflected in their behavior and interactions with their subordinates and even peers. In the rare possibility that they do not get the chance to realise your dreams and hopes, they will always hold that in their heart, even as they continue to carry out their daily responsibilities with efficiency and diligence. They will always be on the look out to make it big and rise above their current standing in life.

Mature, sensible and strong, there will be little that they will not want to take on. Everything will be perceived as an opportunity by them and they will willingly take charge of situations and crises. They will gladly lead the way for others and will enjoy being in command. However, too much of anything will have a negative impact. Therefore, too much of responsibility could burn them out and exhaust them emotionally and physically. They could put a great deal of stress on their nerves and become prone to several ailments.

They also have the inclination to be dominating and controlling without even realising it. They may even want their way in everything and this could lead to problems especially, professionally. It is important that they maintain a balanced approach and not take on more than what they can safely handle. Another thing that they will need to take care of will be their candour and bluntness. They will have the tendency to give their unvarnished opinion when asked and this could hurt quite a few sentiments and feelings. Therefore, it will be nicer and better for them to develop diplomacy and subtlety when advising, criticising or guiding those around them.

Finance

The combination of planets that rule they will ensure that they succeed in life and with success. They will undoubtedly receive money and prosperity. They will do well in a wide variety of professions and hence, will not find it difficult to make money. What is important is that they learn to take things easy and not over-burden themselves. That will only create problems and will ultimately lead to loss of efficiency and therefore, income.

Health

Although they are blessed with a constitution that is strong and healthy, they will, like I said earlier, have the tendency to tax themselves and bring on too much pressure. This is bound to have a negative impact on their health, mental, physical and emotional. Anxiety and stress will be the two main things that will trigger illnesses and will make them prone to headaches, heart problems and hypertension. What is important is that they learn to relax and rejuvenate themselves at regular intervals and take only as much responsibility as they can comfortably handle.

Born on the 4th, 13th, 22nd and 31st

It would be the planets Mars, Uranus and the Sun that would come together to change and influence the personality those who if you were born on any of the dates given above. This particular combination of planetary influences would be responsible in endowing their personality with a strange yet distinctive complexity.

The basic traits and characteristics of their inherent personality have been described in the preceding pages, describing Scorpios. On these pages, we would consider the uniqueness of the individuals born on the above-mentioned dates.

There is considerable evidence to show that Uranus and Mars are two of the most significant planets and when they come together, they can be responsible for bringing about some profound changes in the personality of the individual. Even between the planet Uranus and the sign Scorpio, there is a strong bond and it tends to exert an influence that brings about changes not only in the character but also, in the life of the individual. We would understand this in the following pages.

Number 4 Scorpios have immense potential and can bring about the unlikeliest of results. They have strength of character and willpower that enables them to realise their dreams and aspirations. At the same time, it is essential for them to keep strengthening their determination and self-esteem, so that they are equipped to face the challenges and hurdles of everyday life.

Intelligent and mature, once they decide on something, it becomes a possibility. That is one of the reasons why fame and fortune is not difficult for them to achieve. They have the ideal combination of innovation and practicality. As a result, most of their dreams are achievable and have great goodness in them. The combination of planets would also be responsible for bringing about some amount of unconventional behaviour in their personality. However, this could be controlled by virtue of their own resolution and strength of mind.

They might have to face the hurdles of envy and criticism. This would not deter them and if they use a combination of optimism, spiritualism and pragmatism, they would be able to sail through life with relative ease and success. As a matter of fact, spiritualism would help them to face life with more strength and efficiency. It would help them in their relationships with others and would give them more insight in to their own personality. Even if they do not take to spiritualism in the literal sense of the word, they would have some sort of unifying force that would help them to face reality and at the same time, would keep their child-like optimism and hope alive.

There are indications that if they lose hope and faith in the goodness of life, they may use the powers that the planets have endowed them with in a negative manner and therefore, this could impact their life in many different ways. On the other hand, the possibility of this happening is bleak and that is the reason, they should use quiet moments of introspection to evolve and strengthen their willpower and character.

They would be diligent in whatever they undertake and it would be this loyalty to hard work and perseverance that would bring them good results. They would also, have the same level of loyalty towards friends and family, who support them and stand by them. For them to lead a balanced and content life, it is important that their surroundings be positive and the people they interact with are well-rounded individuals. Only then would they be in an environment that would bring out the best in them. For their personality, inner tranquillity and peace is extremely important and critical and it would go a long way in determining their success.

Finance

For them, money would be something that they would need to spend with wisdom and carefulness. They should try not to place too much hope on the help of others. Since they would be intelligent and practical, making money would not be difficult. However, they would need to practise a reasonable amount of judiciousness when spending and investing it. They should try and avoid unnecessary speculation and if in business, select their partners with great care, or else, they could even go solo. Their talents and abilities would make them a success in the fields of engineering, literature, theatre, management and similar lines.

Health

Positive thinking and a regular routine would work wonders for their health and would keep them in the best shape possible. If their mind is healthy and sharp, there would be hardly any illness

illness that would affect them adversely. Moreover, they would be able to recuperate quickly and efficiently. However, if they succumb to pessimism and negativity, they would be prone to nervous disorders, weakness of the heart, blood infections and digestive disorders.

As far as possible, they should get a lot of sunlight, exercise and humour to keep them in good spirits and great health.

Born on the 5th, 14th and 23rd

For those born on any of the dates given above, would imply that the vibrations of the planets Mars and Mercury would play a critical role in shaping their personality and making them distinct from their counterparts born on other dates.

The basic traits and characteristics of their inherent personality have been described in the preceding pages, describing Scorpios. On these pages, we would consider the uniqueness of the individuals born on the abovementioned dates.

It would be the presence of Mercury that would endow them with an intellect that would be sharp and astute. They would have the ability to think on their feet and would exhibit sound administrative skills. Not only that, they would also be perceptive and would have the ability to form accurate opinions about people and situations. This kind of intelligence would give them the ability to succeed in most professional and personal situations. Candid and profound, they would prefer to keep their opinions to themselves unless asked. They would also, not be the kinds to place their trust in others quickly and easily. They would also want to evaluate the person and see whether he or she is worthy of their trust and also, their respect.

Their mind would be their biggest asset and would hold the key to their success. Their creativity would be unique and would bear their distinctive touch. They will display much imagination and innovation in various fields. Moreover, they would have an innate flair for art and music and would therefore, take to these spheres easily. They would also, have a temperament that would be somewhat restless and would want to explore and see the world. As a result, they would often travel and go to distant places. Traveling would not only satisfy their urge to see a new place but would also, widen their horizon and they would be able to see things from varied perspectives. All this would add to their knowledge and would help them in their journey through life. The opportunity to travel, however, would solely be dependent on their financial and social circumstances.

As far as relationships are concerned, they would be drawn towards members of the opposite sex. Whether they fall in love with them or not would be another question altogether. Their restlessness would be reflected, even in matters of the heart and they would often not be sure about their feelings. However, once they do find someone who would intrigue you and at the same time, support them, they would be a loyal and ardent lover. They would work hard to keep their home safe and secure.

Materialism would not have a big place in their life. However, they would want their life to be comfortable, if not lavish and they would work hard for the same. Their dedication to their goals and their determination to make a name for themselves would ensure that they succeed in life. On the other hand, if they take a dislike to hard work and labour, they would spend a life without any focus and this would, only, make them more discontent and unhappy than anything else.

Finance

Those born on the above-mentioned dates would be very lucky in matters of finance and wealth. They would be willing to put in the hard work that is required to earn money and also, would be intelligent enough to invest that money with wisdom and caution. It is important that they save enough for their retirement since the planetary influences, indicate several ups and downs in their fortune.

Health

Health, for them, would be more a matter of curbing their irritation and anger at others. If they are happy and content with everything around them, they would be in the best of health. Their constitution would be lean and wiry; however, they would have enough strength and stamina in them. They would need to reduce the amount of stress that they take so as to keep their body in optimum condition. As a child, they may suffer from the usual children's ailments; however, nothing would be too serious.

As long they keep a check on the amount of tension that they take, they would lead a life that is happy and healthy. Otherwise, they could be prone to disorders of the nervous system and the digestive system.

Born on the 6th, 15th and 24th

For Scorpios born on the above mentioned dates, the influence of the planets Venus and Mars is significant and this combination would endow the innate Scorpio character with traits and talents that would make the native distinctive in more than one way.

The basic traits and characteristics of their inherent personality have been described in the preceding pages, describing Scorpios. On these pages, we would consider the uniqueness of the individuals born on the above mentioned dates.

The presence of Venus in their sign would endow them with a loving and compassionate temperament. They would take to people easily and would be gentle and caring. Also, they would be willing to sacrifice their own desires and needs for the sake of others, especially, parents, siblings and relatives. Their selflessness would be exemplary and they would feel happy when doing things for others.

They would also have the tendency to control others. However, they would not do this in an offensive and dominating way, therefore, their peers and subordinates would not mind bowing down to their will. Moreover, they would be intelligent and hence, their opinions, views and arguments would always be treated with respect and seriousness. Although they would be a diligent and devoted worker, there are possibilities that indicate that they may have to struggle during their initial years. However, if they would persevere and keep their focus, success would surely, be theirs. Even if they are born in a family that is well-established, chances are that they would still have to struggle in order to create their own identity. They may have to submit to the requirements and needs of society or even, people in their own family. And though, they would willingly carry out their obligations, they would chafe against undesirable restrictions and limitations.

It would be this spirit of independence that would motivate them to travel and also, be unconventional in many ways. When given the chance, they would express their individuality in ways that would be offbeat and at the same time, inspiring. Nothing that they would do would be ordinary. Their intrinsic intelligence and creativity would reflect themselves in everything that they do.

In matters of the heart and marriage, they would be most suitably paired with someone who would not place too many demands on them and let them be the person they truly are. They would be inexplicably drawn towards the opposite sex, however,

however, it would be wise if they take their time and use their discretion in deciding on their marriage partner. Due to the presence of Venus, they would be a passionate and loyal lover; however, they may have the tendency to be somewhat possessive. To enjoy a secure and loving relationship, it would be advisable for them to curb this tendency. The most important thing, however, would be not to rush into things and to think these things through.

Their inherent skills would be more inclined towards the arts and music. They would have the natural flair for painting, writing, music, and dance. However, at the same time, they would be comfortable handling positions of authority and managing teams of people, successfully and efficiently. Their overall personality would be such that they would be able to perform to the best of their abilities in any line, as long as they are interested in it and it gives them a feeling of satisfaction. Even in businesses and routine jobs, they would be an industrious and organised worker and would give their best efforts to the task at hand.

Considering their personality and the special traits that their planets endow them with, it is not surprising that they would be able to succeed in most professions and earn both fame and fortune. They would truly, merit all that they earn and would add to it, by willingly sharing it with everyone around them. They would be loved and admired by friends, superiors and subordinates and would enjoy the limelight when it shines on them.

Finance

In matters of finance, they would be benefited by their instincts and commonsense. Since they would put in the hard work and effort that is required, making money would not be a problem. Even if born in to money, they would be able to multiply it and make it grow. They would also enjoy spending the money that they earn and would want to lead a comfortable life as much as possible. Therefore, it is essential that they maintain a balance between spending and earning and, also, invest their money so that their later years are well provided for.

Health

They would be fortunate since they would be blessed with a strong body and a great deal of stamina. However, since they would be fond of leading a good, easy life, they might not pay sufficient attention to their diet and exercise. As a result, they may be prone to obesity and related problems of heart, liver and lungs.

Born on the 7th, 16th and 25th

It would be the combination of Mars, Neptune and the Moon that would come together to influence those were born on any of the above-mentioned dates. They would benefit from the presence of Neptune, since it is the planet that rules the mind more than the body, and therefore, would endow them with a mind that is sharper and quicker than their other counterparts. Not only that, Mars in the sign of Scorpio is negative and has many mental features and so does the Moon. Therefore, all of them would gift them with a mind that would be imaginative and fertile.

The basic traits and characteristics of their inherent personality have been described in the preceding pages, describing Scorpios. On these pages, we would consider the uniqueness of the individuals born on the above-mentioned dates.

This unique and strange combination of planetary influences would be responsible for bringing about unusual experiences in their life and giving them a personality that would be unconventional to say the very least. They would be deeply impacted by their environment and the people around them. If in an unhappy and melancholy atmosphere, they, too, would become depressed and dissatisfied. There are strong indications that they would reflect too much on themselves and their behaviour. As a result, they would put too much pressure on themselves and would often, strive for perfection.

It would be their innate desire for perfection that would often, make them critical of those around them and they would even, be harsh with them. Their bluntness could hurt people and their offbeat temperament could make them suspicious of them. However, once someone would get to really know them, they would be surprised to find that they are a thoughtful and compassionate person, beneath the rough demeanor.

The influence of Neptune and Mars would be responsible for creating in them an interest in the worlds of mysticism, astrology and even, psychology. They would be intrigued by the working of the supernatural elements and of the human mind. They, themselves, would be gifted with intelligence and would be able to absorb knowledge like a sponge. Moreover, they would have a flair for scientific and other research. Unlike most people, they would not place a high premium on material goods and would be more inclined to look for a deeper meaning of life. Self-improvement and evolution would be one of their keen interests and they would devote considerable time and effort for this purpose.

As far as relationships and love is concerned, they would often, be misinterpreted. Fortunately, for them, these misconceptions would be resolved and people would be charmed by their knowledge and their comfort with themselves. They would need to work on their tendency to be overly critical of others, in order to enjoy relationships that are meaningful and long-term. They would be able to set up a home with a person who understands and accepts them the way they are. Because they would change, only if they feel the need to do so and nothing anyone says would make a difference. Once they find the right person, they would make a good life partner and would work hard to have a loving and warm home environment.

Finance

Despite the fact that materialism would never be on their list of priorities, they would be a conscientious worker and would therefore, earn a decent living for themselves. Also, there are the possibilities that they would come into money through unusual and unexpected sources. Essentially, though, it would be their intellect and the gifts of their mind that would yield the maximum returns for them. It would be in their best interests to invest this money wisely and ensure that they have a comfortable life, even after they retire.

Health

They would have a strong mind and their body would often, struggle to keep pace with their train of thoughts and ideas. It would be beneficial for them to keep a close watch on their diet and also, have a regular exercise regimen since that would help them to build stamina and energy levels. They would also, need to relax and take things easy so that the mind feels lighter and not overly burdened. Although they would not be prone to serious illnesses, they would need to take special care of their nerves and their respiratory system.

Born on the 8th, 17th and 26th

The influence of Saturn and Mars would be responsible for shaping the personality of the Scorpios born on the dates given above. Both these planets are powerful and influential planets. As a result, the native would have to have extraordinary qualities in order to make the best possible use of the influence of both these planets.

The basic traits and characteristics of their inherent personality have been described in the preceding pages, describing Scorpios. On these pages, we would consider the uniqueness of the individuals born on the above mentioned dates.

The presence of Saturn indicates that they would need to build on their willpower and determination so as to prosper and succeed in life. If at any point of time, they are filled with negativity and sadness, they would need to lift up their spirits and keep their focus on their goal. Otherwise, they would not be able to grow and progress in life. Saturn when, used in the proper manner would prove to be more of an aide than a deterrent and would enable them to touch new heights of success.

They would also, have the advantage of Mars, which would support them and give them the strength and the power that they would require in order to deal with Saturn. Mars would endow them with a mind that would be sharp and would give them the ability to soak up all the knowledge around them. They would be able to use their mind to guide them and assist them in every aspect of life.

During their initial years, they may have to struggle and work really hard in order to achieve anything. There may be many hurdles and while overcoming them, may not be easy, they would be able to deal with them, by virtue of their self-control and discipline. Once they learn to control themselves, they would be able to control everything else, easily and efficiently.

They would have a streak of stubbornness and would often, want their own way in most situations. As a result, working in a team is something that they would not really enjoy. They would be more successful when working on their own and would be able to achieve more in less time. However, if compelled to work in a team, they would make a sincere effort to get along and be somewhat adjusting and easy-going. They would also, have the tendency to be more of 'a closed book' than anything else. In other words, they would not wish to divulge their plans and ideas to others. They would keep them to themselves and experiment with them. That is another reason, why working in a team, would not suit their personality immensely.

Their inclination to be obstinate would reflect itself in their tendency to support their own views and ideas completely and refusing to look at a different perspective. They would often, be distrustful of others and would view them with doubt and suspicion. Even when others would act for their benefit, they would feel as if they are trying to place hurdles in their path. This would partly be because they would have had to face many obstacles, early in life and that is why they would be more wary of people than others. However, it is important that they use their intelligence and their perceptiveness to form judgements about others. Rather than simply hold on to past beliefs and opinions. There would be people who may try and oppose them, yet, at the same time, there would also, be those who would support them and help them. It is important that they learn to accept their help graciously and not view them with doubt.

In affairs of the heart, once they overcome their initial mistrust, they would be a loyal and passionate lover, who would be willing to sacrifice his or her own needs for the sake of their love. They should open their heart and their mind to the wonderful world around them and their life would be much happier and fulfilling than ever before surround themselves with positive–thinking people and they would be able to deal with all the challenges of life in a more efficient manner.

Achieving goals and realising dreams would not be difficult for them, once they set their mind to it and persevere despite all odds and challenges. Once they have learnt that dealing with life is not difficult, nothing would be impossible for them. They would be able to dream the biggest dreams and also, realise them in a successful and efficient manner. Simply do not let their failures affect them and try and learn something from everything that happens in their life. They have a strong and magnetic personality and therefore, they would be able to succeed, evolve and grow in the various spheres of life.

Finance

Their money matters are more dependent on how they deal with life than anything else. If they are able to face life positively, they would be a success in any professional field, since they would have the ability and the intelligence to learn and apply their knowledge. Once they have established themselves in any field, they would be able to make money and also, invest it so as to reap the maximum returns. Their determination would be their greatest asset and would enable them to succeed in whatever they wish to undertake.

They would not have the inclination to go overboard with spending; therefore, maintaining a balance between income and expenditure would not be too much of a problem for them.

Health

As far as health is concerned, they would often swing between being extremely healthy and otherwise. It is important to understand that they would have the tendency to be influenced by their surroundings and therefore, if they live in positive environments, they would remain healthy and strong. They would be somewhat prone to skin infections and joint problems. Too much of stress and pressure would have a negative impact on their system, therefore, they should try and relax every now and then. Their health would actually, be totally in their own hands and they should make the most out of it.

Born on the 9th, 18th and 27th

The influence of the planet Mars would be critical for those, who were born on the dates given above. There is something very interesting about the presence of Mars in this sign. It would be called the 'double Mars', since Mars would be present in its own House and therefore, the impact that it would have on their personality would be profound and intense.

The basic traits and characteristics of their inherent personality have been described in the preceding pages, describing Scorpios. On these pages, we would consider the uniqueness of the individuals born on the above-mentioned dates.

Dynamic and passionate, they would be able to rise to any occasion and meet challenges with fiery determination and resolve. they would have the strength to overcome obstacles and would not hesitate in taking risks, in order to achieve their goals. Fighting opposition and criticism would come naturally to them, and the power endowed by Mars would motivate them to give their one hundred percent to all that they undertake.

Considering the fact that they would be imbued with the courage and endurance of Mars, they would be very successful in fields such as the army, politics and other fields where these talents would be appreciated and utilised. They would also, be most comfortable in leadership roles and would be able to carry out responsibilities in an efficient and diligent manner. They would not treat life lightly and would be extremely keen on achieving their goals. Their ability to deal with people and also, organise affairs would be commendable and would often, win them the admiration and respect of their peers, juniors and seniors.

As far as relationships and their personal life are concerned, they would be just as passionate in this sphere as in any other. They would be loyal and devoted. However, they would not place their trust in anyone easily and quickly. They would take Their time to judge people and then, form an opinion about them. Their diligence and commitment would make them a success in most professions. However, they would do really well in fields of medicine, defence, engineering and in any position of responsibility in a business or administrative field.

Their individuality and strength of character would often, be a sore point for people who are envious of their success and prosperity. As a result, they would often, have to stand alone for their convictions and their goals. The positive aspect of all this would be that they would become stronger than ever before and would also; be able to succeed despite all odds.

Their desire to learn would be strong and They would also, want to travel and explore the world. This would not only widen your perspective but would also, help them to relax. They would at times, place too much pressure on themselves and this would make them irritable and moody. Travel would lighten their heart and spirit and They would be capable of handling things in a more effective manner.

Once they would decide on something and would believe in, nothing would be able to stand in their path. They would be willing to overcome hurdles and obstacles and would not be deterred by the opinions of other people. Criticism and rebuke would not affect them greatly and they would be able to deal with life and its challenges in a positive manner. Although their personality would be influential and enthusiastic, they would benefit from being more adaptable and considering the views of others as well. This would help them to be a better team player and would increase their popularity as well.

Finance

Initially, They may have to struggle and overcome odds, however, in the latter part of their life, their efforts would pay off and they would be successful and prosperous. Everything that they would do would bring results and would add to their financial well-being. Once they invest their money, effort and time wisely, it is only natural that they would be able to earn profits and accumulate wealth.

Health

Although they would have a strong personality and a healthy constitution, they would be somewhat prone to colds, cough, fever and even, hypertension. They would need to take care when travelling since they may suffer from accidents and injuries.

SAGITTARIUS

(23RD NOVEMBER TO 21ST DECEMBER)

Sagittarius in General

Sagittarius—the Archer. The Sagittarius persons are amiable, enthusiastic and generous persons who will relate well to people and will often, end up surprising themselves with their natural spontaneity and warm humour. This is a sign that begins at the end of November and continues till the end of December. On these pages, we will try and understand in greater detail the normally misunderstood personality of the Sagittarius person. Ruled by the planet Jupiter, they have many distinctive and lovable characteristics in their personality that appeals to everybody.

Light-hearted, loving and guileless, the Sagittarius is so simply straightforward that he may well be understood as being tactless but not inconsiderate. One should never imagine that the Sagittarius is not intelligent; it is just that he will not think before he speaks. He gets so caught up in the moment that everything else fades away. Ironically, the archer will always think of himself as being diplomatic and sophisticated. It will never be his intention to hurt anyone. And, neither will he be wily, sly or underhand. Those are exactly the kind of things that he detests.

Sagittarians will have a sort of restlessness that will always run through their body and as a result, they will always be moving around and up to something or the other. They will carry themselves with confidence and a quiet pride. One will never find them sitting in a corner trying to avoid meeting people. They will love to be the centre of attention and will often succeed in being just that.

Courageous and positive, they move through life with cheerfulness and a certain amount of recklessness. They enjoy taking risks and love adventure. It will be this spirit of adventure that will also fill them with a fondness for the outdoors and nature. They will enjoy trekking, rafting and all extreme sports which will bring them closer to nature and at the same time, will give them the thrill they crave for.

Benevolent and truthful, Sagittarians will always try and be of use to society and mankind. They will try and lead a life with good values and depending on their background will always try and be as righteous as they can. However, they will never be boring and pious; they will always be fun, high on energy and energetic. On the whole, Sagittarians will be candid and liberal. However, when irritated, they can be quite defensive and brusque.

Even on their off days, it is not very easy for people to dislike Sagittarians. They will often overlook their moodiness and enjoy their warmth, wit and optimism. The Sagittarian sense of humour is quite legendary. It will either be satiric or childish, but it will always be there. Along with their humour, these lovable people will also be quite good at debates and will manage to make their point in nearly every argument.

They will also be endowed with an innate sense of instinct and perception. This will probably account for their interest in spiritualism, occult and related things. They will, in all likelihood, be talkative and decisive, so much so that they will often clash with others over views and ideas. They have plenty of ideas and opinions and will often want to share them with others. There are also chances that one might come across a few Sagittarians who will be quiet and submissive; however, even they will be creative and imaginative.

Ruled by Jupiter, the archers are normally vibrant, imaginative people and will always be ready to devote themselves to the realisation of their dreams and aspirations. Irrespective of whether they like to talk about their ideas and dreams, they will always have a plan to achieve those dreams.

Usually, Sagittarians are amicable and delightful, yet when they are taken for granted and pushed around, they will lose their tempers and flare up. They are also irritated by illogical and worthless rules and regulations. Freedom-loving and brave, they will often, oppose what they feel is wrong and will not hesitate in stating what they think in simple terms.

They will encourage people to be open with them and will always respect and reciprocate honesty. They will also be touched by sadness and will want to help people. However, since they will be so trusting of others they will often be taken advantage of. Their generosity and compassion will flow freely for everybody and they will extend a helping hand without even being asked.

Sagittarians will enjoy travelling and if they have the resources of time and money, they would love to go around the world. They will also have religious inclinations and at many times during their lives, they will try and find a belief that will balance their ideals and their intelligence.

Bubbly, ebullient and spontaneous, they will often be like grown up children in their outlook on life. They will be responsible and mature yet they will always retain a freshness and innocence. Even when they decide to take on more serious endeavours, they will do so with a certain youthfulness and joie de vivre.

In matters of love and romance, Sagittarians often plunge right in. They will fall in love completely and are gentle, loving and passionate. They will think of funny things to do and be expressive about their feelings and sentiments. Yet, they will always dawdle when it will come to real commitment and taking the final steps towards wedlock.

To think that these lovable people will be free of all flaws will be a misconception. They might have an inclination for over-indulgence and being short-tempered. However, like I said earlier, it is very difficult to hold a grudge against these joyful individuals and therefore, one will realise that they never mean any malice. Also, even if they lose their tempers, they will quickly cool down and even more quickly, apologise.

Gifted with sharp memories, they will remember details yet ironically, will forget routine matters.

Outgoing, expressive and generous, Sagittarians will be lively and will be adaptable to the various changes that come about and bravely face all obstacles, never once losing heart or faith in himself and his ability to bring about great things.

Finance

For Sagittarians, money will be earned largely through their creativity and talent. They will need to work hard in order to accumulate wealth and also since they are perceptive, they should trust their instincts more than other people. They should always be wary about who they invest their money with. They will also be generous and giving, therefore, they should always keep a sufficient amount aside for their future.

Sagittarians will have imaginative ideas and most of them will be productive and profitable. Most importantly, they will have the belief in themselves and this will be primarily responsible for their success and prosperity.

Health

Health for these Jupiter-ruled people is more a case of mind over matter. They will be active, energetic and will constantly be occupied with something or the other. Their minds and bodies will always be working and as a result, they will tire themselves out completely. This will make them prone to infections and injuries. Also, colds and coughs will be a common occurrence with them.

Since they will at times go overboard with their food and drink, they will need to keep a check on their weight, blood pressure and overall well being. As long as they keep a balanced approach, they will enjoy a healthy and fit life. Exercise will not be a problem with them, since they will be inherently active and adventurous people.

Sagittarius

Born on the 1st, 10th, 19th and 28th

For all Sagittarians born on the above-mentioned dates, the Sun, Uranus and Jupiter will be influential and will bring about certain distinctive features in their personality. There will be certain features that might be enhanced while others might be subdued.

They will have the characteristic Sagittarian personality. In other words, they will be positive, cheerful and will have a happy-go-lucky attitude to life. There will be hardly anything that will bring them down and depress them. They will take all of life's challenges and hardships in their stride. They will always be upbeat and buoyant about life and the future.

Benevolent and caring, they will be willing to share their time, resources, energy and money with everybody. They will be a good team player and will want to share their ideas and feelings as well. This will make them more straightforward than usual. And, they will also be someone who will not give up easily. Each time they face a block or a fall, they will brush themselves up and get ready to try a different technique. However, once they are convinced about something, they will not rest till you accomplish it. They are very motivated and will have an infectious enthusiasm, which will make everyone around them as focused and positive as they are.

Considering the fact that they are thoughtful and considerate of others, they will be touched by sad stories and will try and make things better for other people. However, they have a good sense of intuition and therefore, will always be able to tell if someone is taking advantage of them. Typically, they will never bear a grudge against anyone and will sincerely forgive and forget. They often, believe that life is too short to bear grudges against others.

Active and full of life, they will always be engaged in something or the other. Sitting idle is just not their style. Once they have a goal in sight, they will be ambitious and driven to achieve it. If not a definite goal, they will keep themselves busy with some hobby or the other. However, their mind and body will always be at work and they will always endeavour to rise and succeed. At the same time, when people meet them, they will never be able to judge how ambitious they are. They will be childishly enthusiastic and energetic and it will be this spirit that will appeal to all those in their company.

Diligent and principled, they always lead a life that will be righteous. For them, it will always be important to do the right thing. They will always try and abide by the rules, as long as they make sense to them. Illogical and meaningless restrictions annoy them and they will never adhere to them.

Their free and happy spirit will motivate them to take up sports and adventuresome activities. They will be talkative and will often be an engaging conversationalist. They will be intrigued by diverse topics and will often be an authority on philosophy, religion and similar subjects. Not only will they be good at talking, they will also be attentive when listening to people whom they admire and respect.

Finance

Number one Sagittarians are capable and efficient. If they are one of them, they will make your money by exploiting their potential, skills and talents. It will be hard, honest work that will yield profits for them. They might face some losses if they invest their money unwisely, however, they will always be able to recover and get back to business. They will not be the sort who will sit and feel sorry for themselves. That is the reason they will always be successful and fortunate in everything that they do.

Health

They will be fortunate in health matters and will have a strong and healthy constitution. As a result, they will be able to ward off most illnesses and infections. What they will need to focus on will be their nerves. They need to keep them relaxed. Too much work and stress will exhaust them and pull their energy levels down. Therefore, they should try and get enough sleep and exercise caution when travelling to avoid mishaps. That, alone, will keep them healthy and fit.

Born on the 2nd, 11th, 20th and 29th

The planets Jupiter, Neptune and the Moon will come together to influence Sagittarians born on the above-mentioned dates. The influence of the Moon and Neptune will make them less dynamic and driven than other Sagittarians. They will, in particular, be softer and somewhat reserved.

They have a more spiritual outlook and will evaluate life on this level rather than on a materialistic one. Also, their sense of intuition and perception will be heightened. They will be able to rely on their instincts and benefit from them as well. However, they should be careful not to misuse or abuse any of the gifts that they may be endowed with.

They will also be quite compassionate and empathetic towards people and will radiate warmth that will draw them towards them. Their inherent simplicity and innocence will be endearing and even though they will not be a true extrovert, they will often have a diverse circle of friends and acquaintances. They will be interested in science and nature. Travelling will be special for them and they will use it as a means to learn more about the world around them. Considering the fact that they are patient and discreet, they will make a good teacher or even diplomat.

Creative and imaginative, they have an inclination for the arts, music, poetry, theatre and literature. They will also be somewhat excitable and will enjoy spending time on their own and nurturing their creative spirit. There are strong chances that, unlike most Sagittarians who have simple wants and tastes, they will have sophisticated preferences and inclinations. They will also be very particular about the food they eat and their health.

They will be happy with who they are and will be satisfied with life in general. This should not mean that they will be complacent. They are not the kind who will crib about what they don't have and feel sorry for themselves. They will be hopeful and confident about being able to build a successful life for themselves. They will be more mature and responsible in their outlook and will be able to handle positions of authority with ease and efficiency.

Finance

For those born on the above-mentioned dates, money will not be the top-most priority. They will tend to treat it with a sense of detachment and will work more for their satisfaction than for the money involved. However, they will be a diligent worker and there are strong chances, that they will rise and be a success in all that they do.

They are generous and will often support charities. If they invest their money wisely and judiciously, they will lead a comfortable life and not want for anything.

Health

They will be concerned about their health from an early age and will ensure that they do the right things to keep fit. Although they will not have a strong disposition, they will often work hard to give it strength and endurance. They will need to take good care of their respiratory system and the joints.

Born on the 3rd, 12th, 21st, 30th

It will be the influence of the planets Jupiter, Venus and Mars that will distinguish Sagittarians born on the above-mentioned dates. While they will be as cheerful and enthusiastic as their other counterparts, these fortunate individuals have a powerful planetary combination that supports them and will bring about sweeping changes in their life.

They will be lively and fun-loving with a special fondness for the outdoors. They will enjoy exercise and will spend a great deal of time engaged in some sport or the other. Even if they do not actively pursue sports, they will enjoy reading about them or watching them. Their sense of humour and warmth towards people will make them popular and they will be able to get out of sticky situations with just a warm smile.

There is very little that they will not be able to accomplish. Although they will not have brutal ambition in their nature, they will have a quiet determination. Once you decide what they want from life, there will be little that will be able to hold them back. Also, they will have an inherent optimism that will enable them to overcome all odds and learn from all setbacks. They will be strong and yet will not seem to throw their weight around. Arrogance and cunningness will be absent from their personality.

The presence of Venus in their planets will make them warm and approachable. They will have an inherent attractiveness that will draw people, especially the opposite sex, towards them. In matters of love and romance, they will be very successful and will enjoy the attention and appreciation of many admirers. Once they find someone they truly love and respect, they will be loyal and passionate. Even with friends, they will be someone they will look forward to meeting.

They will not be the sort who will hold grudges against people or life. They will simply move on and start afresh. It will be this approach combined with their determination that will enable them to succeed in all their endeavours and bring prosperity to their life. There are strong possibilities that they will have quite a few talents and whether they use them for profit or not, will solely be their decision.

Capable and confident, they are cheerful and will find happiness in doing what they do. They will not want to sit and feel sorry for themselves. If stuck in a job that they dislike, they will still find reasons to be happy and this will reflect in their work and help them in building a secure future for themselves. Their outlook on life will be contagious and they will therefore, do quite well in a people management role. Although they may not be discreet, they will never be deliberately rude or hurtful. And, when made to realise their blunder, they will never hesitate in apologising. It will be this openness and freshness that will appeal to everyone they meet and interact with.

There will be quite a few changes in their life and social situation, however, they will be able to deal with these and turn them to their advantage. They will also have a strong faith in spiritualism and will rely on it for strength and sustenance. Creative and artistic, they will enjoy reading, music, painting and the like. They will also be a good speaker and when talking about a subject of their choice will be fluent and lucid.

On the whole, their personality is generous, warm and compassionate. They will be successful and hard-working and at the same time, will not be too serious or gloomy. They will look at life as a journey that will involve adventure, exploring and learning.

Finance

For Number three Sagittarians, fortune will play a strong hand in matters of finance. They will be prosperous, and irrespective of whether they are in business or in a profession, they will be able to earn a good amount and lead a comfortable life. They will never want for anything and at the same time, will be a generous and giving soul. They will always try and help those in need and will do so selflessly.

While they will lead a life of comfort, it is also essential that they save and invest money for their future. Considering the fact that their life will be filled with changes, it is important that they keep some money aside since after they retire, there will be some tight times.

Health

Generally, Sagittarians born on the dates mentioned above will have strong and healthy constitutions. They will be lucky not to suffer from major illness and disease. However, after the age of sixty, they might have to take special care of their joints and also their nerves. Since they will always be involved in something or the other, they may put too much stress on their nervous system and this might lead to ailments and illness.

Born on the 4th, 13th, 22nd and 31st

Jupiter will combine with Uranus and the Sun to influence the personality of Sagittarians born on the above-given dates. This particular combination will make their life an eventful one, one which will have many sudden changes and upheavals.

Extremely intelligent and talented, they have a fertile, imaginative and aesthetic mind. Even they will not be aware of the full strength and potential of their mind. They will have great ideas and most of them will serve to bring them profits and gains.

It will be their intelligence and their distinctiveness that will compel you to think 'out of the box'. They will not conform to the traditional modes of thought and will be highly individualistic in their leanings and preferences.

Although they will have the typical Sagittarian fondness for people and gatherings, they will often, spend time on their own because of their different and unconventional thoughts and ideals. They will be perceptive and will be sensitive to the vibes that others will give. Hence, they will always know how people feel about them and will react accordingly. It will be their intuitive nature that will predispose them towards mysticism and occult. They will be intrigued by it and will often study it in detail.

Rules, regulations and routine will certainly not be meant for them. They will love freedom and will always want to live life on their own terms. They will not interfere in the lives of others and will expect the same from them. That is probably the reason why they enjoy being on their own more than in groups. They will have a select circle of friends and these will share their personality and preferences.

As far as marriage is concerned, it is critical in their case that they marry only when they meet someone who will be able to adjust to them and give they all the space that you need to express their individualism and creativity. If they do not have such a partner, they will always feel stifled and unhappy.

They have a spirit for adventure and will love to travel to unusual destinations. They should be careful when travelling since they might meet with accidents and mishaps.

Liberal and benevolent, they will speak their mind and will not be afraid of anything. They will also be fortunate professionally and will be able to earn their living by using their talents. Their creativity and independence will often, bring them great returns. There is no doubt that they will have a life that will be unusual. They might often encounter changes when they least expect them and there could be quite a few hurdles on their path to success. However, they will be able to deal with these in an effective and positive manner. Due to their unconventional standpoint, they might earn the rebuke and censure of traditional bodies in the fields of religion and politics.

They will lead a life that will be different from most Sagittarians born on other dates. They will be intelligent and independent and will not want to be answerable to others for their actions and decisions.

Finance

For them, money will be a controversial subject. They will never be too sure about whether they really want money or they just need it to survive. However, they will put their intelligence and their talents to good use and will be able to earn a decent sum for themselves. With diligence and luck, they will be able to accumulate wealth. However, there will never be a set pattern in their life. There will be times with lots of money and times with very little. Yet, they will not be disillusioned and will always retain their inherent optimism.

They should invest your money with care and wisdom and there will be little difficulty for them once they retire.

Health

In matters of health, Sagittarians born on the 4th, 13th, 22nd and 31st can be divided into two categories. The first category will consist of people who will not be very strong however, will lead a relatively healthy life, free of disease and illness. Yet, they will be prone to accidents and injuries. On the other hand, there will be another category of people, who will be somewhat frailer and will be prone to colds, fever, stomach ailments and respiratory infections.

Born on the 5th, 14th and 23rd

For Sagittarians born on the dates given above will be influenced by the planets Jupiter and Mercury. As a matter of fact, the influence of Mercury will be vital in their life and will gift them with a keen intelligence and a strong, underlying restlessness.

They will have a strong desire to always be on the move and hence, will keep themselves occupied, either mentally or physically. They will have a constant flow of ideas and thoughts that will run through their head and they will also try and find things to do. Idleness will never be in their dictionary. Even when not doing anything, they will be thinking up new things and it will be this desire to keep occupied, that will make them quite successful professionally.

Sports and adventure will be a good expression for their restlessness. They will also have a slightly reckless attitude and will not care much for danger or risks. They will enjoy moving fast and therefore, cars, planes and anything that will have speed will fascinate them.

They will be independent and confident about themselves. Their sunny optimism and good natured humour will win them many friends. They will also be spontaneous and will express themselves beautifully. However, they will also form strong preferences and will not be able to justify these preferences.

Despite the fact that they will be restless, they will also have a strong sense of determination. Once they decide to do something, they will be quite successful. When they find their true calling, they will be capable and will make a niche for themselves in fields such as literature, arts, management and even teaching.

The combination of Mercury with Jupiter will endow them with good reasoning and logic. They will be quite proficient when arguing and will be able to hold their own in any debate or argument. However, they will be fair and will not hold any grudges against anyone.

They will also have a penchant for love and romance. The opposite sex will often, be drawn towards them and there are possibilities that they will have many affairs. It will be favourable for they to settle down a little late in life, since they will have had enough time to mature and decide on what they want from their partner.

In a nutshell, they will have a restless yet determined personality; one that will be able to accomplish anything as long as it knows what it wants from life. It will be this focus and passion that will make them a success in all their endeavours.

Finance

They will have the good fortune of being able to make money by virtue of their talents and skills. Not only that, they will make profits by investing their money wisely. Their intuition and intelligence will go a long way in helping them to build their wealth. However, it is important that they value money and do not waste or squander it away.

Health

Number five Sagittarians will be blessed with good health and will not be prone to many illnesses and diseases. However, they will need to take care of their diet and sleep in order to retain the strong disposition that they have been endowed with. Irregular routines will harm their digestive system and putting too much pressure on their system will affect the nerves. Therefore, it is important that they calm their inherent restlessness and lead a slightly relaxed life.

Born on 6th, 15th and 24th

It will be the influence of Venus and Jupiter that will be critical for Sagittarians born on the above-mentioned dates. This combination will be significant since it will enhance the usually buoyant Sagittarian personality even more and give it a 'softness' that will be unique and endearing.

They will have a positive, radiant and warm temperament that will be appealing and winsome. They will be able to make friends wherever they go. They will spread their good hearted cheer and happiness with generosity and genuineness. There will be nothing fake or insincere about their attitude. People will be touched by their benevolence and there will be hardly anyone who will hold a grudge against them.

They will be a gracious host and will enjoy socialising. They will be openhearted and will enjoy spending time with Nature. They will also have a special love for animals and will often have a pet or two. Although they will have a wide and varied circle of friends, they will also enjoy spending time on their own. This will give them the chance to reflect and introspect. It will be their love for nature that will motivate them to travel and see the world. If they have the time and the money, they will surely spend a lot of it on exploring unusual destinations.

Balance and tranquillity will appeal to them and they will not enjoy disarray. They will enjoy moving through life with a smile. Difficulties and troubles will all be treated lightly by them and they will be able to overcome these by the sheer strength of their optimism and attitude. They will even try to pass this on to those who are depressed and pessimistic about life.

They will often, be drawn towards members of the opposite sex and will have them as friends, if not as lovers. They will be high on integrity and will be a loving and dependable friend. Their company will be enjoyable and their conversation interesting.

Although they will be loving and generous, chances are that they might be perceived as snooty and therefore, they might be friends with people who belong to a social class that is higher than their own. Nevertheless, their personality will be such that no one will be able to get really angry with them or hate them.

Original and imaginative, they will be able to generate creative ideas and will be able to use them in a most productive and profitable manner. As a matter of fact, they should trust their instinct and use their talents to help they build their wealth. Their inherent intelligence will draw them towards people who also are intelligent and creative. They will be quite comfortable interacting with writers, actors, musicians and such. They have a personality that will enable them to climb the social ladder and carve a niche for themselves.

Finance

They will be lucky in financial matters and will often, come into money through marriage, inheritances and other unexpected sources. However, they should also make use of their talents and abilities in order to keep up a steady source of income. They should do not share their money with everybody and always maintain a balance between spending and earning.

Health

Health, too, will be good for them and they will have a constitution that will be able to withstand a lot of wear and tear. However, they will need to look after it by leading a lifestyle that is healthy and balanced. Too much of anything will be harmful, therefore, they should always keep a moderate approach.

Born on 7th, 16th and 25th

For Number seven Sagittarians, Jupiter, Neptune and the Moon will come together and influence their personality in a distinctive and interesting manner. They will blend together to make the inherently energetic Sagittarius intriguing and different from most other archers.

The combined influence of all three planets will make them stronger and more aggressive. Ambition will also be more significant in their personality and will motivate them to achieve great things. They will also be more focused on what they want from life and will spend a lot of time and effort in accomplishing their goals and realising their dreams.

The presence of Neptune will have an influence on their mind. As a result, they will be more perceptive and intuitive than others. When combined with the influence of the Moon, their creative senses will be heightened and they will be able to realise their potential as a writer, poet, dramatist and the like. However, unlike most people, the presence of Jupiter will bring about the ambition that is needed to realise the potential and transform it into a reality.

Ironically, this will be a conflicting aspect of their personality. Like a typical Sagittarian, they will be fond of dreaming big dreams, yet they will also have the necessary drive to act and realise those dreams. They will be ambitious to the extent that they will want to rise up at all costs. They will love to win and prosper and they will do that, regardless of the circumstances that they are born in.

It is also a possibility that they might belong to a category of people who will have a philosophical bent of mind and will be more generous than ever with their money, talent and resources. Regardless of the category that they belong to, they will be famous and successful in everything they do. Their persistence and patience will pay off and bring them prosperity and fame, just as they will desire.

It is important that they learn to be balanced and not become ruthless in their desire to be successful. While ambition will take you places, it will be emotion that will sharpen their creativity and make them a more sensitive person. Therefore, it is important to have both in order to be a complete individual.

Finance

For Number seven Sagittarians, finance will be an unusual matter. They will be able to make a lot of money; however, they must be careful of unscrupulous people and schemes, otherwise they will lose the wealth that they have accumulated. A large chunk of their earnings will come from unexpected and unusual sources.

Health

Typically, Sagittarians born on the above-mentioned dates will not have the best digestive systems. They will be prone to acidity, indigestion, and similar ailments. As long as they take good care of their eating and sleeping habits, they will be able to keep most illnesses at a distance.

Born on the 8th, 17th and 26th

For Sagittarians born on the 8th, 17th and 26th, the influence of the planets Jupiter and Saturn will be significant in shaping their personality and giving it a unique character, distinct from other archers born on different dates.

The presence of Saturn will make them a strong-minded and resolute individual. Even if they have to struggle at the beginning, they will do so and overcome odds in order to reach their goal. It will be their strength of character and willpower that will give them the ability to succeed, regardless of the hurdles in the way. They will not be disheartened by temporary setbacks and will be able to look at them in a positive way. Therefore, they will continue working and in next to no time, they will reach their goals.

They have good perceptive skills and will be quite proficient at reasoning. They also have a strong sense of duty and will be devoted to their work. There is the danger, however, that they might be perceived as too laidback and unsure. Therefore, they should try and develop more faith in themselves and show others that they believe in their abilities. That will enable them to make a favourable impression on business associates and the like.

Unlike most Sagittarians, they will be somewhat reserved, quiet and sensitive to the opinions of others. They will often, feel hurt if spoken to rudely or ignored. However, they will not hesitate in voicing their opinions in the face of prejudice and biased treatments. They will not be afraid of criticism and reprimand. In this aspect, they will be a strong and independent person.

They will also have a tendency to be bitter towards those they don't like. And, it will be this quality that they will often use when arguing or in a conflict. Other than that, their character will be like most Sagittarians in general and they will reflect that in most aspects.

Considering the fact that they will be a diligent and devoted worker, they will be able to rise high and will often, win the admiration and appreciation of seniors, subordinates and peers.

However, they should be careful to continue the good work and also be approachable and warm towards others. They could have a lot of people who influence them significantly in the course of their career.

They will be quite charming to those you consider friends and will also be loyal and trustworthy. However, in matters of all relationships, they will take their time and be quite wary of who they will confide in. Even in matters of love and romance, they will need a partner who will be able to win and retain their love, trust and respect.

Finance

For Sagittarians born on the 8th, 17th or 26th, building up wealth will be more a matter of time than luck. They will persist and endure upheavals and change as they move from one stage to another. They will be generous and therefore, will often willingly support needy friends and relatives. Also, their intelligence and instincts will hold them back from indulging in reckless speculation and gambling. They will be judicious when spending and will invest their money with wisdom. All these habits will ensure that they earn profits and eventually, are able to reach the stage of financial security and contentment.

Health

They will be fortunate when it comes to their health and well being. They will have a robust constitution which will be able to withstand quite a bit of wear and tear. They should however, be careful when travelling and also ensure that they get regular check-ups done, since they will be the sort who might look healthy but will have some hidden ailment.

They will also have the ability to recover quickly from any illness and this will primarily be due to their innate strength and will-power. They will also lead a regulated life, in terms of health and hygiene and will never be reckless about such matters.

Born on the 9th, 18th and 27th

Sagittarians born on the dates given above will be highly affected by the vibes of the planets Jupiter, Saturn and Mars. These planets will come together and in their own unique way influence Number nine Sagittarians. While the inherent personality will remain the same, there will be certain changes that will be brought about due to the presence of these three planets. These individuals will be highly motivated, focused and responsible and this will enable them to reach great heights.

They have a strong belief in themselves and their abilities. Nothing will be too difficult or impossible for them. Even failures and setbacks will be treated with a sense of optimism, as if they are a promise for better times to come. Their efficiency and capability will shine through during tough times and they will be the person people will rely on during a crisis.

Their courage, endurance and determination will be inspirational and will often, serve as motivation for those working with them. They will be charged up to take risks and lead the life that you visualise for themselves. Their strength will not just be mental but also physical and they will greatly enjoy roughing it out and being as adventurous as possible. If born in a wealthy family, they will often, spend a great deal of time travelling and enjoying adventure sports.

Benevolence and compassion will run deep in them and even though, they may not be aware of it, they will have a sensitive and humane aspect to their personality which will emerge when faced with a touching situation. They will willingly give their money to charity and in case, they do not have enough of that, they will give your time and energy to them. They will, however, also be quite bossy and authoritative and will often want others to follow their way. Qualities such as these will make them a good leader and this will be more so, because they will compensate for their authoritativeness by their good heartedness and their love for humanity.

There will be a profound intelligence in everything that they do and while they may not conform to the traditional views of intelligence, they will show their wisdom in their actions and in the success story of their life. Their talents could be mechanical, literary, creative or aesthetic. They will explore and discover their strengths in a reflective manner and once aware about them, will use them to prosper and progress.

As far as affairs of the heart are concerned, they will be able to attract and draw members of the opposite sex by their intellect, wit and goodness. They will have a cheerful temperament and this will only make them more popular. Also, considering the fact that they will be ambitious and energetic, they will achieve a great deal in life and hence, add to their attractiveness and esteem. Their confidence and independence will give an extra appeal to their personality. There are strong indications that they will be lucky in love and even if they marry someone they do not really love, they will lead a life that will be content and peaceful. Their domestic life will have some ups and downs but there will hardly be anything that they will not have the strength to deal with.

Integrity and righteousness will also be high on their priority list. However, this will largely be influenced by their background. They will always try to do the right thing, as they know it, and will try and keep the larger interest in mind. Whether in business or in a job, they will rise high due to their conscientiousness and their desire to succeed.

Finance

Fortune will smile on them in financial matters and they will be able to earn and make a lot of money. Their hard work and perseverance will pay off as they reap the profits. They will also come into money through unusual and unexpected sources, such as legacies, marriage and gifts. They will be generous and will support charities and people in need. However, they will also invest their money and multiply it.

They will do well in fields where both their mind and body are used rather than in a business where their contribution is minimal. However, there are also possibilities that if they find the right area, you will do well in business as well. The key is in their hard work and this will surely bring rewards.

Health

Although they have a relatively strong constitution, they will be somewhat neglectful of their health and will often, suffer from hypertension, blood pressure, injuries and infections. They will always be on the move and hence, will hardly ever look after themselves. This will surely have an impact on their overall well-being and therefore, it is important for them to take care of themselves.

It will be after their eighteenth birthday that their disposition will gain in strength and endurance. At the same time, it should be kept in mind that they must follow a regimen of diet and exercise to keep their body and their mind in good shape.

CAPRICORN

(21ST DECEMBER TO 20TH JANUARY)

Capricorn in General

Capricorn, symbolised by the ram, is a sign that is endowed with considerable determination and willpower. The sign of Capricorn commences on the 21st of December and continues till the 21st of January. It is ruled by the planet Saturn and is the Third House of the Earth Triplicity.

In order for us to understand the characteristics that distinguish Capricorns from other signs, we will have to apply our minds and learn that the first thing about these individuals is their capability to attain anything they set their eyes on. Life for Capricorns is a journey of improvement and advancement. They will never be able to rest till they have bettered themselves and then, they will move on, yet again. Driven by goals and aspirations, they will be high on motivation and ambition. They will set high goals and given their capability, they will achieve them, too.

Ruled by the planet Saturn, they will be gifted with a flair for diplomacy and carefulness. They will be able to keep their plans and schemes to themselves and will not be the kind to glorify themselves. Their achievements will speak for themselves and they will end up enjoying the limelight eventually. One thing that is distinctive about them is that they will never rush into anything. Every step of theirs, even if it seems spontaneous, will be well thought out and planned to the last detail. That is probably also the reason behind their eventual success and prosperity.

Though somewhat of a contradiction, Capricorns will often be liberal and sincere, yet they will also be wary of others and will not be quick to form judgements or opinions. They will have a strong, stable, mind that will have both philosophy and science as its key traits. They will rely on both reason and intuition to plan and form their strategies. They will have sharp perceptive skills and will be able to sense vibes and attitudes of people around them.

They will be intelligent and wise, in their own special way. They will respect intelligence in others and will be willing to listen to reason and fact, simply because it will be one way of improving their own knowledge and acquiring additional information. They will also be able to make their point with tact, yet firmness. Although they have immense determination, they will also tend to get discouraged easily. However, once they see reason, they will be able to get back on their feet and start afresh.

Self-reliant and original, they will often, start a trend and will be able to come up with ideas and plans that will be creative, innovative and profitable. They will also have a firm belief in their own abilities and potential and nothing that anyone will say will be able to change their opinion about themselves. They will be their best judge and will not be complacent. On the contrary, they will always be looking around for ways to improve themselves and their personalities.

They will not believe in rash action and regret. That is the reason you will often, find that they do not react to harsh words and talk easily. They will simply wait for their chance and then prove their point effortlessly and graciously. Obstacles, oppositions and hurdles will not deter them and they will always be focused on what they want from life and how will they achieve it.

They will also be born leaders and even if they do not take a position of authority initially, they will work towards it and will eventually reach it. Unnecessary rules and regulations will not go down well with them. They are free spirited and will be willing to stand up for what they firmly believe in. Mature and sensible, they will always have an original way of looking at things. Even at their most low moments, they will be able to derive strength and will never go down without a fight.

Diligent and dedicated to their goals and dreams, they will even be on the verge of becoming workaholics. Their rise up the social and economic ladder will be more due to their own efforts than anything else. Irrespective of the background in which they were born, they will be able to accomplish all they want by their hard work and wisdom. They will, however, have a tendency to view life with a great deal of seriousness and therefore, it is essential that they surround themselves with happy people and positive situations since the latter will lift their spirits and enable them to view life in a lighter vein.

There are also indications that people may often, misinterpret their intentions and views. Hence, it will be better if they are straightforward, as far as possible. Tact will be good, but only in certain situations. They will have a select circle of friends who will be able to see who they really are who are also on the same wavelength as them. Though they may not consciously realise it, they will have a fondness for being in the limelight and will eventually get to be in it.

Professionally, they will do well in most fields where they are given a position of authority and responsibility. They will be able to handle emergencies and manage people and situations with effectiveness and ease. Capricorns pretty much keep to themselves. In other words, they will not interfere in the lives of others and will not appreciate undue interference in their own lives. Even giving advice to others is something they will not do unless asked to. However, one can trust them to give solid, sound advice and they will want you to follow their counsel.

They have unique and original views on subjects of love, religion, society and money. As a result, they will often, be viewed as eccentric or quirky by their peers and acquaintances. However, in true Saturn style, they will often, not be bothered by what others think of them and they will continue to endorse views and opinions which they feel are right by them.

They will certainly not be showy and ostentatious; however, they will be able to create an impression of steadfastness and persistence. They will meet life head on and will be willing to handle challenges with their steady, deliberate hand. To be in the company of a Capricorn will enrich your life as much as it will enrich his own. Their efficiency, quiet strength and sound wisdom will be a guiding light for many.

Finance

They will have to work hard in order to build up their financial situation. However, their efforts will pay off and they will be able to accumulate a great deal of wealth and enjoy a life that is comfortable and even luxurious. They will also be judicious when spending and will be able to invest their money with caution and care.

Investing in land, real estate, factories, transport and agriculture will turn out positively for them. They should also avoid lending money and should ensure that they invest in firms and establishments that are stable and secure. Speculation and risk-taking will not be something that they will take to easily. Therefore, they should stick to the more traditional forms of investments and professions since they will be bound to yield profits from them.

Health

The Capricorn is influenced by the planet Saturn and this will have an impact on his health. They will be blessed with a sound, robust constitution and will have enough energy to tackle all that they want to. However, they will also be prone to mood swings and it will be in their best interest to surround themselves with cheerful and positive people, relationships and environment as far as possible. That will enable them to be stronger mentally and hence, combat most stress related disorders, such as, digestive ailments, hypertension, ulcers and the like.

They will also be affected by cold weather and humidity which will have an effect on their joints. On the whole, living in a dry climate will suit them better. Also, they should keep a close watch on their diet and exercise. They get bored by monotony. Therefore, they should alter their routines every now and then to keep the interest alive. A positive attitude, a light-hearted approach and a regular exercise plan will keep them in the best of health. They should try and stay as cheerful as possible. Being too serious will never suit them, from a health point of view.

They should also guard against injuries, accidents and rheumatism. They should stay in moderate climates and not over-indulge in food, drink or sleep.

CAPRICORN

Born on 1st, 10th, 19th and 28th

The planetary combination of Uranus, Saturn and the Sun will be vital in shaping the personalities of all of those who are born on the dates given above. This will be a strong and potent alliance that will bring about certain changes in their personality and make them carve their own identity, distinct from all other Capricorns born on other dates.

They will have a considerate and sombre personality. They will want to ensure that everything they do is complete and methodical in all respects. Doing things half-heartedly is not their style. They will devote their attention and efforts to the task at hand, no matter how small or big it may be. If they decide on something, they will ensure that they see it through and will not let minor or major hurdles stand in their way.

They are confident and well-grounded. Pride and egotism will not be something that they display. They will think about things and will not be affected by what others say. Their own opinion will matter to them and they will indulge in introspection and reflection to constantly better themselves, as a person, friend and professional.

Everything they do will be motivated and driven by a larger goal. Right from an early age, they will know exactly what they want and will be ready to take on any challenge to achieve the same. That will also be the reason why they will not be disappointed by failures and setbacks. They will always be ready to deal with them and move on, rather than let them hold them down. It will be this ambition and fire that will motivate them to work hard and rise above all those around them. However, they will not be condescending; rather they will be quite unassuming and modest about their achievements. This should not imply that they will not enjoy being recognised and appreciated; it is just that that will not make a big deal out of it.

Benevolent and compassionate, they will have a soft corner for those in distress and trouble. However, they will not be willing to be taken for granted. They will be generous with their time, money and efforts for a genuine cause and will be glad to be of assistance to others. However, they will also be sensible and realistic and will not squander away all their wealth for noble causes alone.

Their greatest strengths will be their endurance and persistence. They will be able to achieve all that they want simply by virtue of these two. They should try and look at life from a lighter point of view as well, since that will help them to remain more positive and cheerful. Professionally, they will have quite a charismatic and influential personality. While they may not be flamboyant, they will have a quiet grace that will motivate and inspire all those around them. Given the fact that they are hard-working and committed, they will do well in nearly all professional fields, especially, in roles where they will have some amount of responsibility, authority and trust invested in them.

Finance

They will adopt a careful and simple approach when dealing with money. They will nearly always believe in saving first and spending later. Moreover, they will feel safer when investing their hard-earned money in companies that are stable and solid. Speculation and risky ventures will seem fatal to them and hence, they will not be comfortable putting their money into things like stocks and shares. Their intelligence and astuteness will enable them to take advantage of all the opportunities that come their way and hence, they will be able to profit from them. As long as they continue to maintain a sensible attitude towards spending and saving, wealth accumulation will not be a problem for them.

Health

As a Capricorn born on the dates given above, they will be bestowed with a good amount of energy and strength, which will be vital in helping them to accomplish all that they want. It is essential that they continue to build on their inherent strength and not ruin it by an over-indulgent temperament. Moderation in all aspects will suit them and will also help in keeping illnesses and infections at bay. They will, however, need to guard themselves against aches and pains of the joints, rheumatism and the like.

Born on the 2nd, 11th, 20th and 29th

Capricorns born on any of the dates given above will be influenced by the radiations of the planet Neptune in conjunction with the Moon. This planetary alliance will be responsible for giving their personality a certain tenderness and a keen perceptiveness that will make it stand apart from the personality of fellow-Capricorns born on different dates.

Original in thought and artistic in actions, they will have a temperament that will nearly always respond to the environment. Hence, if they are in the midst of sadness and despair, they will become unhappy and pessimistic themselves. For someone of their nature, it is important that they learn early on that life is made up of both ups and downs, and hence, they should not get dejected by set-backs and failures, since they will only be temporary in nature.

Also, they will have a personality that will be affected to a certain extent by what people say and think of them. Harsh and critical words will hurt them and they will retreat into their shell to brood about things. This approach will only aggravate the pain and not alleviate it. It is essential for their well-being that they learn to face the reality of life and not run away from it.

All this should not imply that they will be weak and fragile. They will have the inherent strength of Capricorn and will be able to accomplish their goals. It is just that they will be more susceptible to words and feelings than most other Capricorns. They will have a fertile imagination and will be able to come up with unusual and productive ideas that will yield good results. Once they strengthen their belief in their own potential and talent, they will be able to achieve nearly everything that their heart desires with ease and capability.

They are gracious in their mannerisms and will take their time in making friends and forming relationships. They will not be the kind to rush into things and will often, wait and watch to see how things turn out before arriving at any conclusion about them. Even with people, they will not make hasty judgements and will often observe them before forming an opinion. They will have high aspirations and will get fidgety and impatient if they feel that they are being held back from achieving them.

Since they place quite a premium on the opinions of others, encouragement and praise will mean a great deal to them. They will not consciously wish for the limelight, however, they will want to be acknowledged and appreciated. Neglect and rejection could hurt their feelings and their pride. They will have a tendency to think too much and to place a great deal of pressure on their mind. Nearly every little thing will be processed, analysed and evaluated by them. Also, they will be influenced by the vibes that others will give to them and all this could lead to undue pressure and strain on their mental make-up.

They are gifted in ways unlike others and it is important that they learn to value themselves and respect all that they have. What others say should not matter to them; rather, they should have confidence in themselves and be happy about it. Only then will they be able to make the most of their latent potential and achieve all that their heart desires.

Finance

For them, money and wealth will not be of much importance. They will be more of a necessity than anything else. They are intelligent and hard-working and as a result, will always be able to earn a good income and lead a good life. However, they will not place too much value on money. That is probably the reason why they will often indulge in generosity and give away money for causes that they believe are worthy and noble. However, while this is a good gesture, it is important that they also learn that money will come in handy during their retirement years and therefore, they should save some of it.

Health

Although they will have good health and energy levels, they will have the tendency to pressurise their nervous system by thinking too much. Therefore, they should learn to relax and not push themselves so hard. If they take regular breaks from the tension and anxiety of life, they will be able to handle almost anything and will feel much better. They will be prone to aches and pains as well as some amount of trouble in the eyes.

Born on the 3rd, 12th, 21st and 30th

It will be the predominant influence of Jupiter that will play a vital role in their life who were born on any of the dates given above. This powerful planet will endow their already strong personality with more endurance, persistence and aggressiveness.

Everything they do will be filled with fiery ambition and an unwavering motivation to excel and succeed. They will have a strong desire to rise above their current standing in society. And, for that they will be willing to devote themselves tirelessly to their goals and dreams. They will work hard and will not rest till they reach your destination. All they want is to succeed, prosper and grow. Considering the fact that they are intelligent and conscientious, they will not have too much of a problem in accomplishing their aims and ambitions.

They are candid and straightforward in their views and opinions. As a result, they will often meet with opposition and envy. However, they will not let such things deter them and will continue to move towards their goals. They will be naturally comfortable handling positions of responsibility and trust and will do their best to execute the trust that is put in them.

So strong is their self-esteem and confidence that they will firmly stand by what they believe in and will not be affected by the thoughts and ideas of others. It is not that they will be intolerant of others; however, they will not change simply because someone else wants them to. They will listen to reason and logic and will alter their views only if they see the sense in doing so.

As far as relationships are concerned, they will need to curb their forceful temperament and see things from a different perspective. Only then will they be able to compromise and make things move forward. Adjustments and changes will have to be made to enjoy a relationship that is mature, intelligent and emotionally satisfying. In marriage, they will need a partner who will be able to respect their intelligence and capability, as well as be a support system for them.

They will have the ability to dream big and to execute those dreams with efficiency and ease. Their plans will always be well thought out and detailed to the last bit. They will not make rash decisions and act in an impulsive, thoughtless manner. As far as possible, they should try and remain self-reliant, instead of relying on the support and assistance of others. That will enable them to handle things in a much better and effective manner.

Another interesting facet of their personality will be that they will not be self-centred, even though it may seem so. They will have a strong desire to be of help and support to others, especially the underprivileged and the needy. They will often give their time and resources for the benefit of others. Reforming and improving the conditions of others will be something that will be close to their heart and depending upon their circumstances, they will try to do as much as they can.

They have a tendency to be really hard on themselves and will push themselves to the limit in order to realise their dreams and goals. They will believe in resting only after they've accomplished all that they had set out to do. While this will be a good approach, it is also important that they learn the importance of rest and relaxation, so that their body and mind stay in optimum condition at all times.

Life for they will be a constant journey to achieve, accomplish and attain. They will be able to go to great heights if they develop and hone the talents they have and make the most of their ambition and intelligence.

Finance

It will be their aim to earn a lot of money and lead a life that is comfortable, if not luxurious. It is important that they stick to safe methods of multiplying their money, rather than speculating and risk-taking. Also, they should try to maintain a balance between earning, spending and donating. Only then will they be in a position to save and accumulate enough for a rainy day.

Health

They are gifted with a strong and healthy body that will be able to endure the tensions and worries of life. However, it is important that they give it a break once in a while, so as to recharge it. Otherwise, they will be affecting it negatively. Even their heart and limbs will need frequent attention and care.

Born on the 4th, 13th, 22nd and 31st

Capricorns born on the dates given above will be influenced by the planetary combination of Saturn, Uranus and the Sun. This particular alliance is unique and the influence of Uranus will be dominant in shaping their personality and bringing out the distinctiveness of certain traits more than the others.

Highly individualistic and independent, they will be their own person in all respects. They will have offbeat and unconventional views on nearly everything and will not conform to tradition simply because they have to. They will rely on reason and logic and will go by what they will feel is right. They will have a sharp, keen mind and will want to use it in order to rise and prosper.

There are chances that because of their rebellious temperament, they may have to work harder to maintain relationships and will also have to learn how to make adjustments and compromises with people who are important and integral to their well-being. Diligent and motivated, they will have to make their own path to success and avoid being dependent on others for help and support. However, since they have an independent spirit, this will not be a problem.

Although, they will enjoy light-hearted moments of fun and frolic, yet deep within, they will be a serious and mature individual who will tend to think about things deeply and analytically. All their actions will be motivated by a desire to control and dominate either themselves or others around them. They will not be bitter or cynical, yet they will have their own unique way of looking at things and they may even be termed as a staunch realist.

They will be able to use words to influence and inspire people. They will often, be a good leader and will be able to command the respect and admiration of their followers and even their superiors. They will do well in positions of authority and will want others to give their hundred per cent to the task at hand.

All that they do will have their uniqueness stamped all over it. Being distinct will suit their personality and they will always try to stand out in the crowd. Being a trailblazer than a follower is something that they will endeavour to do. Their desire for novelty will motivate them to travel and experience life in different lands and societies. This will also help to broaden their view on life and relationships.

They will see life as a drama that has different scenes which must be played out by them. Nevertheless, they will not take it all that seriously and will try to blend wry humour with irony and sobriety. It is not surprising that they will enjoy the journey of life and will gain great advantages from it.

Finance

Since their life will be a series of strange and surprising occurrences, financial affairs will be no different. They will come into money through unexpected sources. However, they will need to learn how to manage their finances. Balancing income and expenditure will have to be learnt and they must, under all circumstances, save a sufficient amount for their old age. Professionally, it will not be difficult for them to earn and lead a comfortable life, since they will be a sharp and eager individual.

Health

They will be one of those fortunate people who will have immense amounts of energy and strength. They will just need to realise that and make full use of it. They will be filled with creative ideas and will be able to work endlessly in order to make those ideas materialise. However, they will at times, suffer from vague and mysterious ailments and accidents that could harm their lower limbs, knees and feet.

Born on the 5th, 14th and 23rd

Number five Capricorns are influenced by the vibrations of the planets Saturn and Mercury. This combination of planets will bring about quite a few changes in their personality and give they certain advantages over the other Capricorns born on different dates.

They will be quite adaptable and will be able to fit in with any section of people or activities. Such a multi-talented temperament will be a gift, if they are able to figure out what it is that they want from life and what their real goals are. Once they have that in place, everything else will be easy. They will be able to adjust to any kind of situation and people. As a result, their circle of friends will be diverse. They will also have the ability to mould themselves to any situation; hence, they will do well in difficult times as well as in days.

Restless at heart, they will often want to travel and explore the unknown lands. If they have the resources of time and money, they will fulfil their deep desire to see the world and learn about people and different societies. Learning will also be one of their passions and though they may or may not conform to the traditional form of learning, they will always try to absorb new information and use it in an appropriate form and fashion. They will at times, put too much pressure on their mind and try to do too many things at one time. Remember, it is always better to do one thing properly and then take another task in hand.

Luck and fortune will also play a strong role in their life, though their belief in their own abilities will be stronger. There will be some good chances that could come their way and they will be able to take advantage of them and profit from them. They will have an astute and gifted mind that will be able to analyse and evaluate things with accuracy. Although they have a wide circle of acquaintances, they will trust individuals only after they have proven themselves in their eyes. Otherwise, they will be quite wary of them. They will be moved by thoughtfulness and compassion.

Discreet and subtle, they will keep their plans and actions to themselves and at the same time, be able to be a confidante for others. People around them will find it easy to tell them their troubles and secrets, since they will be a responsible and wise friend and a guide. When asked for advice, they will always give sensible and sound counsel in a frank and candid manner. They do not believe in sugar-coating words, however, they are not blunt or crude. They will have a fondness for reading. Literature, science, philosophy, and mechanical things will often, engross them and capture their attention.

There are chances that they may be perceived as being too mature for their age. Therefore, they should try and cultivate a sense of humour and cheerfulness that will lighten their heart and lift their spirits whenever they are feeling low or depressed. Positive people and surroundings will give them a boost whenever their morale is low and things are not going the way they should be. Therefore, whatever they do, they should try and make friends who are optimists and have a good sense of humour.

Finance

They will be quite sensible and shrewd when spending their money. Lending and borrowing is something that they will not favour and hence, they will not incur debt of any kind. Even if circumstances compel them to take a loan, it will be their top priority to repay it at the earliest. As far as investments are concerned, they should be too careful. Therefore, they should take the counsel of trusted sources and if investing in a speculative market, be prepared to take risks. Their maturity and flexibility will make them successful professionally and hence, they will be able to accumulate enough money for themselves and their family.

Health

They will have a lean constitution but will be able to ward off any ailments with their strong immunity. However, they should always try to give their mind and body a break from the hectic activities of everyday life. That will give them a chance to recharge themselves and be better equipped to face the world and its hurdles.

Mood swings will be something that they will be susceptible to and therefore, they should try and spend as much time as possible in positive surroundings. Also, they will be somewhat prone to acidity, digestive problems and joint pains.

Born on the 6th, 15th and 24th

Capricorns born on the dates given above, they will be influenced by the planetary alliance of Venus and Saturn. The influence of the planet Venus will be responsible for endowing their personality with a softness and romantic outlook that will affect their life in a variety of ways.

Their life will be deeply influenced by the affairs of the heart, emotions and sentiments. They will be compassionate and empathetic to those around them and it will be their constant endeavour to use these positive traits to build their own self-esteem and confidence. They have a strong personality; however, it will have the tendency to be influenced by their emotions and feelings.

They will have an exciting but hectic professional and personal life that will bring out various facets of their personality. As a matter of fact, they will grow and evolve with the passage of time and become a better and stronger person in the process. They have a charismatic personality and will be able to influence and inspire others to deliver their best.

Also, they have a creative temperament and will do well in artistic lines, such as painting, music, literature and the like. Even if they do not take them up professionally, they will have an inherent flair for them and will be able to use them in their home and surroundings.

Since they are strongly influenced by their family and relationships, there are chances that they may sacrifice some of their dreams and aspirations for their sake. However, later in life, they may be able to achieve them and be able to reach the goals that they set for themselves. There may be hurdles in their path to prosperity; however, they will be able to overcome most of them. Also, they are not the kind to lose heart easily.

Even though the initial years may not be easy for them, they will be able to conquer and prevail, irrespective of everything. This will strengthen their character and give them more belief in themselves and their potential. They will also have a strong desire to improve themselves and will constantly be on the path to achieve fame and fortune. It will be their willpower and their determination to excel that will lead to success, while their gentleness and graciousness will increase their popularity.

Finance

In matters of finance, they will have the tendency to go overboard with saving and will often, not maintain a balance between spending and saving. Therefore, it is important that they strike a balance and while they save, they should also spend their hard-earned money to lead a comfortable and relaxed life.

Health

Capricorns born on the 6th, 15th and 24th will have a reasonable amount of strength and stamina. They will be able to lead a healthy life and if they keep an eye on their diet and exercise, they will enjoy good health for a long time. However, they need to stay on guard against fire and accidents.

Born on 7th, 16th and 25th

Capricorns born on the dates given above will be influenced by the planetary combination of Neptune, Saturn and the Moon. This particular combination will be responsible for endowing them with characteristics that will make them somewhat more spiritually inclined and highly perceptive. We will look at more distinguishing features of their personality in the next few pages.

While they will be philosophical and even spiritual, they will also be motivated and driven to excel in whatever they take up. This attitude will stand them in good stead in many professional and personal situations. Their approach towards religion and devotion will be original and unique. However, they will definitely have an inclination towards such beliefs and ideas.

They are highly imaginative and will have creative and innovative ideas. Also, they will be idealistic and will have their own firm principles and ideologies. Their approach towards life will be an interesting blend of modernism and traditionalism. They will be able to maintain a balance between these two dimensions with ease and efficiency.

While they will have a special fondness for their own company and being by themselves, they will also have friends who are on the same wavelength as them and who will enrich their life in various ways. They will also enjoy travelling and will also like to experience changes as much as possible, in occupation or residence. They will try and bring about as much newness as and when they can. They like meeting people from different cultures and learning more about them. There are also indications that they may even settle in a place that is away from their native place.

Dependable and responsible, they will have a personality that will attract positions of authority and trust. The best part is that they will do well in such positions and will be able to carry out their duties in a capable and mature fashion. As a matter of fact, most of their behaviour will be mature and sensible. Behaving in a reckless and irresponsible manner is not their cup of tea. That is the reason why from an early age, they will be able to handle the ups and downs of life with a positive and optimistic outlook.

There are many things that will occupy their mind and at any given time, they will always be thinking of what could be done next. As a result, they will often, come up with ideas that are creative and useful. However, this might put some amount of stress on their system and also they might push their body to its limit. Travelling and going on breaks is something that will be therapeutic as well as relaxing for them.

Their personality will have the inherent Capricorn traits; however, they will be softened by the spiritual inclination and the gentleness of their mannerisms. Beneath their matter-of-fact attitude, will be an idealism that will be dreamy with thoughts that will be romantic and colored by sunny optimism.

Finance

They are diligent and conscientious and therefore, earning money will not be a problem. They will also not have materialistic perspectives. Therefore, they will be able to save a reasonable amount for their future. They have the strength to withstand times with little money and will not be disheartened by temporary losses and set-backs.

Health

Although they have enough stamina and energy to tackle with their many duties and responsibilities, they will have a certain frailty in their appearance. They may suffer from certain illnesses that will be difficult to pinpoint. Yet, it will not be a problem and they will be able to take care of their health without much problem. Their respiratory system will be somewhat prone to infections and ailments.

Born on the 8th, 17th and 26th

Capricorns born on any of the dates given above will be influenced by the planet Saturn. This single planet will actually, be a 'double Saturn' and this will have a strong and powerful impact on their personality. Not only that, they will have a lot of responsibility to take care of from an early age.

There are people who triumph against all odds and use difficult times to show the strength of their character. They will be one such person. Hard times will bring out the best in them and they will not be disillusioned by failures and obstacles. Rather, they will use them as learning tools and will move forward with more grit and determination. Independent and confident, they will have a firm belief in their own abilities and talents. As a result, they will not seek help from other sources, but will always first try and get things done on their own.

Everything that they do reflects the great amount of tolerance and steadfastness that they possess. There could be chances that they may not have realised it till now, however, there will come an occasion when they will find themselves exhibiting these traits beautifully. Every experience in their life will lead to revelations about their own personality and as a result, they will be able to face life with courage and resilience.

Their desire to achieve will be great. Once they set their mind to something, nothing will be able to take it away from them. They will pursue their goals with dogged determination and will not rest till they have achieved what they set out to do. There could be problems along the way, however, even if they hit a low point, they will always be able to bounce back and take things ahead.

Since they are one of those people who may have to handle a great deal of trials and tribulations, there could be instances in their life when they feel sad and miserable. However, they will be able to handle these periods of sadness. They should try not to feel depressed too often, since that could have negative impact on their health and well-being. Forever on the move, their thoughts will move faster than their body. They will enjoy action and hence, will always be thinking of something or the other to do or get. At the same time, they will not be a rash, irresponsible soul. Rather, they will be known for their mature and sobre approach towards life, society, relationships and the like.

Their ability to reason and rationalise will be very good and they will often, be able to make the other side see their point of view in a calm and logical fashion. They will also have the graciousness to accept a perspective different from their own. They will have a meticulous and industrious temperament and as a result, will often push their body to the limit in trying to execute something.

Benevolence is also something that will be close to their heart and if they have the resources, they will take great pleasure in sharing them with those who are needy, weak and underprivileged. Being of help to others will give them joy and they will often, support the underdog, thereby, inviting criticism for themselves. However, they will not be affected by what others think of them. They will hold themselves up to their own ideals and will live life by their own standards.

They will also have a strong faith in the goodness of mankind. While they are not naïve, they like to give people a second chance and try and give them the benefit of doubt, rather than blame them for anything. This should not imply that they will not see what they are doing, it is just that they will be willing to let their mistakes go by and see if they learn something from it. Hence, forgiving and forgetting is something that they will practise sincerely.

As far as relationships are concerned, they are intelligent and interesting company and hence people will enjoy spending time with them. Also, they are sensible and mature in their outlook and will not be amused by juvenile humour and pranks. They believe that life is a learning experience and hence, everything should be viewed with an open mind and heart. Their circle of friends will be composed of people who appreciate and value their uniqueness and individuality. Marriage will also be a happy affair and will bring warmth and contentment to the domestic front.

Irrespective of what they do professionally, they will always manage to make a mark. Stagnation is something that they dislike and this could throw them into moods of despair and desolation. Hence, it is important that they should always be fascinated by their job and that it should offer them plenty of room to grow and evolve.

Although they will have a sensitive heart, they will not be the kind to display their feelings or their weaknesses. They will keep them hidden in an effort to shield themselves from hurt and rejection. While this will be good at times, at other times, they may lose someone precious due to this. Continue to take life head-on and educate themselves about the intricacies of living. However, build on their confidence and feel secure enough to let people in on their true self.

Finance

It will be their constant effort and tireless labour that will help to bring the money in. Even if they are born rich, they will need to work hard in order to add to the wealth. They will make money by making the most of their intelligence and talents, as well as by investing in industries related to minerals, real estate and construction. Professionally, if endowed with responsibility and authority, they will be able to deliver their best.

Since they are generous and giving, there are chances that they may give away a significant portion of their wealth. While a spirit of charity is commendable, they should also ensure that they save enough for their old age, since that will be essential and critical.

Health

Their energy and strength will be fairly good and they will be able to handle the pressures of life with ease and effectiveness. However, they will also have the tendency to contract infections and ailments of various internal organs as well as injuries to the lower limbs. It will be a good and wise step for them to take care of their diet, exercise and relaxation regime. Other than that, they will be able to enjoy good, robust health for the most part of their life.

Born on the 9th, 18th and 27th

For all Capricorns born on the above-mentioned dates, the influence of the planets Saturn and Mars will be vital in shaping and defining their personality. The influence of Mars will endow them with a strong belief in destiny or fate. There will be many instances in their life over which they will have little or no control. Over the next few pages, you will learn more about the ways in which their personality will be influenced by these planets.

The journey of life for they will be an eventful one, with many ups and downs. There will be many times when things will go their way and then, there will be times when all their efforts will be obstructed by the hands of fate. Even if they are born in a rich family, they will have to work hard in order to make a name for themselves and be recognised for their abilities and potential. They will be hard-working and will not shy away from responsibility. However, there are chances that they may have to take up jobs that they don't really enjoy, simply for the sake of making money. Nonetheless, they will be able to carve a niche for themselves and eventually, get what they really want.

Highly motivated and driven, they will have goals set for themselves and they will be focused on them and will not rest till they achieve them. They will want to rise and grow and they will not rest till they do so. Their confidence and individualism will help in their endeavours to hone their inherent potential and make the most of what they have been given.

They will also have a quiet grace and poise that will make them comfortable in any society or company. They will always have the ability to find order in disorder and will be adept at managing people and situations. This will help them in positions of authority and dependability. However, they should try and widen their perspective and for this, travelling and meeting people from various cultures will be ideal. Also, it will give them a chance to rest and rejuvenate, since they will always have plenty on their mind.

Stubborn and insistent, there will be times when they will hold firm and stand their ground, irrespective of everything. Another thing that they will need to control will be their temper and not risk losing it, easily and quickly. Therefore, the best thing for them to do will be to try and be more level-headed, this will bring them greater success and popularity. They will also not be bothered by the opinion of other people, at the same time, they will enjoy being in the company of friends and family. Therefore, it will be in their best interests to become more approachable and adaptable.

For them, being outdoors will be the greatest thrill and they will have a lot of fun indulging in adventure and similar sports. However, they will not be reckless. They will be responsible, and at the same time, they will enjoy the adrenalin rush that being adventurous and dangerous will give them. A word of advice thus, they should always exercise caution and restraint when indulging in such sports and activities, since they could result in mishaps.

As far as relationships are concerned, they are candid and hence, people will like them for their honest and frank attitude. Marriage will also be beneficial for them and they will bring stability and security into the home. At the same time, it will be advisable for them to marry someone who understands their personality and is also willing to support their dreams and ambitions. Therefore, a late marriage is not a bad idea. While they will enjoy the company and camaraderie of friends, kith and kin, there will also be some people who may be hurt by or resentful of their straightforward approach. Therefore, they should try and develop tact and diplomacy, to assist them better in a professional and personal manner.

Finance

They will not have a problem in earning and multiplying money. However, they will need to exercise prudence in spending and saving. While they could spend their hard-earned money, it is also viable that they save some for their retirement and secure future. Most professions will suit them and they will always give their hundred per cent to whatever they undertake. However, they will excel when in positions of conscientiousness and trust. As far as businesses are concerned, they will be able to devote their thoroughness and eye for detail to the growth and development of the enterprise and hence, ensure its prosperity.

Health

It is their good fortune to be blessed with a sound and robust disposition that will be able to withstand the stress and strain of life. They will be able to make the most of it and regular exercise and a well-watched diet will yield great benefits. Towards the latter half of their life, they may develop some cardiac-related problems. However, they will be able to take care of these by leading a balanced and regulated life.

AQUARIUS

(21ST JANUARY TO 19TH FEBRUARY)

Aquarius in General

Enigmatic. That is the one word which will describe the sign of Aquarius. It begins in the month of January on the 21st and continues till the end of February. However, the sign attains full potency sometime around January 28th and stays that way till the 19th of February. Thereafter, it starts becoming weaker since it gets shadowed by the incoming sign of Pisces. Similarly, before January 28th, the sign is influenced to quite an extent by the earlier sign of Capricorn.

Aquarians are sensitive, intuitive and intelligent souls. In the next few pages, we will learn more about the general characteristics of Aquarians and what makes them unique.

They are often perceived to be aloof and distant, simply because they do not express their emotions in an overt manner. However, Aquarians are deeply emotional and devoted to their friends and close ones and will never back away from taking a strong stand for them. They will do so, irrespective of what society will think of them and even if it means becoming unpopular. This also goes to show their independent thinking and their tendency to be non-conformists.

Ironically, Aquarians, though restrained in emotional expressions, will often feel isolated and hurt. Despite the fact that they will have a seemingly good circle of friends and acquaintances, there will be instances when they will feel all alone and sad.

Their tendency to bottle up their feelings and sentiments at times lead to great stress on their nerves and hence, it will be better if they learn to relax and express their feelings.

Aquarians also have an inherent curiosity about people and will often be intrigued by them. However, the interest they have will be as dispassionate and rational as that of a scientist. They will not be extremely enthusiastic yet you will never be able to label them as downright lazy. They will always have something or the other on their mind or at the very least, they will give that impression to others.

Aquarians are extremely perceptive and will be able to judge the thoughts and personalities of their acquaintances with uncanny accuracy. They will have the ability to somehow sense what the other person is feeling or thinking and this will enable them to react accordingly. Hence, there could be instances when they will hide their real views and spare hurting someone close to them.

There could be instances however, when their deep sense of honesty and integrity will compel them to state the truth. Yet, even when they do so, they will often feel remorse over trampling the feelings of others and will try and make amends.

Intelligent and interested, Aquarians will move through life with an open mind and absorb all that they can. They will be quick to grasp and apply new concepts and test out new principles. Their sense of logic and reason will be profound and hence, they will enjoy being reasoned with rather than just accepting what is in front of them.

Most Aquarians are blessed with a spirit of goodness and benevolence. They will get great gratification from helping others out and providing hope to those who are suffering. Quite often, they will do so and not expect any credit for it which makes the entire action so beautiful. Their first instinct to someone in difficulty will be to help and not to turn their back on the unfortunate soul. As a result, we will often find them either being associated with charitable organisations or simply doing good whenever it is called for.

Quite a few Aquarians will also have a keen business acumen and one will often find them giving sound counsel to others. However, for the most part, they will occupy responsible posts in companies and industries. There will be a fair percentage of them who will venture into business, and once they figure out what will work for them, there is no doubt that they will succeed.

Some people may be of the opinion that Aquarians are laidback and too easy going. That is not entirely true. When an Aquarian realises his true calling, he will be quite an achiever and display all the latent talents and skills that he possesses.

Aquarians will often, be a bundle of contradictions and oddities. To begin with, they will enjoy being on their own and at the same time, will want to be a part of the larger society. Hence, one will find them frequenting exhibitions, theatres, amusement centres and similar locations. Not only that, while on the one hand, they will be unexpressive about their emotions and somewhat highly strung due to their restrained feelings, on the other hand, they will be quite capable when calming people down and giving them a sense of balance and harmony.

Professionally, it is evident that Aquarians will do very well when involved in a field of their interest and calibre. However, they will be exceptional when involved in a movement that will cater to the benefit of humankind. They will be natural at fund raising, administration and organisation.

Also, since most Aquarians are sharp and intelligent, they will often, think out of the box and come up with unique, offbeat and worthwhile ideas and opinions. They will not just walk the usual path. Rather, they will try and see what will be better, simpler and quicker. As a result, they will do very well in any role and organisation.

Aquarians may also be thought of as reticent and low on self-esteem. That again, is partly a misconception. Aquarians will build their self-assurance and poise slowly and steadily through life. They will be constant observers and students of the human psyche and will try and inculcate all that they admire and consider worthy and right in their personalities. Hence, it will only be a matter of time, before an Aquarian will turn out to be one of the most self-assured people you have ever known.

There is a possibility that if an Aquarian is born in a well-to-do family and has every need taken care of, he or she might not develop all the qualities that will lead to a wholesome personality. There might be the tendency to take things for granted and not try and evolve with time and learning.

Although Aquarians will be idealists most of the time, however, they will not try and push their views on other people. Live and let live—will be their principle. They will follow their ideas and let the rest of the world follow their own. If they wish to join this intelligent thinker, he will be happy to include them.

Finance

In money matters, Aquarians will often find that although they try and be judicious about spending, saving is not easily possible. On the brighter side, it is quite possible that they will profit from windfalls in terms of investments, trusts, insurances and the like.

Most Aquarians will swing between two extremes of being lavish or miserly to a fault. This will, in part, be influenced by the state of income at that point of time. If the money is flowing in freely, they will spend. If it isn't, they will skimp.

There is also a strong probability of them coming into money from some completely unexpected and unforeseen sources. That is something that most Aquarians experience at some point or the other in their lives.

Health

Although Aquarians will be relatively healthy people, they will have the tendency to develop nervous disorders simply because they will keep everything inside them. Also, the upper respiratory system and the digestive system will be somewhat susceptible to infections.

Headaches, colds, backaches and some amount of physical exhaustion might also bother them from time to time.

Aquarius

Born on 1st, 10th, 19th and 28th

Individuals born on any of the above dates will be ruled by the planet Saturn (Negative). When a particular sign starts, the initial 7 days are called the cusp. The cusp signifies the part where one sign is overlapped by another sign and therefore, individuals born during that period will have characteristics of both.

In this manner, the period from the 21st of January to the 28th of January is the cusp for Capricorn and Aquarius. Starting from the 21st of January, Capricorn begins reducing in strength while Aquarius keeps gaining. And, this continues till the 28th of January, which is when Aquarius attains complete power and retains it till the 19th of February, after which the cusp of Pisces begins.

Aquarians born on the above-mentioned dates will have a strong streak of independence and will enjoy being on their own. However, they will also appreciate the fact that they are part of a larger society and will endeavour to observe it and learn from it.

Innovative and idealistic, they will be thinkers of new and unconventional ideas and views. They will be the ones to come up with original, yet practical schemes and plans. They are also adaptable and will be able to adjust to change with relative ease and flexibility.

The initial years of their life will be filled with activity and adjustments. They might have to deal with new developments on the home and professional front. There is also the possibility that their family might not be able to execute the plans they had for them and as a result, they might have to become independent at an early age. This will only be the starting point and they will go on to enhance this self-reliance as they move through the various stages of life.

The aspect of change will remain with them even when they move into a career. There could be instances when people will be envious of your intelligence or independence or any one of their various features and compel them to switch jobs or professional streams during the beginning of their career. Later on, they might understand the inherent nature of certain individuals and refuse to be overwhelmed by them. This constant learning, introspection and evolution will be another one of their characteristic traits.

While they are keen and perceptive, they might not be extremely fortunate when dealing with people in business or trade. Therefore, it will be better for them to either be on their own or choose their partners with great care and caution. They should not rush into anything before thinking it through.

For someone of their competence, they should always aim high and be with people who will inspire and motivate them. There is a strong possibility that they will achieve all that they will aim for, provided they put in the hard work and dedication that is asked of them.

Finance

In Aquarians born on any of the above-mentioned dates, there might be a slight tendency to try and make money as quickly as possible. Therefore, it might be advisable that they try and avoid all forms of risky speculation and gambling.

For those Aquarians who are engaged in trade or business, the month of February will be a beneficial one as far as income is concerned. However, the reverse will be true for those following professions. This month will be an expensive one, in all likelihood.

For those born on the 28th, they will be on the cusp, hence, the limitations will be relatively lesser and they will be able to earn a good amount of money and experience more prosperity than their counterparts born on the 1st , 10th and 19th. That should in no way imply that the latter will not have a fair amount of wealth, it is just that they will have to work harder in order to earn it. However, even they will lead fairly comfortable lives, in all.

Health

Aquarians born on the 1st, 10th and 19th will be blessed with an immense amount of energy and will be able to deal with many things at the same time, on the mental level.

Since these individuals will be prone to develop digestive problems, it is advisable that they eat simple food and follow an exercise regime. Also, they will want to sleep more than other people and also have the ability to recover quickly from any ailment whatsoever.

Those born on the 19th or 28th will be even more agile mentally and hence, will achieve slightly more than individuals born on the other three dates. They will also have the tendency to tire themselves out due to working excessively or mental exhaustion. However, a good night's sleep will ensure them refreshed and rejuvenated. They might be susceptible to blood and liver disorders. Also, they will catch colds easily and will need to take care of their upper respiratory system.

Born on 2nd, 11th, 20th and 29th

Aquarians born on any of the above dates will be influenced by the vibes from the planet Neptune and the Moon. Also, Saturn will have an influence over their personality. Since this will be Saturn Negative, the influence will be positive and will give them the ability to implement all that they want and plan.

They are quite a dreamer and an idealist. Therefore, it will not be surprising that they will get involved in quite a few affairs before they finally find the one they truly love.

Strangely, along with being a romantic, they are also quite determined and driven to realise their goals and aspirations. One of their constant endeavours will be to improve upon their lifestyle.

There is the possibility that they will want more than what was provided to them as a child. Hence, they will decide to become independent and take life in their own hands. They will also realise that that will be a good and more certain way to prosper and achieve. It is essential, however, that they work on their self-esteem and have complete faith in their abilities and talents.

There will be many ups and downs in their life. However, they will be able to overcome all odds and learn something from them. As a matter of fact, it will be this spirit of learning that will create in them a wish to travel to foreign and unknown places. They will want to widen their perspective and one way to do that is travel.

Benevolence will also be an integral feature of their personality. They will gain a lot of happiness from doing good and being of value to the society, especially the underprivileged and needy. While on the subject of interests and inclinations, they will be at their best on stage or in the fields of writing, music and a arts. These will be the lines where they will definitely create a niche for themselves.

They will have a gifted imagination and will be able to spin interesting and innovative ideas, opinions and views. The offbeat path is what will appeal to them. Their inherent curiosity will demand that they question all that is put in front of them and they will accept only that which meets their logic and reasoning.

Finance

For all Aquarians born on the above-mentioned dates, money will not be too strong a worry. They will be able to accumulate quite a lot of it in the later years of their life. There is also a chance that they will come into money through real estate or an inheritance.

Aquarians born on the 2nd, 11th or 20th might have to endure some tough times money-wise, especially during their early years. The exception to this will be their being born in wealthy families. However, even if they do face some financial hardships, these will be smoothened out as they grow in their field and start applying their innate intelligence and sharpness.

In the event that they are a professional, they might face some problems in trying to maintain a balance between income and expenditure. However, if they take up some form of business, they will do quite well and may never have to worry about money. In either case, however, it is extremely important for them to think things over and then invest. Otherwise, things could become difficult.

For those Aquarians born on the 29th, there will not be that many limitations and life will be easier.

On the whole, though, Aquarians born on the above-mentioned dates will simply need to trust their instincts and their intelligence while earning, investing, and there will be very little reason for them to be anxious about money matters.

Health

Aquarians born on the dates given above they will be fortunate to have a sound disposition and by simply following a healthy diet and exercise routine, they will be able to keep most illnesses and ailments at an arm's length.

Born on 3rd, 12th, and 21st and 30th

Aquarians born on the above-mentioned dates will be under the influence of the planets Jupiter and Saturn. This particular combination will endow them with certain unique features in addition to the ones they already have. Moreover, this combination will bring about a softening effect in certain negative features as well. Let us go ahead now and take a deeper look at the characteristics and traits of all Aquarians born on the 3rd, 12th and 21st. They will also have the benefit of experiencing the sobering influence of Saturn (negative) and this, when combined with the effects of Jupiter will bring about a subtle yet definite change in their personality.

A deep determination and a flair for administration will characterise their personality. They are honest and uncomplicated. When asked, they will give their opinion without mincing any words. However, with time, they might understand the importance of tact and start to be a little diplomatic, so as to avoid hurting people's feelings.

However, chances are they will be a strong individualist, and therefore, they will not appreciate the notion of others telling they how to run their life. By the same principle, even they will not give out advice and opinions, unless asked. Prejudices, interference and nosiness are things that they will stay away from.

They will enjoy being with people who are on the same wavelength as them. Even in the rare circumstances where they mix with people who will not have much in common with them, their adaptability and inherent interest in people will give them the ability to interact with them, observe them and even derive some learning from them.

Also, they have a strong yet subdued streak of rebelliousness which will not be displayed in an overt fashion. They will display this by refusing to conform to rules and regulations which do not make any sense to them. They will want to see the reason behind things before they decide to inculcate them in their life.

Despite the fact that they, themselves, will be fond of solitude, they will be good at dealing with people and handling teams of individuals with ease. Since they rely on their innate intuition and the knowledge gathered from observing those around them, their understanding of the human psyche will be unique and profound.

Finance

For Aquarians born on the 3rd, 12th and 21st, money will not be much of an issue. They will achieve prosperity and fame in whichever field they adopt. They will be gifted with an extremely sharp mind, therefore all that has to be done is to apply that mind and then enjoy the results.

At the same time, it is important that they should be judicious in their spending and save some for the future. There might be instances where they might have to bear some losses as well, especially in business and trade. As long as they maintain a balance between spending and saving, there will not be anything to worry about.

Health

As far as health is concerned, they have a strong disposition. However, they may tend to push it to the limit by working too much, either physically or mentally. Hence, their nerves will need much rest and relaxation. They should take good care of their heart, liver and blood pressure. Reduce stress and ensure that they eat wholesome food to benefit their digestive system as well. Sleep will also be extremely important for them. Therefore, they should try and get as much of it as possible.

Born on 4th, 13th, and 22nd and 31st

All Aquarians born on the 4th, 13th or 22nd will be influenced by the vibes from the planet Uranus along with Saturn (negative).

This combination of planetary influences will bring about a personality that will retain many of the essential Aquarian traits, yet have its own distinctiveness.

Polite and well-mannered, they will have a certain sense of detachment, even when in a crowd. They will take their own sweet time in opening up to people, so much so that certain people might even perceive them to be aloof and cold. However, this will, in all likelihood, be a mask to hide their own reticence and hesitations. Society will always interest them and they will try and learn from it. Whether they will apply the learning to their life remains to be seen.

When they spend sufficient time in the company of people whose ideas and views interest them, they will be a friend they can depend on. Devoted and loyal, for them the word 'friend' will have great meaning and depth. They will never hesitate from doing a good deed and standing by the people they value.

They will also be the sort who will not really be influenced by what people think of them. They will be their own person and hence, their ideas and views will be their own. They might have taken some inspiration from others, however, what they will finally believe in will be their own creation. Intelligent and rational, they will be an asset to whichever field they take a keen interest in. It is essential for them to be intrigued by what they do; otherwise chances are that they might not even want to do it. Therefore, make their career choices with thought and deliberation.

Intuitive and perceptive, they have a thoughtful outlook and will often be in deep thought about something or the other. These issues need not be related to their daily life. They could be vague and not part of your life at all, yet they will be interesting enough for them to think about them. That is part of the education that they will receive throughout life.

If your child is born on any of the above dates, be extremely careful that you treat the young mind with great care and tenderness. They will have extremely sensitive and perceptive minds and any form of harshness will mar them completely. They will also need to be gently shown the art of expressing their thoughts and emotions. Try and understand them and give them the right direction so that they will not be misinterpreted and hurt as grown ups.

They will have the inherent dislike for any restriction that is not based on sound reason and logic. As a result, they will be a trailblazer without even intending to be one. If something does not make sense to them, they will refuse to toe the line, even if it means being punished for it. Simply put, they will do what appeals to their rationale and values. They are not very expressive about their innermost thoughts and feelings.

Unpredictable and enigmatic: Those are the words that will best explain individuals born on the above dates. One will not be able to decipher their thoughts since they will run deeply and rapidly. They will also be the kind who will not let many people in on what they are thinking. That is, again, part of their enigma and allure. Odd, unconventional and practical, they will be a fascination for most people.

Finance

Money for Aquarians born on the above-mentioned dates will be an issue that they will not really enjoy. They will not be the kind to worry about the future and save all that they earn. For them, money will be earned and spent in a relatively smooth cycle. There are chances that they will come in to money through unconventional sources and there are also chances that they will spend it in the same unconventional manner.

It will be advisable for them to spend only some of what they earn. Otherwise, the future could become somewhat uncertain and insecure.

Health

For all Aquarians born on the 4th, 13th and 22nd, health will be a question of how well they feel mentally. If they are involved in things that interest them and make them happy, they will be healthy and well. On the other hand, if they are saddened by anything that happens in their life or are trapped in a boring job, they will be susceptible to digestive ailments, nervous illnesses and the like.

Born on the 5th, 14th and 23rd

Aquarians born on the above-mentioned dates will be influenced by the vibes from the planets Mercury and Saturn (Negative). This is a favourable alliance of planetary influences and will result in an extremely sharp mind and a flair for human psychology.

Aquarians born on the 5th, 14th and 23rd will be gifted with a sharp mind, as mentioned before. What will make them unique will be their ability to understand the depth and intensity of the human psyche and this will have an impact on their relationships and their interactions with the world, at large. This understanding will also provide them with the uncanny ability to influence others without trying too hard.

Therefore, it is not surprising that these Aquarians will have the ability to soothe hysterical and excited souls and also make them see logic, thereby, becoming quite successful as counselors, doctors and teachers.

Their memory could be called 'photographic', since they will be able to retain nearly everything that they will merely read, with amazing accuracy. As a result, they will enjoy reading and spend quite a bit of their time in going through articles and books of diverse streams and spheres of knowledge.

Perceptive and analytical, they will enjoy scientific problems and will also be quite successful in untangling puzzles, etc. Facts are what they will believe in and although they will not trust vague theories and hypothesis, their inherent curiosity will compel them to unravel these and even study them.

While Aquarians born on the above-mentioned dates will not be mercenaries, striving for wealth will not be at the top of their list of priorities. They will want to be recognised for their efforts and accomplishments. They are a bundle of contradictions. For instance, while they will be quite happy on their own, they will be extremely pleased when someone compliments and motivates them.

For these people, it is critical that they get to accomplish all that they want. Otherwise, they might sink into depression and loneliness. They will thrive on the feeling of having accomplished something, and this is what will keep them going. Since Aquarians, in general, are quite affected by their thoughts, it is important they always remain positive and upbeat.

Finance

For Aquarians born on the dates given above, money will be something that they will be good with when counseling someone else. On the contrary, when it will come to themselves, they will not be all that financially savvy. While they will often, make a fair amount of money during their lifetime through their hard work and intelligence, chances are that they will not invest it very wisely. Hence, they might even lose some of their money.

My advice for all of them will be to avoid stepping into any investment which relies mainly on speculation. For in that case, there will be strong chances that they will not be able to make any profits and may even lose the money invested.

As they are the quiet sort, people will often try and borrow money from them. However, they might find it difficult to either get the money back or get similar help when they need it. Therefore, make the decision to lend only if they really know the person in question and after having given it some thought.

Health

Aquarians born on 5th, 14th or 23rd will be relatively healthy and energetic. Illnesses and ailments will not bother them to a great extent. However, it is adviseable that they take care of their back and the digestive system, including liver, kidneys, etc.

There might also be instances when there is an excess of money and certain individuals born on the dates above might become addicted to either drugs, drink or such substances. It is important that they be given some purpose or goal in life, else they will continue to drift and move away from society.

On the whole, though, there will not be much cause for worry and as long as they lead an active and full life, health will remain in an optimum state.

Born on 6th, 15th and 24th

All Aquarians born on the 6th, 15th and 24th will be influenced by the planetary vibes of Venus along with Saturn (Negative). This particular combination will endow the individuals with a sensitive temperament where love and affection will take precedence and influence their day to day living as well.

Number six Aquarians will be quite emotional and dedicated to the love of their life. So profound will be their feelings that they will willingly give away all that they have for the sake of their happiness. While this is indeed a noble sentiment, they also run the risk of being taken advantage of. It is important that they realise that the world is not all rosy and certain people may not be worthy of the love that they are willing to shower on them. Hence, it is advisable that although they may not have any control over the emotion of love, they should never let go of their intelligence and rationale. This is what will prevent them from getting hurt in a relationship.

There is no doubt about the fact that most Number six Aquarians will value love greatly and will wish to both give and receive love. On the other hand, there is also the great possibility that so blind will be their love that they will marry people who are not on the same wavelength as they are or are simply not deserving of their love.

They will also be gifted with a creative streak and will be quite successful in all those lines where they could be in the limelight. Art, music, cinema, and theatre, all these will be suitable for them. In short, any field where they are able to experience the love of the public will bring out the best in them and they will shine gloriously.

Their love for people will also result in a fondness for surrounding themselves with friends and acquaintances. Socialising and mingling with others will bring them happiness and they will often be seen in the company of friends. Not only that, they will also be quite good at making friends and relating to others. With the kind of personality that they have, they will often, be admired by their subordinates and even their superiors will be able to trust them and favor them.

They will not be very materialistic or money-minded. As a result, they will often spend all that they earn. This large-heartedness could result in the depletion of their bank balance, if they do not maintain a healthy equilibrium between spending and saving.

Their inherent idealism will often, lead them to dream lofty dreams and aspirations. They will, as a matter of fact, enjoy the struggle of being able to realise all that their heart desires. Hurdles and obstructions will not pull them down, rather they will motivate they to try harder. There is no doubt that they will be successful in all that they endeavour to do. For they, the word 'impossible' will cease to exist and therefore, they will make all their dreams come true. Risk will not scare them and so they will simply take the plunge and enjoy the fruits.

Since they are also a die-hard romantic, their love life will be full and offbeat. Though they love their partner dearly, they will often let their work or social service take precedence, leading to some difficult situations.

Lavishness will appeal to their senses and more often than not, they will spend nearly all that they earn. Typically, they will live in the present and not think of the future. Fortunately for them, they will often find people going out of their way to help you and pull them out of financial debt. Again, this will be related to the fact that they, themselves, will be a benevolent soul and will not hesitate in helping others.

Finance

Initially, they might face some problems with cash flow and might not have the amount of money that they truly need. However, as they progress professionally and personally, this will ease out and they will have a sufficient amount of money.

If in business, they will have to be extremely prudent and not jump into things without thought. With their luck, they will be able to bounce back and recover from anything that comes in their way.

If engaged in business, they will do well, as long as the public is involved in the business that they do. They will have a good head for planning and strategising and will also be able to win over others with their persuasive skills. As far as possible, they should not be over ambitious else they could get into some financial difficulties.

Health

They will be fortunate since they will have a healthy and strong constitution. Also, they will hardly ever have reason to worry about falling ill. Primarily, they will need to protect themselves from change in weather and becoming negligent about food and sleep. They may have some upper respiratory ailments and it is important that they keep their chest protected. Also, ensure that they take enough time out to relax and not over burden their nerves with stress and exhaustion.

Born on 7th, 16th and 25th

Aquarians born on the 7th, 16th and 25th will be influenced by the vibes from a combination of planets Uranus, Neptune, Saturn and the Moon. This unique combination of influences will bring about certain distinguishing characteristics in the personality of the individual.

They are highly perceptive and intuitive and therefore, every thing will make a difference to their state of mind. People and situations will have a lot of impact on how they feel and react. Therefore, it will be important for your well-being to surround themselves with cheerful and positive company and environs.

Highly imaginative, creative and idealistic, they will move through life on a level that will be entirely their own. Their imagination will prove extremely helpful when planning for the future and working out strategies. They will also want to do the right thing at all times and will try to live up to high ideals as far as possible.

They will also have a deep sense of duty and will often, suppress their own desires in order to attend to your work. There are also the chances that you will need to start working on your self-esteem from an early age and continue building on it through adulthood. Everything that you succeed in will add to your confidence.

For you, it will be extremely important that you have a goal, since that is what they will remain focused on. Their personal profit is not that important for them. What will be important will be doing the job well. Their innate curiosity in astrology, spiritualism, occult and the like will lead them to study these subjects with great interest. The mind and its workings will intrigue them and combined with other interests will make them quite an authority on the psychology of human beings.

Generous and charitable, they will have a strong compassion for those individuals who are not mentally stable and are less fortunate than them. As a matter of fact, they will spend quite a few of their resources in bringing relief and reprieve to these souls.

Most Number seven Aquarians will be known for their unique approach to life. All of them will have their own way of dealing with life and will not be swayed by people whose advice has no reason or logic behind it. They will also enjoy reading and being in the limelight and hence, anything that is dramatic or connected with literary activities will interest them and they will do quite well at it.

So unique will they be that even when it comes to questions of religion and faith, they will not be able to conform to convention and tradition easily. They will often, question everything and believe only in that which will have some sound rationale behind it.

On the whole, Number seven Aquarians will be interesting to be with and will, invariably, be able to provide a fresh approach to most issues and questions.

Finance

In money matters, Aquarians born on the 7th, 16th and 25th will be relatively laid back and will not be bothered about finances too much. They will need to work hard and build up their bank balances. Speculation and risky investments will not turn out too favorably for them.

As they are generous and large hearted, they will often give away money and not ask for it back. This, again, could result in depletion of resources. However, since this act of giving will bring great joy to them, they will be still happy and content with what they have.

Health

Aquarians born on the above-mentioned dates will be relatively healthy, yet will also have some unique and unconventional ailments every once in a while. As children, they may be somewhat sensitive and as such will often have to be treated for allergies, coughs and colds.

As adults, they will be stronger, more energetic and more capable, however, they will often have to deal with gastric ailments and will more often that not, believe in curing themselves. Also, these individuals will be very intuitive and will be able to feel the vibes from those around them; hence, it is important they mingle with happy, positive and cheerful people.

Overall, they will not suffer from anything which a good diet, exercise and sleep regime will not be able to take care of. They will be able to deal with anything as long as these three things are met with properly.

Born on 8th, 17th and 26th

Aquarians born on 8th, 17th or 26th will be influenced by the vibes from the planets Saturn and Uranus. Their is a combination of planetary influences that will endow them with a personality that is decidedly unique and not only that, even the life style that they will enjoy will be different from most people. They will be in a niche of their own.

Profound and intense, they will often be engrossed in deep thought and irrespective of their professional interests, they will surely have an idealistic bent of mind. They life will be an interesting one and various unusual and surprising conditions will come into their life and have an impact on them and their lifestyle. These conditions will be both positive and negative. However, given their personality, they will be able to deal with everything with a strong outlook and viewpoint.

Their planetary influences will also result in them having a comfortable life and most luxuries that their heart desires. There will be little that they will want and despite the fact that they may have to work really hard in the initial years of their life, the latter half will be spent enjoying the fruits of their labour. The only exception to this will be cases where individuals are born into wealthy and rich families.

They are a benevolent and charitable soul. This quality will develop more so once they start making a reasonable amount of money. However, even when they do not have that much, they will try and help those in need. They will be a loving and affectionate person and will spread warmth everywhere they go. People will value them for the person they are and everyone will enjoy being in their company. Moreover, they will extend their hand of friendship to everyone, irrespective of their social status or mental wave length. This will be another aspect of their versatile and adaptable personality.

As far as home and domestic life is concerned, they will need to work on marrying the right partner so that their marital life does not have too many ups and downs and their partner should be able to understand them completely. They will enjoy being married and will try their best to be an understanding and loving parent.

They will be contented with what they have and will not be the kind to unduly exert themselves for more money or possessions. They will be happy and satisfied to have the love and affection of their dear ones and will value the ties of family and friends. Despite the fact that they will consciously not run after money, there are strong chances that owing to their diligence and determination, they will make quite a bit of money and will go on to live a satisfied and fruitful life.

Finance

Aquarians born on the above-mentioned dates will not have many worries about their financial state of affairs. Although they might have to struggle quite a bit during their initial years, with time and experience, they will be able to build up a decent bank balance for themselves. They should, however, guard themselves against people who are jealous of them, since these individuals will attempt to pull them down and cause them harm.

Health

From a health point of view, Aquarians born on 8th, 17th and 26th will be quite fortunate. They will nearly always seem healthy and strong. However, they should take adequate measures regarding diet, drink and exercise and protect themselves from the risk of coronary diseases and similar serious ailments, which could strike them without any warning.

Born on 9th, 18th and 27th

For all those Aquarians born on the 9th, 18th and 27th, the planetary influences of Mars and Saturn will affect them and their personality. These influences will bring about an independence of thought and a distinctiveness of character in the individual to a great extent and will enable them to carve out a special niche for themselves in the greater fabric of the society.

It has been observed that in case any of the Aquarians born on a date that adds to nine and is close to the cusp, the uniqueness of the personality is greater than in any other date. Moreover, the planetary influences will bestow these Number nine Aquarians with an abundance of energy and enthusiasm for life and living. They will have the drive that is needed to realise all dreams, big or small and will devote themselves tirelessly for their goals and aspirations.

Number nine Aquarians will have a personality that will always stand out irrespective of the role they play in life. Their superiors and peers will always be able to talk about them with admiration, and everything you do will bear their trademark, even if it was part of teamwork. This will be the strength of their personality and will enable them to climb up the social and professional ladder with ease.

Another distinguishing feature of Aquarians born on the 9th, 18th and 27th is that they have highly developed mental faculties. Their intellect and sharpness will allow them to grasp and understand new and complicated concepts and theories with relative ease. What is important is that the subject should interest them; otherwise, nothing can bring them to apply their minds to it.

So strong and keen is their perception and intuition that they will be able to bring about any change that they want in their life, simply by concentrating and focusing on the goal. They are able to form an idea of how they will achieve their dreams by simply thinking about it and more often than not, their plan and strategy will work out to their advantage. Even in the rare cases where they might meet with opposition or failure, it will nearly always be a temporary set-back and they will recover from it with characteristic composure.

They are also highly independent and will be their own best friend and advisor. Their thoughts will be their own and so will their actions. They might listen to others but ultimately will rely on your own intelligence to make the proper decision. They will also be gifted with a strong sense of determination and if they set their mind to something, they will very nearly do it. This will be highly exemplified in cases where they will support someone or something. Even if the entire world does not stand by it, if they will have the belief that it is the right thing, they will go ahead and support it.

This brings us to another trait of them which is the lack of concern about what society or people may think. They will firmly believe in going by what they believe in. The opinions of others will hardly ever matter to them. They will try not to offend the feelings and sentiments of others by being tactful and diplomatic, yet they will eventually do what they believe in. High on self-esteem and spontaneity, they will often, win hearts wherever they go and people will be drawn towards their freshness and novel ideas and views.

Right from childhood, they will have the ability to leave their distinct impression on everything they do. They will have an inherent flair for logic and analysis. As a result, they will be able to see all aspects and angles of any issue or problem and deal with them accordingly. Even in an argument, they will try and see all the angles before reaching any conclusion. As a result, there could be cases where they might come to realise that there is another way of thinking that is better than their own. They will display humility by accepting it and changing rather than by being egoistic. Therefore, while they may be individualistic, they will certainly not be an ego driven person.

Their ability to analyse an argument or problem will also benefit them when opposing someone. They will be able to see the loopholes in their argument and make their case stronger. This will give they a strong advantage if they are in the fields of law where they will need to argue their point and weaken the other side.

Their spontaneous nature will also reflect itself in their speech and they will be known for being absolutely candid when stating their views and thoughts. This straightforward temperament may not appeal to a lot of people and they might be scolded for this by elders and superiors. However, this is an inherent trait so they will not be able to do much about it. Yet, they will also have a charm about themselves which will endear them to people and they will not be able to stay annoyed with them for long. Their personality will have an intense charisma which will, invariably, pull people towards them and enable them to have quite an influence over them.

Charitable and compassionate, they will always be willing to dedicate themselves to the cause of the needy and underprivileged. Supporting a worthy cause will be something that they will strongly believe in and will generously give their time and money for helping out those who need it. Even if they do not have a lot of money, they will still try to make some contribution or the other and do their bit for the sake of the weaker section of people.

They have strong administration skills because of which they will be able to organise people and bring order to chaos. Another favourable feature will be their innate understanding.

Their self-confidence and bluntness will at times hurt people or make them envious, because of which they might make things difficult for them. However, they will be able to overcome most hurdles with ease and will not let anything or anyone pull them down. As a matter of fact, they will be often able to show your opponents the goodness in their actions and bring them over to their side. Even if that does not happen, they will not be subdued by them for long.

From a professional point of view, they will do well in nearly everything as along as they have an interest in the subject and it appeals to their intelligence. Diversity will appeal to them and they will try their hands at many things before settling down for the career that really suits their personality and their intelligence.

One thing that will nearly always be certain is that whatever they do, they will be closely involved with the public. They will either be helping them or will be interacting with them on a day to day basis. Whatever may be the case, they will be closely related to them. This will be true, despite their independence and individualism. They will also be close to friends and loved ones. They will have an important place in their life. They will not give their trust and love easily, but once they find people that they can really relate to, they will be a dedicated and loyal ally.

Finance

Aquarians born on the 9th, 18th and 27th will have little to worry about with regards to finances. They will be able to build wealth by working hard and making use of their intelligence. Even if born into wealth, they will continue to multiply it and only if influenced by the wrong counsel, will they bring about the depletion of the family bank balances.

Number nine Aquarians will need to ensure that they maintain a balance between their spending and earning. There could be instances where they might, in a fit of generosity, give away more than they can afford. Therefore, it will be essential that while they help others, they also help themselves. They should build up enough so that their life will be comfortable even after they retire from whatever profession they are engaged in.

They will be one of those lucky individuals who will not have many health related worries. They will keep themselves engrossed in their work and humanitarian activities, as a result, their focus will not be their health. This could be one of the reasons why they will not have many health problems in the first place. Their sensitive areas will be the heart and the respiratory system. As long as they have enough exercise and wholesome food, they will be fine. They should stay away from too much of dust to protect their respiratory system.

PISCES

(20TH FEBRUARY TO 20TH MARCH)

Pisces in General

The sign of Pisces is indeed, a fascinating and intriguing sign that never ceases to amaze by its powers of intuition and perception, amongst other things. Beginning on the 19th of February, it gains complete strength around the 26th of February and then retains it till the 21st of March. It is ruled by the planet Jupiter and during the period of Pisces, the influence of Saturn is on the decline. It is essential that we remember that Jupiter in Pisces is in its negative House in the Zodiac.

Pisceans have the ability to learn and acquire knowledge with relative ease. While they may or may not take to academic endeavours, they will still be interested in knowing about topics that intrigue them and widen their perspective. As a result, they will always be comfortable in any company or circle and will always be able to appear learned and knowledgeable. Traditional education may not always be their mode of learning and they will look for innovative and unique methods to develop and hone their intellectual skills.

They tend to have a deep-seated ambition to excel. However, their ambition will be focused on areas in which they have expertise and skill. They are not the kind to put their efforts into fields about which they do not have much knowledge. They will also have a strong regard for traditions and principles that have some logic and reasoning behind them.

Symbolised by the pair of fish swimming in opposite directions, Pisceans will be able to fit in with a wide variety of people and this will be one of the reasons for their closeness with their friends and family. At the same time, it is important that they feel wanted and secure. While they are comfortable handling positions that require them to be accountable, they will normally not volunteer their opinion or efforts, and will wait till someone calls upon them.

Most of them will be fond of comfort and ease and will often, be susceptible to over-indulgence in food, drink or rest. In this particular case, they will be laidback and complacent, with a tendency to be swayed by their friends and a tendency to get influenced by the wrong schemes and plans. However, this will be true for only a percentage of Pisceans. Most others will be active and energetic, with integrity and dependability as their core strengths.

Pisces is a sign whose element is Water, and therefore, there is a strong role that is played by their emotions, feelings and imagination. They, indeed, have a fertile and creative imagination which, if used productively, can come up with some profitable and useful ideas. Sensitive to vibrations, they will be receptive to their surroundings and the people around them and will respond accordingly. It has also been seen that they have a method to their madness. In other words, they will find order in disorder and will not always be known for their meticulous nature. Only a few rare Pisceans will exhibit an orderly, organised temperament.

While most individuals will think of Pisceans as happy-go-lucky souls who are content with their state, they will be surprised to see them cope with crises and tough times. If a Piscean can find a strong goal or focus for his life, he will exhibit great determination and strength that will amaze all those who know him. They will be able to cast away all frailties and rise to the occasion in a brave and passionate manner.

Just like their symbol of the fish swimming in opposite directions, Pisceans will at times, be known for the duality. This does not mean that they will be two-faced, it is just that there will be times in their life when they will have to make tough choices and also that they will be able to fit in with pretty much any category of people, without any problem. It will be their adaptability that will draw people towards them and make them popular as entertainers and social beings.

They will have a fondness for travel and will often, want to experience life in different countries. Change will appeal to them and they will take to it like 'a fish to water'. Meeting people from various cultures will appeal to the scholar in them and they will use these chances to widen their horizons and also add to their repertoire of skills and knowledge. Quite naturally, they will be drawn towards water and if they have the resources, will take voyages across the seas. Even if they lack money, they will have a strong desire to make their house somewhere around a water body.

Their seemingly easy going temperament will have a mature and responsible side to it. Also, there are indications that they may be interested in spiritualism and mystical topics that will intrigue them and give them something to think about. Routine life and everyday occurrences will tend to bore them after sometime and this interest will keep the fire of inquisitiveness alive and burning.

Professionally, they will do well in fields where they have a strong interest. It is extremely important that they should develop a strong sense of diligence so that they can sustain their interest and productivity. The fields of transportation, imports and exports and related trades will be beneficial for them. They will also have a profound generous streak and will always want to be of assistance and help to friends, family and even complete strangers. They will extend money, time and their help to whosoever needs it, yet at the same time, they will not want to be taken for granted.

When in love, they will be tender and compassionate lovers and will be willing to give their partner everything. They will also be the kinds who will be happy to be with their partner the way they are, without wanting to change anything. It is not that they are passive, it just that they are happy accepting people and situations as they are, since there is a reason behind everything. They will also want others to show them the same treatment and not try to change them. While they will be happy with the process and idea of change, they will do so only when they feel like. Marriage will make them secure and comfortable and will appeal to the emotional side of their personality.

They are also intrigued by the unknown and will often, spend a great deal of time and energy in trying to figure out concepts and ideas. Not the kinds to accept things at face value, they will often, want to find out what lies beneath the surface. Investigating, probing and inquisitive, they will be fascinated by things that are vague and mysterious. However, their desire to probe will not extend into the lives of other people. They are relatively non-interfering and will appreciate that others give them the same kind of space.

Most Pisceans will be gifted with a unique sense of humour and will always have the ability to make you smile. Entertaining and witty, they will be the life of parties and even if they don't talk much, they will be able to make people feel warm, comfortable and wanted. Since they will be able to adapt, one could put them anywhere and be secure in the knowledge that they will be able to interact, have fun and all in all, let everybody enjoy a good time.

Life for them will be an experience to be enjoyed, utilised and valued. They will do all that and much more, enriching their own life and that of others.

Finance

Once the desire to excel arises in the hearts of the Piscean, nothing will be able to stop them. However, it is important that they realise what their goals are and what they really want from life. Since Pisceans have an idealistic temperament, they will often dream big and will want to reach a certain ideal. At the same time, though, they will not be able to sustain their efforts in reaching that ideal or goal. It is for this sustenance of attempts that they will need constant motivation, either from themselves or from other external sources. They will have to drive themselves to make the physical efforts that are required to achieve what they dream of.

Due to their inconsistent efforts, individuals in this sign often, witness a great deal of change and upheaval in their financial status. It will be best for them, if from an early age, they learn to complete the task at hand and ensure that they see their goals and targets through. Once they have learnt to, Pisceans will have no problems in attaining all that they want and will be able to take advantage of all the opportunities that come their way. They will be filled with the fire to reach their destination and will be willing to put in all that is required for the same.

When Pisceans have settled into their careers and businesses and found what they really like, they will be able to make a fair amount of money and lead a comfortable life. However, they will need to balance the earning and spending scale, so that they also save enough for the future. The inclination to save will not be seen in all Pisceans. It is something that they will have to consciously work upon in order to ensure a secure future. Since they are generous and benevolent, they will have to additionally see that they do not end up giving more than they actually can afford.

The most important thing for them will be their ability to sustain their focus on their goals till completion. Once that aspect is taken care of, life for Pisceans will be more stable and financially secure.

Health

For Pisceans, health is more a matter of mind than body. They will have a lot of energy and enthusiasm and will be able to deal with life in an effective and capable manner. However, they will have a tendency to worry and hence, will overload their mental make-up. It will be in their best interests to enjoy everything that life offers them and give their mind and body adequate rest and nourishment.

An excessive amount of tension and worrying can make them prone to nervous disorders and that of the digestive system. They will be sensitive to their surroundings; hence, it will be adviseable that they remain in the company of positive and cheerful people as much as possible. They should also take adequate care of their respiratory system, particularly the lungs.

Pisces

Born on the 1st, 10th, 19th and 28th

Pisceans born on the dates given above will be influenced by the planetary combination of the Sun and the planet Uranus. This particular combination requires some explanation. The planet Uranus takes eighty four years to make one revolution around the zodiac. It forms a favourable aspect to the Sun every fourteen years. This is an estimate, as close as can be made. It is also known to have a profound and far-reaching impact on Piscean individuals born on the above-mentioned dates.

Their sense of perception and intuition will be heightened due to the influence of Uranus. They will have the ability and the confidence to trust their instincts and go with their 'gut-feeling'. More often than not, they will be right. Inventive and impulsive, they will be quite successful in pretty much any professional line. They will have a tendency to be somewhat stubborn and stick to their own viewpoint with loyalty and tenacity. Something that they should try and develop will be more confidence and belief in themselves and the ability to carry their plans and schemes through.

Idealistic and positive, they will always try and look at the brighter side of things. Seeing the good in people and the lighter side of situations will help them to cope with many of life's ups and downs. Once they are equipped with the confidence and the inner strength that they need, they will be able to meet challenges and obstacles in a manner that will reflect determination and persistence. They will have a good amount of energy and mental strength that will enable them to deal with the pressures and stresses of life in an effective and sensible manner.

They do not like to be held back. After they have developed their own system of belief and values, they will be focused on their goals and ambitions and will not rest till they achieve them. There are indications that they may not have high self-esteem as a child, however, they will be able to acquire it with age and maturity and will soon be able to use it in a worthwhile manner.

Loving and compassionate, they will have a fondness for home, family, kith and kin. It will be their earnest endeavor to keep the ties that bind and be a part of a loving and nurturing circle. However, due to their stubbornness, they may often be at odds with parents, siblings or relatives. While this may not be serious, it will sadden them; yet, they will want to hold their own ground also.

There is no doubt about the fact that their life will be exciting and hectic with many things going on at the same time. The best part is that they will be able to manage the various dimensions of their life in an effective manner. Irrespective of what profession they choose, they will be successful and will enjoy the love, respect and admiration of friends, family, peers and superiors.

Finance

Number one Pisceans will be quite lucky as far as financial affairs are concerned and will often get new and unusual chances to earn money. Quite often, they will also be given positions that require trust and responsibility and they will be able to execute their duties in a mature manner. Number one Piscean, you will have a good amount of prudence and will be able to make wise decisions in matters of business and money.

What they will really want and thrive on is recognition and the chance to be 'boss'. Although they will have to start at a lower level, it will be their burning ambition to rise as high as possible and to do it quickly. That is the reason they will probably take to business and will go solo rather than in a partnership. While there is no doubt that they will make money and will lead a prosperous and comfortable life, it is also essential that you should balance their spending and earning and also watch their career graph carefully.

Health

It will be their good fortune that they will be blessed with a robust and healthy constitution. Their energy levels will be high and they will be able to withstand considerable wear and tear, physically as well as mentally. They will have a tendency to push themselves to the limit and burden their nervous system with stress, tension and anxiety. It has been indicated that they will be one of those who will have to be on the go pretty much always and will not be kept down for long. As a result, they will often, tire themselves out and use up the abundance of energy and stamina that they have been endowed with.

It will be in their best interests to relax and not put too many things on their platter. While it is a good thing to be active and energetic, it is another thing to deplete themselves of their inner energy. Therefore, frequent periods of calm, peace and relaxation will do them wonders.

Born on the 2nd, 11th, 20th and 29th

For all Pisceans born on the dates given above, the influence of the planet Neptune in conjunction with the Moon will be vital. It will be this planetary alliance that will shape their personality and give it the distinctiveness from other Pisceans. The effect of both these will bring about an enhanced sense of creativity and imagination.

They will have a sensitive temperament, in the sense that they will be able to pick up vibes around them and respond accordingly. Hence, being in positive, cheerful and uplifting environments will suit they much more than anything else. Like I said earlier, they will have a greater gift of creativity than their other counterparts; therefore, they should try to make the most of it. By developing a stronger sense of determination and strength of character, they will be able to focus on a definite goal and ensure that they work towards realising it.

Their prolific and rich imagination will seek expression in many forms and some of them may be traditional while others could be modern. Hence, they could have an interest in poetry, drama, music, writing, and similar arts. Or else, they could use it in planning, improvising and producing business and professional strategies. They will also have a fine eye for beauty and will be especially fond of loveliness in Nature and her various aspects.

There is a strong indication that due to the influence of the Moon, they will have astute perceptive skills and will be able to sense things that others seem to overlook. They will be intrigued by mysticism and similar subjects and may take either a keen or passing interest in them.

As far as relationships are concerned, they will be happy with a small circle of friends who give them a sense of stability and security than with a huge group which annoys them and grates on their sensibilities. They will be loyal and devoted to those whom they care about and will try and make life as comfortable for them as possible.

Since they have a temperament that will be more idealistic than realistic, they will not place a heavy premium on wealth and materialistic possessions. What they will enjoy more will be harmony, beauty and simplicity in their surroundings and a warmth and closeness in their relationships. Therefore, while they may take up professions that will yield good incomes and also be of their interest, their real goal will be to lead a life filled with all that they really crave for. Accumulating wealth will not be their top priority.

Their life will be filled with interesting and educative experiences. Everything they do will teach them something about themselves, about others or about life itself. And, they will have the intelligence to be able to absorb this learning and use it in a wise and sensible manner in all their future endeavours.

Finance

Money matters for them will be related closely to their temperament. They will have the ability to make money and earn a good living for themselves; however, there will be instances when they may not be able to hold on to it for too long. Their financial state will be greatly helped if they develop the ability to save and budget with prudence and judiciousness. They will have the tendency to dream big and sometimes they may not be able to realise all their dreams. It is essential that they seek the help and guidance of someone while investing their money and secure their future.

Health

They will be quite a mystery as far as health is concerned. The mind will be the chief concern. Most of their illnesses will be related to the mind and therefore, when they are upbeat and cheerful, everything will be well physically also. However, when sad and despondent, they will suffer from various aches and pains.

Most importantly, they will need to guard themselves against spinal injuries, blood disorders and renal ailments. Other than that, they will be able to keep off most illnesses and as long as they keep their mind healthy, the body will take care of itself.

Born on the 3rd, 12th, 21st and 30th

Pisceans born on any of the dates given above will be significantly influenced by their own planet Jupiter. This will imply that these dates come under a 'double Jupiter'. This will be a potent and influential alliance which will endow them with immense vitality and a lot of drive and motivation.

Their fiery ambition and immense stamina will be their strongest features. Irrespective of what they focus on, they will concentrate all their energy into its realisation. It will give them a lot of satisfaction to be able to rise above their initial status and make a mark for themselves in social and business circles. they will not be happy until they have accomplished all that their heart was set upon.

In them, one will be able to find a unique and excellent example of realism blended with idealism. They will be able to think practically and at the same time have a strong emotional perspective as well. It will be the latter that will motivate them to indulge in charity and benevolence while the former will ensure that they are not taken for granted and that they provide for their own future as well. They will be more inclined towards helping organisations. However, deserving and worthy individuals will also receive their compassion and assistance.

As far as relationships are concerned, they will be able to get along with a wide variety of people. However, they will be happier with those who will let them have their say and acknowledge their dominance. While they will not be condescending or arrogant, they like to be given control and authority. Being a subordinate is not something that they will relish and this will be reflected in most of their personal and professional relationships.

Professionally, they will do well in nearly all fields, since they will have the diligence and the intelligence needed. However, it is essential that they be interested in the field and also that it provides them with enough mental stimulation. Monotony, stagnation and the like are things that they will abhor and hence, may take up business in fields such as mining, transportation and other forms of industry.

Not only are they intelligent, they are also instinctive and perceptive; with the ability to 'know' people and things. They will also be known for their social graces and their ability to make people feel at home and comfortable. Not the kinds to throw their weight around, even when they reach the top, they will always have an approachable and unpretentious manner.

Their prosperity lies in their hands. They will be the maker of their destiny and with their efforts be able to chart their growth, rise and development. On the other hand, if they do not use the ambition that they have been endowed with, they run the risk of becoming complacent and too laid-back for their own good. Therefore, it is important that they learn to make full use of all their potential and reach for the stars.

Finance

Fueled by ambition and charged up with the desire to achieve, they will be able to fit into nearly any professional field and make money. Their hard work and sincerity will not go unrecognised and they will not let temporary setbacks disillusion them. By investing in and establishing stable businesses, they will be able to build up a good amount of wealth for themselves. They will have good business acumen and will be able to use it profitably. There is hardly any reason why they will not be able to establish themselves firmly and successfully in any professional or business field.

Health

Their physical health will be largely determined by their perspective and views on life and living. Since they are endowed with a considerable amount of energy and stamina, it is important that they keep themselves occupied and busy. Otherwise, they will get restless and the mind will become inactive. In such a state, they will be prone to lethargy and hence, suffer from the illnesses that it brings. Other than that, there will be nothing extremely serious that they will have to worry about. They should keep their mind and their hands busy and there will be little else that they will need to do.

Born on the 4th, 13th, 22nd and 31st

The planets Jupiter, Uranus and the Sun will come together to influence them who were born on any of the dates given above. The significant influence of Uranus will be responsible for endowing them with a greater degree of originality and unconventionality.

They are imaginative and unique. Gifted with a strong sense of self-reliance and confidence, they will do what they will feel is right and hence, will often invite the disapproval.

There are strong indications that they may have to struggle during the initial years of their life and may have to overcome many hurdles and obstacles as they move towards their goals. However, this period of struggle will toughen them up and make them a more secure and well-centred individual, who has greater confidence in his or her self. They will have to develop tact and a subtle discernment about the people they interact and associate with. They will nearly always have to stand up for themselves and be independent rather than relying on those around them.

Temperamentally, they will be fond of things which touch them emotionally and move them in a myriad of ways. Literature, art and music will all have a special place in their life. They will also be inclined towards mysticism and related subjects such as, astrology, etc. A keen perception will help them to deal with the ups and downs of life in a more capable manner.

As far as relationships are concerned, they will have a small and intimate circle of friends who will be on the same wavelength as them. They will be able to understand and respect their uniqueness and their quirks. More often than not, they will like to be by themselves and will develop a fondness and attachment for a select circle of people.

They will be judicious and wise when handling money and will not squander it. They will believe in valuing it and using it in a proper and sensible manner. Overall, they will be somewhat laid-back and will want to lead a relaxed and easy-going life, without too much pressure or stress that is normally associated with modern life.

Gifted with talents and potential, it will be up to them to utilise these and create the life that they want. Though they will not always walk the traditional path, they will be able to blend modernism with conventionality. This will help them to cope better and also give them more skills to succeed and prosper, professionally and personally.

Finance

Like I said earlier, they will display a sensible and mature manner when dealing with money. Not only that, they will not be the sort to trust anyone and everyone. They will hence, be able to shield themselves from risk and ensure that the money they earn is safe and secure. Creating a stable future for themselves will be their concern and you will endeavour to make this a possibility. There are chances that they may come into money through inheritance, legacies, gifts, etc.

Health

As far as health is concerned, they will often trust their own opinion more than anyone else's. While they will have a fair amount of stamina and energy, they will often feel tired and sad. This will only be due to their own mental makeup. Hence, they should surround themselves with happy thoughts and people who make them smile. That will be the best thing for them.

Also, they will have the tendency to follow their own ideas about food, exercise and overall lifestyle. There will not be many health problems that will plague them, however, they should try and remain active as well as cheerful to lead a fulfilling and enriched life.

Born on the 5th, 14th and 23rd

The planet Mercury will be responsible for influencing them and shaping their personality. In conjunction with their native planet Jupiter, Mercury will endow them with the ability to shape their personality and make the most of their latent potential and talents.

Number five Pisceans have the tendency to take to either one of two extremes, as far as their personality is concerned. They will either be strong or weak. Moderation is not something that they really know about. If they take the decision to work on their strong aspect, they will be able to achieve a great deal in life. They will be intelligent, ambitious and will have a good amount of originality. There will be hardly anything that they won't be able to achieve. Life will offer them plenty of opportunities and they will be willing to make use of all of them.

Their energy, sense of humour and their quiet strength will be their greatest assets. They will not be bogged down by the pressures of life. Rather, they will try to turn the impossible into the possible. Hurdles and obstacles will be dealt with in an effective manner by them. There will be little that they will not be able to accomplish and even then, they will manage to turn the tide in their favor.

Professionally, they will do well in a variety of areas and given the fact that they will be diligent and motivated, their growth will be definite and steady. They will have a knack for multiplying their money and will do it with expertise. However, they will need to keep an eye on spending and not let all their money slip away.

In the event that they decide to develop the weaker side of their personality, they will have the tendency to be too laidback and will not be able to focus on things for long. However, this is something that they will be able to reverse whenever they take a firm decision to do so. They will be able to change for the better and develop the stronger aspect of their personality.

It will be their strength and their determination that will be highlighted, when they build on the positive aspects of their personality. Not only that, they will also have sharp perceptive skills and will be a keen and observant learner. Their mind will constantly active and they will be constantly picking up information about people, life, and society from all that goes around them. It will be this diverse knowledge that will help them to interact with and associate with a cross-section of people.

Finance

They would have a gift for trusting their instinct and handling money matters with sense and intuitiveness. However, since number 5 Pisceans have a tendency to splurge and go overboard with spending, they normally don't save a great deal. Therefore, they would need to make a conscious attempt not to do so, and put some money aside for a rainy day. When considering new ventures, plans and schemes, it would be a good idea to consult an expert and only then, they should put their money into it.

Health

Adaptable and flexible, they would be able to adjust to most situations and circumstances, however, they may be prone to anxiety and irritation, especially, when opposed or criticised. They would need to take special care of their nerves and prevent themselves from getting unduly stressed or worn out, mentally. Other than that, they would be a lively bundle of energy and stamina and when, occupied with work that thrills them, they would be able to show a great deal of potential and promise.

Born on the 6th, 15th and 24th

In the event of those being a Piscean born on any of the dates given above, they would be profoundly influenced by the planet Venus and also, by Jupiter to some extent. As a matter of fact, it would be the influence of these two planets that would protect them from any negativity and adverse circumstances that may befall other native Pisceans.

The basic traits and characteristics of their inherent personality have been described in the preceding pages, describing Pisceans. On these pages, we would consider the uniqueness of the individuals born on the above mentioned dates.

The influence of Venus would endow within them a penchant for all beautiful and comfortable things. As a result, they would have a fondness for art, music, literature, poetry, drama, and may even, carve a special niche for themselves in any one of these fields. The overall planetary influence on their life would be positive and fortunate; therefore, if things don't go as planned, they would have to take a close look at their own efforts.

Sensitive and thoughtful, they would have a nature that is supportive and helpful and hence, would often be a good friend and relative. If financially capable, they would also, be willing to share their time with those in need and would not hesitate from lending their time and money.

Sociable and cheerful, they would win friends and since, they themselves would be loyal, their friends too, would stand by them and admire them for their genuineness and warmth. The Venusian temperament would show itself in their love for parties and gatherings and they would try and create as much beauty and aesthetic appeal around them as is possible.

Chances are they would cash in on their innate fondness for the arts and even, make money out of it. They would also, do quite well in fields such as entertaining, fine dining, antiques, or any such are where they would be able to indulge their creativity and love for luxury and fine things. As far as romance and marriage are concerned, they would enjoy the attention and company of the opposite sex and some of them may even, have more than one affair before they finally settle down. However, once they marry, they must try and be diplomatic and discreet as well as thoughtful about their partner and his/her needs. Some of they may also, have to face some opposition to their alliance from relatives.

Their tendency to pamper themselves, indulge and even, suffer from occasional laziness would tend to pull them down, professionally and personally. Therefore, it would be wise to guard against these habits.

On the whole, they would be a person whom most people would love or admire and would be drawn towards their magnetism, sincerity and sensitivity. Affectionate and romantic, their optimism and hopefulness would be endearing and inspiring. At work and at home, they would enjoy surrounding themselves with beautiful and comfort-giving things.

Finance

Pisceans born on the 6th, 15th and 24th would usually, be quite fortunate in financial matters and hence, would be able to lead a life that they would like and enjoy. Unforeseen monetary gifts and legacies would ease any financial burden whatsoever and give them the ability to indulge their extravagant tastes. However, they would need to consciously work on saving prudently for their retirement and not relying on speculation alone. Being generous and amiable, they would often, give away large portions of money without a thought and this may lead to some difficulty later on.

Health

Gifted with strength and stamina, they would be able to make the most of their inherently healthy constitution right from the beginning. However, keeping in view the fact that they would be predisposed towards god food and drink, they may need to pay special attention to their weight, blood pressure and cholesterol levels. Negligence would result in cardiac and similar problems, later on in life. Regular exercise and moderation in diet would be extremely helpful and would enable them to lead a long and fruitful life. They should also keep themselves active and alert since indolence would only lead to obesity and lack of energy.

Born on the 7th, 16th and 25th

Number seven Pisceans are influenced by the planetary combination of the Moon, Jupiter and Neptune. This alliance will bring about significant changes in the Piscean personality and will lead them through a life that will be eventful and interesting, to say the least. Everything they do will have a reaction in their life and they will be able to derive some learning from it.

They will have a temperament that will be somewhat conflicting. They could be decisive as well as indecisive. Similarly, they could exhibit the greatest strength and the biggest weakness at the same time. In the same way, they will have a strong sense of idealism and yet will be practical and grounded.

They will be motivated, ambitious and at the same time, will have a strong value system. In all likelihood, it will be a system that they will have arrived at by themselves, after much deliberation and thought. They are not the kind who will just accept what others have to say. They will be independent, intelligent and individualistic. Life for them will be a learning process and they will move through it, acquiring and discarding concepts, ideas and principles.

Liberal and unconventional, they will have strong beliefs about certain things and will not be willing to change them for anything. Only when they will feel it is necessary, will they be willing to reconsider their stand on anything. Religion, politics and similar subjects will demand utmost loyalty from them, in terms of opinions and ideas. In some matters, they will be more stubborn than otherwise and nothing will be able to change them.

They will have a sense of creativity that will be passionate and sensitive. Indulging in activities such as writing, poetry, music, drama and the like will inspire and soothe them. Their surroundings will also have a profound impact on them. There will be times when they will be able to think of the most wonderful things, however, this will be when they are peaceful and relaxed. Disharmony and chaos will jar their senses and they will find it difficult, if not impossible, to think in such circumstances.

Relationships will bring excitement and newness into their life. As a friend, they will be loyal and warm to those who respect them and give them their space without neglecting them. They will be willing to support their friends and will expect them to do the same for them. Their sense of idealism could at times set them up for disappointment. Therefore, it will be favourable if they learn to lessen their expectations of others and of themselves. Leading a life under pressure and stress will not do them any good. As far as family relationships are concerned, they will be fond of their kith and kin, however, due to a slightly stubborn nature, they might get into arguments and conflicts with them.

Marriage will bring security and stability into their life. They will need a partner who will be empathetic and understanding. Since change is not something that they will be comfortable with, their partner will need to adapt to them and their lifestyle. Once they find someone who matches their wave length and gives them the respect, space and love they need, they will be a sensitive and caring partner.

There will be a strong streak of benevolence in them. They will find joy and contentment in being able to help those who are in need. Whether they're wealthy or not will not be the point, they will try and spare time and effort in trying to make life better for the poor, weak and underprivileged sections of society. Promoting artists and people who need their support will be something that they will be passionate about and will willingly share their resources with them.

All in all, they will lead an enriched life on their own terms. They will follow conventions and at the same time, will be a broad-minded, modern individual with a thinking mind. They will not be content to simply sit back and let the world pass them by. In their own quiet way, they will reach forward and make use of the opportunities that interest them the most.

Finance

Their mind will be their greatest gift and they will be able to see the proof of that in their financial matters. Irrespective of what professional line they adopt, they will be able to succeed in it and establish themselves firmly in it. They may get carried away and become too benevolent. However, once they learn to walk the balancing act of spending and saving, life will be very different for them.

Due to their strong sense of idealism, they will not be the sort who will place a heavy premium on wealth. At the same time, they will want a comfortable life and will work towards it with diligence and dedication. If they take an interest in business, transportation, real estate, foreign trade etc. they will all prove profitable for them.

Health

As far as appearances go, they are physically strong. However, they will need to take special care of their mental health and ensure that they do not put too much pressure on themselves. If they push themselves too hard, they will be prone to suffering from tiredness, exhaustion and nervousness. While change in themselves is not something that they will always want, they will, on the other hand, enjoy a change in scenery and hence, will try and travel as and when possible. This break from routine will serve as a good medicine for their frayed nerves and will refresh and relax them completely.

Born on the 8th, 17th and 26th

Pisceans born on any of the dates given above will be significantly influenced by the planets Saturn and Jupiter. It will be the influence of Saturn that will develop the mature aspect of their personality and make they view life with more sobriety than most other Pisceans.

They will lead a life that will enable them to build their willpower, determination and strength of character. They will learn not to be overcome by difficulties; instead they will conquer them and learn from their mistakes. They may have to shoulder plenty of responsibilities and this will help them to learn how to lead life in a dependable and mature fashion. They will become more prudent and worldly wise in their dealings with people from various walks of life.

There will be many times in life when their good intentions will be misread by those around them and they will have to spend a lot of time in explaining their position. However, this will help them to develop tact and discretion and as a result, they will often, keep their plans and ideas to themselves and share them only with a select few.

Independent and self-reliant, they will have the ability to manage their life and all its ups and downs in a capable and sensible manner. They will not want to place your burdens on the shoulders of other people. As a result, they will keep to themselves and believe in sharing their joys but not their sorrows. They will be extremely fond of their family, kith and kin. They will hold an important place in their life and they will be bound by a sense of duty towards their well-being and comfort. There are strong indications that they might even sacrifice their own personal goals for the sake of the larger family.

Idealistic and principled, they will try to lead a life that is exemplary. However, they will not blindly conform to the standards laid down by society and at times, will have their own unique value system. They will believe in helping the needy and will also not want to be taken for granted. They will be sensitive and compassionate and will always try to make a difference.

Marriage and other relationships will bring a lot of change and upheaval in their life. However, they will be able to cope with it with a great deal of maturity. Being serious and sobre will never be a problem with them. Life should always be a blend of joviality and maturity. They will be a sensitive and caring partner; however, they will have a tendency to view life in a very somber and grave manner.

As far as their professional life is concerned, they will be able to carve a niche for themselves in whichever field they opt for. They should work towards maintaining a balanced approach and not push themselves to the limit in trying to fulfil all their duties and responsibilities. Their perceptive skills and their sharp learning abilities will make it easy for them to deal with the day to day routines as well as manage people with diplomacy.

Finance

Number eight Pisceans will have to work hard for money. While they will be willing to put in the efforts required, they will not have a strong regard for money. Therefore, they will want money to fulfil their needs but it will not be their ambition to amass wealth. In all likelihood, they will normally have a certain desire for which they will need money and then they will work towards it.

It is important that while they keep an idealistic attitude towards finance, they also provide for their future. It is with this purpose in mind that they should rely on sound advice for investments and work towards establishing a secure future for themselves and their family. They should not let their generosity be affected by people who simply want to take them for granted. They should use their fine judgement and accordingly, decide about what they feel will be a worthy cause.

There could be plenty of ups and downs in their financial status and this highlights the importance of saving and keeping aside a sufficient amount for their lean days.

Health

Frequently it has been said that the mind is more powerful than the body. And, this is true for them. Their mental state will pretty much determine the state of their body. Although they will have a good system of immunity and will be able to ward off almost any disease, it will be worry and tension that will affect them adversely and increase their susceptibility to illnesses and infections.

They will have the tendency to contract colds, coughs, infections of the blood and periods of depression and sadness. Therefore, it is best if they learn to look at the lighter side of their life and spend a good amount of time in the company of cheerful and fun-loving people who will add to the vitality and overall well-being of their life.

Relaxing and refreshing breaks will help them to recharge their mind and body. They should try and take these as frequently as possible and not burden themselves with too much responsibility. They should spend time in the lap of Nature and exercise regularly, since they will have joints that could give them trouble in the form of arthritis and rheumatism.

Born on the 9th, 18th and 27th

Jupiter and Mars will come together to influence and bring out the distinctiveness in the personality of those who were born on any of the dates given above. It will be the influence of the planet Mars that will be responsible for endowing them with spontaneity and a certain recklessness in their temperament.

It will be easy to classify their personality as 'fickle'; however, it will be much more than that. They will be someone who will thrive on change and will try and bring about as much of it as possible in their personal and professional life. They will be quick to think and react. While this will be good in many situations, it will also be worthwhile for them to learn how to think things through and not be totally reckless and rash.

Strong, steadfast and brave, they will have the ability and the efficiency to deal with tough times and hurdles that stand in their way to success and prosperity. However, they will have a tendency to be hard on themselves whenever they will fail and this will lead to periods of sadness and loneliness. At the same time, this will not be something that they will experience always. There will be instances when they will be able to derive extra strength and learn from their mistakes.

They will have a quick and fiery temper that will rise whenever they will see anything not going the way it is meant to. Patience is a virtue that they will need to work on. They will be able to use it in many personal and professional situations. They will also be candid and blunt when voicing their views and opinions. As a result, they may end up stepping on some toes and hurting the feelings of others. Along with patience, if they could hone their diplomatic skills, they will be equipped to handle any position of trust and responsibility.

Professionally, they would do well in most fields. If they decide to set up a business, they should try and be careful of business partners, since there are chances that they might try and take advantage of them. They would do especially, well in government jobs and also, in industries where some amount of responsibility is entrusted to them. Any career that would put them in the middle of people or in the limelight would suit them and they would shine brilliantly.

As far as love and romance are concerned, they would have to overcome some obstacles in this field, but would meet the right person and lead a fulfilling and enriching marital life. Children would bring joy as well as a fair amount of anxiety to them.

Indulgent and charitable, they would be willing to share their time and money with anyone who would express a need for it. They are not the kinds to hold grudges and would be willing to mend bridges with old friends and acquaintances. Since they would be helpful and sociable, they would often, have friends placed in important positions and these would come in handy someday. However, their natural frankness may not go down well with many people, and hence, they may even make some enemies.

In their young years, they may be tempted to succumb to peer pressure and experiment with alcohol, drugs, tobacco and the like. However, they should try not to get addicted to them and if possible, stay away from them, as these may become crutches for them later in life.

Finance

Just as their temperament is fickle, so would be the case with their finances. There would be plenty of ups and downs; however, they would be able to lead a relatively comfortable life, without much money trouble. They should try and avoid speculating, unless they have sound advice and guidance. In order to build a safe and secure retirement plan, ensure that they save regularly and take expert help in planning their investments.

Health

Number 9 Pisceans are generally, gifted with strong resistance to most diseases and therefore, can cope quite well, especially till their thirties. Towards the forties, however, they would need to pay special attention to their health and wellbeing. Prudent changes in diet, exercise and sleep patterns would yield long lasting benefits and protect them from the usual gamut of illnesses. However, some of them may be prone to disorders of the liver, kidneys, digestive system, cardiac ailments and may even, need some surgery. Other than that, minor injuries and infections may bother them, but things wouldn't get very serious.